INVOLVING CUSTOMERS IN
NEW SERVICE DEVELOPMENT

Series on Technology Management

Series Editor: J. Tidd (Univ. of Sussex, UK) ISSN 0219-9823

SERIES ON TECHNOLOGY MANAGEMENT – VOL.11

INVOLVING CUSTOMERS IN NEW SERVICE DEVELOPMENT

Editors

Bo Edvardsson
Anders Gustafsson
Per Kristensson
Peter Magnusson
Jonas Matthing

Karlstad University, Sweden

ICP

Imperial College Press

Published by

Imperial College Press
57 Shelton Street
Covent Garden
London WC2H 9HE

Distributed by

World Scientific Publishing Co. Pte. Ltd.
5 Toh Tuck Link, Singapore 596224
USA office: 27 Warren Street, Suite 401-402, Hackensack, NJ 07601
UK office: 57 Shelton Street, Covent Garden, London WC2H 9HE

British Library Cataloguing-in-Publication Data
A catalogue record for this book is available from the British Library.

ISBN 1-86094-669-0

Typeset by Stallion Press
Email: enquiries@stallionpress.com

Printed in Singapore by B & JO Enterprise

Preface

In a service-driven economy, companies must develop new and better services to stay competitive and make a profit. Service competition and development of new services which create customer value are major challenges not only for service companies, but also for manufacturing companies and public service providers. Since services are activities and interactions and not physical objects, we cannot apply concepts, models and techniques developed for product development *per se.*

New service development calls for concepts, models and techniques based on the logic of service and it emphasizes value creation through services. Service management theory implies that value is co-created with the customer and is assessed on the basis of the value in use. The customers are directly involved in the value creation process in different ways. Customers can also contribute in the development and design of new services and products. New service concepts and service offerings are also developed together with customers. Customer involvement in service development—the theme of this book—is a relatively new area. Customer involvement refers to becoming close with customers in order to learn from and with them.

This book is the first to address management issues in the area of customer involvement, where internationally leading scholars and consultants contribute and share their knowledge and insights. The book gives readers an overview and understanding of the business potential of learning with customers, an overview of concepts, models, strategies and techniques for involving customers in a fruitful way in the business development process, results from empirical studies and a number of cases as well as guidelines on how to organize and manage customer involvement.

This book is suitable for executive and management development programs at business schools and institutes, as well as for masters programs at business schools and technical universities. It is also relevant to reflective managers and executives working in areas such as marketing, business development, strategy and service and product development in both service organizations and manufacturing companies.

We would like to express our gratitude to many who have contributed to this book in different ways. We particularly acknowledge the efforts of the contributors of the different chapters, as without their contributions and feedback, this book would not exist. This book is part of a research program at the Service Research Center (CTF) focusing on user-driven service development. Our sincere thanks to the Swedish Knowledge Foundation for its financial support. Our colleagues at CTF have provided us with inspiration and critique during seminars and informal discussions. We appreciate the supportive academic culture at CTF and we feel privileged to be part of CTF.

Bo Edvardsson
Anders Gustafsson
Per Kristensson
Peter Magnusson
Jonas Matthing

Service Research Center (CTF)
Karlstad University
Sweden
August 2006

Contents

1

Introduction

The Editors

1.1. Introduction

Services are one of the main bases for profitable businesses today. In the service-driven economy, companies try to increase their competitiveness by introducing new products and services that create value for existing customers and that attract new customers (e.g., Edvardsson *et al.*, 2000). Service Management theory implies that this value is defined by and co-created with the customer on the basis of value in use (Vargo and Lusch, 2004). The term value in use refers to the fact that customers often perceive or experience the richness of a service during and after its use or consumption. This also applies to many manufacturing companies that now include value creation through services and are faced with the challenge of developing service concepts. New service concepts are created, for example, by involving existing or potential customers in new and fruitful ways during different phases of the service development process.

1

Within the market-oriented approach, customer orientation has emerged as an important point of departure when developing new products and services. Involving customers is a relatively new area within customer orientation, which ensures that the services being developed attract customers and create value when they are used. Customer involvement in service development and business development is the theme of this book. The term service development refers to further development of existing services in a company, new services for the company, or services that are "new to the world." We also include issues linked to business transformation where manufacturing companies become service companies, and products are viewed as platforms for services.

Customer involvement for us means "coming close to customers" in order to learn from and with them in new and fruitful ways using methods beyond traditional focus groups, questionnaires, and interviews. The perspective is thus value creation for, by, and with customers. The intensity of involvement may vary based on various aspects such as type of business, level of complexity, or simply the routine behavior of a company. For a thorough categorization of user involvement, we recommend Alam (2002).

The use of customers as co-developers, co-creators of new services, and as co-producers is a relatively new, important, and growing field in service and management research. The research propositions and results to date have had clear and rather far-reaching managerial implications. This can simply be stated as a recommendation to companies to get into the game or be left behind! Use your customers' expertise in newer and better ways! If you choose to follow this trend, there are potentially large gains in terms of better services, more satisfied customers, and consequently larger profits! We recognize, however, that there is a need for more research, knowledge, and guidelines on how to develop new and attractive services by means of involving customers.

This book is the first comprehensive and thought-provoking answer to this need and it includes contributions from the leading scholars and consultants in the field. The book elaborates on how to involve customers in order to learn with them to co-opt customer competence when developing new services. The purpose is to give the reader the following: (1) an understanding of the business potential of learning with customers and other users, (2) an overview of the field's new service development and customer involvement when it comes to concepts, theoretical frameworks, and models as well as strategies and techniques for involving users in fruitful ways in the business development process, (3) results from empirical studies as well as illustrating cases, and (4) managerial implications and guidelines on how to organize and manage customer involvement in different phases of the new service and business development process.

1.2. An Emerging Theme in Management

The competitive situation today has emerged out of deregulations in many sectors (e.g., financial, telecom, transportation, and energy services), the globalization of enterprises, new technologies, and increasingly volatile customer demands. Today, services are infusing into our daily lives in many different forms. Through technology, customers are able to utilize services from all around the world. New service concepts, such as coffee shops, fast food, and small shops, are shifting from a local business to a global competitive business. Technology is also starting to shift the power from companies to consumers. One manifestation of this is when users join forces and develop products on their own. Operation system Linux, for example, is a project that was initiated by Linus Thorvaldsson but involved people from all around the globe and is under constant development by involving users. This shift has also brought turbulence and complexity to business, leading to uncertainty and increased competition. In its most extreme form, the situation is denoted as hyper-competition. Products quickly tend to become commodities. Services can be used to differentiate products, hence enhancing the delivered customer value and creating a competitive advantage. Companies need to develop the service activities and components of the overall customer offering, which implies realizing a service perspective as a strategic approach.

A service perspective is fundamentally a management perspective which offers an insight and assistance for any type of organization that needs to expand their competitive advantage beyond the core product solution to a customer problem. Furthermore, it emphasizes on a deep understanding of the internal value-generating processes of the customer, which will render services that match customer needs. A true understanding of the customer is the driver of competitive advantage in today's business environment. The service perspective consequently refers to a focus on business from a customer's point of view, focusing on how to create customer value when using or consuming the service. It is a challenge for many organizations to become truly customer-oriented. No company would declare that they are not customer-oriented, but when they are studied in detail, the opposite may be true. Very few companies have access to their customers' true needs and wants, and even if they have this knowledge, this information is not disseminated throughout the organization and it does not lead to appropriate actions. This is thus a challenge for the management. Customer involvement could be viewed as a tool to help become more customer-oriented.

1.3. Getting Closer to the Customer

Research studies have also shown that market fit, that is, the correct understanding and translation of customer needs, is one of the key ingredients in new service development. Hence, as the service-profit chain stresses a customer-oriented point of departure, researchers have repeatedly argued in favor of a customer orientation approach in product and service development. A market-oriented company thus seeks to understand not only the expressed needs, but also the latent needs of their customers, and collectively share information among departments. To comprehend unarticulated customer needs, it is suggested that companies need to create processes that facilitate learning early in the innovation process. Learning goes beyond merely asking customers what they want. As some companies have discovered, customers find it difficult to imagine what it would be like to use something that does not exist at the moment — an innovation. Consequently, they will give you their best guess about usage, likelihood to buy, etc. Some companies claim that their customers are not truthful. Our experience is that customers do not normally lie; they provide you with their best guess, and maybe, it is the company's inquiry approach that is wrong.

New service development thus relies on the difficult task of understanding current customer needs and anticipating future needs, which cannot be achieved by means of traditional market research. Hence, merely listening to the voice of the customer is seldom sufficient; interacting with potential customers in the development process becomes critical to understanding the customers' true needs. By getting close to their customers, it is hypothesized that firms will reach a deeper understanding of current as well as latent customer needs. Closeness is rarely achieved by interviews; we need to have a deeper knowledge of aspects such as our customers' values, networks, and habits. A customer involvement approach has therefore been suggested.

1.4. What is Involvement?

This book covers essentially two types of customer involvement: First, there is user involvement to learn more about the customers, that is, their stated and latent needs, preferences, wishes, and values and thus to understand more deeply what creates value for them. Companies do this in order to design new services and customer solutions that will create an attractive customer value and thus a demand. This is related to traditional marketing research activities. We do, however, want to emphasize that these research activities cover a larger span of methods and techniques than just in-depth interviews and focus groups. Advanced customer involvement is trying to capture more than just attitudes toward an existing service.

Second, there are new and pro-active techniques of customer involvement that advance the frontiers of not only exploring customer needs, but also using customers and consumers as innovators. This means creating ideas, assessing ideas, and maybe even developing or designing new solutions to existing needs, as well as re-designing service processes to make them more customer friendly. Customers might thus be seen as service and business developers, with the companies utilizing their customers' expertise. This second type of involvement is characterized by customers actually participating in the development of services, customer solutions, or their own experiences by for instance being a member of a project team. There is a wide variety for this type of involvement. New technology, as with Linux, also helps companies to get in touch with their customers that form user groups helping one another to solve problems. Other examples are companies that offer the customers different kinds of toolkits for creating their own innovations (von Hippel, 2001), or just adapting their half fabricated products (mass customization).

This book discusses customer involvement for different purposes. The purpose may also be linked to a specific stage in the service development process as illustrated in Table 1.

In the beginning of the development process, the purpose of involving customers is to generate ideas or to help a company decide where to focus their business development. It is a creative phase and a company wants help to create solutions for future needs. Later in the product development process, customers may be involved in testing and debugging a new product. A customer experiences the value of a service first when it is consumed, making it difficult, or even impossible, to test it before purchase.

Table 1:   Different purposes and stages for customer involvement (examples).

Purpose of customer involvement	Stage of customer involvement
Acquire information about users/customers	Business planning
Get new ideas	Innovation, idea generation
Adapting products/services	Prototyping
Debugging	Testing
Control the customers' experiences	Usage
Teaching customers and learning from them	All stages

Customers are thus co-producers in their own service process of fulfilling their needs. In every interaction between supplier and customer, there is a potential knowledge exchange where the customer can be taught more about possibilities, and the supplier learns more about customer needs.

1.5.   Who Should Read This Book?

The purpose of this book is to provide an understanding of state of the art in the field by presenting results from service management research and business development emphasizing customer involvement in action.

The book is suitable for executive and management development programs at business schools and institutes as well as for MBA and masters programs at business schools and technical universities.

The book is also of distinct interest for reflective managers and executives working with marketing, business development, strategy, as well as service and product development. The broad span of the practitioner target group reflects that customer involvement efforts are multidisciplinary and cross-traditional functional boarders in companies and other organizations. As a consequence, we have outlined the articles in four sections, which can be read in order or as the reader's interest follows.

1.6.   Outline of the Book

The first section begins with a discussion on customer involvement in service innovation by introducing the field, and presenting overall pictures, examples, and data. The next section focuses on customer involvement project in the early phase of innovation. The third section illustrates a number of cases of customer involvement from a method point of view. Lastly, three cases from different businesses are presented.

1.6.1. *Perspectives on customer involvement*

Ian Alam provides an introduction to the interaction with customers by looking at the reasons behind this interplay in service innovation. Although he makes a clear case of the importance and potential benefits of interacting with customers, he moves on to present a framework. The framework touches upon several issues such as how interaction occurs, which customers should be involved, and also problems related to interaction. He concludes that organizations need to adopt a customer interaction strategy as a key element in their innovation activities.

Next, Bodil Sanden, Anders Gustafsson, and Lars Witell present interesting data on how companies interact with their customers. They argue that even though customer involvement for the purpose of customer input in the service innovation process had many advocates, little is actually known about what companies do. Their survey of 366 Swedish firms aims at providing a basic knowledge about the customer's role in new service development. Most companies involve their customers, but there are large differences between various companies and industries. It is also a question of how they involve the customers, and the survey shows that this involvement varies. The chapter finally reveals motives and issues on the difficulties with customer involvement practices, as well as some interesting performance measures.

Ulf Mannervik and Rafael Ramirez offer a strategic perspective on customers as co-innovators. Their chapter presents a typology of different approaches to customer co-innovation, and then suggests a strategic and systematic model for managing co-innovation. The typology forms four archetypes for customer involvement: form filler, interactive co-designer, real-time field source, and integrated co-designer. The archetypes are then described with illustrative examples. Even though their typology is tentative, it shows that customer co-innovation needs to be treated strategically, for which they then offer a framework.

Evert Gummesson departs from a network approach to marketing in his chapter. This places an emphasis on all relationships that are entered into a marketing process. As a result, there are many customer-to-customer interactions that need to be further explored. The chapter offers several thought-provoking examples of these types of relationships from a customer involvement perspective. Evert Gummesson shows a special ability in pointing out to interesting phenomena and delivering interesting reflections. He concludes that companies can use the customer-to-customer interaction as a potential arena for service design.

1.6.2. *The CuDIT studies*

The next section is devoted to a project called the CuDIT (Customer Driven IT) studies. This was a joint project between CTF in Karlstad and major telecom companies in Sweden for several years in the early millennium. The CuDIT project has thereafter continued with new studies to focus customer involvement in service innovation.

The first chapter by Jonas Matthing, Bodil Sandén, and Bo Edvardsson is an enhanced version of a paper published in the International Journal of Service Industry Management. The chapter draws upon theory from market and learning orientation in conjunction with a service-centered model and reviews the literature on involvement of the customer in innovation. To facilitate proactive learning about the customer, recent findings stress on the involvement of customers in the development process and observations of customers in real action. Thus, a field experiment was conducted in Sweden with end-user mobile phone services. The design departs from the nature of service that precepts value in use and borrows from relevant techniques within product innovation that supports learning in customer co-creation. The experiment reveals that the consumers' service ideas are found to be more innovative, in terms of originality and user value than those of professional service developers.

In the next CuDIT chapter, Per Kristensson presents some of the theoretical issues on which the CuDIT project was based. He argues that traditional methods often do not perform well in their search for innovative ideas. To find innovative ideas in customer interaction is a matter of how and where you ask. The chapter offers some basic principles for customer cooperation in market research. These principles are founded on psychological theories that underlie many market research methods. The chapter also demonstrates how and why customers in the CuDIT study generated creative ideas that stretched beyond what in-house developers were able to achieve.

The third chapter in this section of the CuDIT study is written by Peter Magnusson. His article studies the benefits of user involvement in the ideation phase. The chapter discusses the effects of involving users in creating new service ideas for mobile telephony in three themes: The first concerns whether or not services developed with user involvement are better than those developed by professionals alone, and if so, in what way. The second theme investigates whether or not user involvement can be optimized, that is, what is the best way of involving users? Finally, the chapter discusses how the product development process needs to be adapted when users are involved. The results indicated that the benefit of user ideation is heavily dependent on how it is executed rather than on who is involved.

1.6.3. *Empirical illustrations focusing new methods*

Per Echeverri poses the question of when to collect data—before, during, or after the customer's experience, and furthermore, what to collect involves an assessment of the relevant factors and social mechanisms to explore. He also questions as to how to collect empirical data as it involves assessments of methods that provide a realistic representation of what really happens "out there." The chapter illustrates some of these problems through a study of passengers using a public-transport service. In particular, the interactive process aspects of the service are examined. The chapter also uses a case study to comment on some theoretical problems in understanding customer satisfaction and perceived service quality. Finally, it discusses some methodological problems such as the need for more accurate methods of data collection in service research and in the service industry.

The contribution of Fredrik Dahlsten analyzes customer involvement from within the new product development process at Volvo Cars. The study shows that customer involvement success is highly contextual and needs well-adapted management attention. The author argues that there needs to be a willingness to experiment in the development work, allowing for customer involvement to complement conventional market research. Innovation is facilitated by an understanding of what constitutes customer meaning. With as much emphasis on customer creation as product creation, the resulting customer-value will improve. For customer involvement methodology to develop, knowledge needs to be transferred among projects and then managed and adapted.

The chapter by Hans Björkman addresses the issue of managing user ideas. He suggests there is a need for prescriptive models and methods for enhancing the organizational utilization of knowledge attained from users. The initial emphasis lies in the problematization of the utilization of knowledge acquired from users. It shows that the toolbox for listening to users is more developed than the toolbox for using what is learnt. The chapter then describes the utilization of information acquired from users as a managerial challenge involving a set of specific capabilities. It is based upon evaluations of the role played by task forces/project groups in the Sif (a white collar union) setting, where they have been responsible for organizing Design Dialog Groups with members/users.

1.6.4. *Special topics on customer involvement and service engineering, IPR, and supplier involvement*

Rainer Nägele provides a case study on customer-oriented service engineering procedures and methods. It is often stated that this will offer promising potential and competitive advantages, but it is not clear in which phase of the service development and performance process. This uncertainty is analyzed in a case study. Based on the findings, the paper describes the first draft of a maturity model of customer orientation during the service development process. This draft will later be evaluated and specified in a broader empirical survey among 5.050 German companies.

Because of the interactive nature of services, it has become more and more common that services are co-developed by the producer and the intended user or customer. Christiane Hipp and Cornelius Herstatt state that co-development raises important issues concerning intellectual property rights (IPR). User involvement within service innovation induces the risk of unintentional knowledge spillovers. The protection of innovation and knowledge in service-intensive industries is important to guarantee monopolistic structures for a certain time period and to achieve an adequate return on investment for innovation expenditures. Traditional patent protection is not easy to apply for most services. The authors derive five different protection strategies within service innovation. The chapter is based on a German empirical study on service-intensive companies.

Frank Hull, Bo Edvardsson, and Chris Story's chapter elaborates upon a model of internal product development by adding measures of co-involvement by external companies. The test of this proposition was positive. Adding co-involvement to internal elements of product development explains additional amounts of variance in multiple regression analysis. However, internal elements of the model provide the capability for effective integration of external companies in NSD decision making. These two elements are organic team structure and in-process design controls. In conclusion, the chapter tests how contingencies, such as a strategic focus on novel service development and exploitation of tacit knowledge, moderate the predictors of product development performance. Such environmental uncertainty proves to be a consistent moderator of an internal element of product system design and organic team structure.

1.7. The Future of Customer Involvement

There is a general trend of companies wanting to become more customer-oriented. Involving their customers may be one approach to accomplish this goal. Research shows that there are several benefits to customer involvement, including better products, more satisfied customers, increased loyalty, and higher profits. It is, however, a relatively new research area, and many questions still remain to be answered. For example, as is the case with any other approach, there are limitations to the extent which customers should and can be involved. This is related to the classic dispute between market pull and technology push. For certain products in certain phases of the development process, it may be difficult for companies to involve customers. For example, the development of IP-TV, which is the ability to transmit TV through a phone line, was initiated 10-years prior to its release. It may have been possible for end users to be involved in the early phases of a project like this, but when technical solutions are developed and discussed, they may be of limited use. Instead, it may make sense to involve the end user later on again when this new service is further developed in order to get their opinions on, for example, usability issues. In other words, market pull, illustrated by customer involvement, is applicable and useful in this case during certain phases of the development, whereas in other phases, technology push maybe seen as more useful.

Another issue is which customers should be involved in the process? There are many opinions on this: Should it be the leading customers based on some aspect, that is, customers that are likely to be the first ones to adopt the new service, or are ordinary users better? Many companies, especially in a B-2-B context, are using financially strong customers in their customer involvement efforts. Just as in the case with market pull versus technology push, it is not a matter of choosing one alternative but of making a deliberate choice. For some applications, lead users may have already developed a new innovation, and the company has only to find it. The discovery that lead users often are the actual innovators was made by Eric von Hippel in his seminal research in the 1970s (von Hippel, 1978). When trying to generate ideas for new innovations, ordinary users may be useful as well, since they do not limit their thoughts to what is possible to implement with today's technology. Research studies indicate that these users are more useful when a company wants to think outside the box. This is one of the findings of the CuDIT studies accounted for in this book. Finally, a new innovation may be expensive to implement, and the number of customers that can carry that investment may be limited making it logical to involve financially strong customers.

A further question is what happens once companies start to involve customers. Research shows that there are significant difficulties in adopting ideas from the outside; we are stuck with the "not invented here" problem (Katz and Allen, 1997). If an idea originates at a company, there are people there to defend and explain it. This may not be the case if a customer is the origin. Another difficulty is who actually owns the rights to the idea: Is it the inventor, that is, the customer or the initiator, that is, the company? This implies that IPR is an important issue for service development. Many companies also complain that it is generally not a problem to generate ideas for new services; the problem is selecting the best ideas. One of the questions then is, "In what way should an idea be evaluated, and maybe even more importantly, who should evaluate the idea?" Is it possible to develop a process for this purpose?

Another issue involves the need to know more about different approaches, methods, and tools to involve customers such as the lead user approach, emphatic design, and user developer. There is some research that has been carried out to understand to what extent some of these approaches lead to innovation in the form of novelty of the service. The effectiveness of different methods is difficult to investigate, but there is a need for such research.

Finally, we will emphasize that customer involvement is not the ultimate solution to all challenges that companies face when developing services. We need to know more about the downside of customer involvement and when not to involve customers. A risk might be that focusing on customers will result in "customer nearsightedness." Finding a fruitful balance between technology push and market pull when it comes to customer involvement needs to be researched on more in the future.

As previously stated, our aim is to provide the reader with an understanding of state of the art of the field. As the space is limited in a book like this, there are of course areas that we have not been able to cover. We have, for example, not been able to give much attention to the research claiming the downside of user involvement. These critics mainly state that involving customers for innovation can lead to a stalemate, since innovative ideas rarely arise from customers. "Stay close to your customers" might mislead suppliers into *avoiding exploration* of the opportunities provided by new disruptive technologies (Christensen and Bower, 1996). We think that the warnings are justified, but we further mean that *if* customer involvement is to be successful, it has to be conducted in a proper way. If a company involves ordinary users to develop or evaluate new advanced technology, it will certainly fail. But involving the same users to come up with good creative *use* of new technology can certainly be a good strategy, as can be seen from examples in this book.

While working on this book, we have realized that much is yet to be researched on. We have pinpointed some areas that we think will be especially important. To our delight, we have also discovered that there is a growing research community that is eager to learn more about this thrilling field.

We hope that you will find this book as interesting to read as we found editing it. This book is a tool for learning more about this dynamic evolving field. We hope we will have many more years of continued research in the field of user involvement for service development. Borrowing a quotation from Sir Winston Churchill, we hope that this book "... is not the end. This is not the beginning of the end. But it is, perhaps, the end of the beginning."

References

Alam, I (2002). An exploratory investigation of user involvement in new service development. *Journal of the Academy of Marketing Science*, 30(3), 250–261.

Christensen, CM and J Bower (1996). Customer power, strategic investment and the failure of leading firms. *Strategic Management Journal*, 17(3), 197–218.

Edvardsson, B, A Gustafsson, MD Johnson and B Sandén (2000). *New Service Development and Innovation in the New Economy*, Lund: Studentlitteratur.

Katz, R and TJ Allen (1997). Organizational issues in the introduction of new technologies. In *The Human Side of Managing Technological Innovation: A Collection of Readings*, R Katz (ed.), pp. 384–397. New York: Oxford University Press.

Vargo, S and R Lusch (2004). Evolving to a new dominant logic of marketing. *Journal of Marketing*, 68(1), 1–17.

von Hippel, E (1978). Successful industrial products from customer ideas. *Journal of Marketing*, 42(1), 39–49.

von Hippel, E (2001). User toolkits for innovation. *Journal of Product Innovation Management*, 18(4), 247–257.

2

Process of Customer Interaction in New Service Development

Ian Alam

Jones School of Business, State University of New York, USA
alam@geneseo.edu

2.1. Introduction

Customer interaction has been advocated as a potentially powerful tool for developing successful new services. Specifically, it is seen as an effective tool to jump start the idea generation process for new services, to create value for customers, and to effectively manage the overall innovation process in a firm. Despite the powerful benefits of customer interaction, there are a majority of service firms that are unwilling to expose themselves to the perceived costs and risks of customer interaction. Besides a lack of confidence in service managers' own ability to consistently interact with customers, the risks of confidentiality and a possible lack of customer cooperation are the key reasons why service firms hesitate to use customers for their innovation programs. Yet, service managers are partly to blame for this controversy because they do not know how to interact with the customers correctly (Ulwick, 2002). For instance, scholars argue that despite a significant amount of research into why new services fail, managers have not learned their lesson and continue to make the same mistakes that lead to new service failure. One such mistake is that *customer input* is still missing in most new services. Hence, the method of customer questioning and the overall approach to customer interaction are important considerations in New Service Development (NSD). The objective of this chapter is to outline the strategies needed to effectively interact with customers and to obtain the necessary input from them for an NSD project. The process and techniques discussed in this chapter should be applicable to both business-to-business and business-to-consumer services.

2.2.   Why Interact with Customers?

The first question a service manager might ask is why should we spend our time and resources on interacting with customers? The answer to this question can be gleaned from the success stories of several innovation-vanguard firms, particularly IBM who relies primarily on customers for innovation for their global service division. For example, once positioned as a maker of computer hardware, the company now obtains 65% of its revenue from services (Teresko, 2003). This happened in part due to an extensive interaction process among IBM research scientists and customers of the company's global services division. On average, IBM researchers spend about 25% of their time with customers compared with 3%–4% as recently as 8 years ago (ibid.). This example and several empirical studies suggest that customer interaction in NSD can offer many benefits. Notable among them are the following.

2.2.1.   *Superior and differentiated service*

With customer interaction, it is possible to develop a differentiated new service with unique benefits and better value for the customers. It is a key issue because today's customers are more sophisticated and demanding and search for superior value in a new service. According to Nicholas Donofrio, senior VP of IBM global services,

> *Our interaction with customers gives us a more refined process for identifying problems that will fulfill our purpose of providing competitive value faster.*

2.2.2. *Reduced cycle time*

Customer interaction may help shorten development cycle time, also known as "time to market." The process of customer interaction may yield the most up-to-date information about customer preferences and needs that are changing fast. This potentially reduces the need for alterations in service delivery process in the later stages, because a firm can collect and process customer information for its NSD projects on a concurrent basis. Consider an example suggesting the importance of a quick cycle time. A major on-line retailer suggested the idea for a new insurance product to cover the risks of lawsuits against a firm's online advertising and e-commerce delivery problems and also provided other input for the new service. As a result, an insurance firm could develop the new service in a rather short cycle time. Within a few months, a host of other firms started offering similar types of coverage, but by then, the pioneering firm's product was fully entrenched in the market. Thus, a quick cycle time allowed the firm to reap the reward for its innovation.

2.2.3. *Rapid diffusion*

Customer involvement in the NSD process helps in rapidly diffusing innovation. This may help accelerate the market acceptance of a new service. This "time to acceptance" is key success factor for many new services. One rationale for this assertion is that the interaction process may educate a customer about the specifications, attributes, and use of a new service which in turn helps in building a quick support for the innovation. Customer interaction also provides crucial assistance in the diffusion of many technical oriented services mainly in the financial services industry.

2.2.4. *Long-term relationships*

Providing potential customers with the experience of participation in the NSD process helps win their loyalty and can improve a customer-service producer relationship. It can also be seen as a public relation exercise. For example, the customer may feel that the firm listens to what he has to say and may decide to buy the new service or may even promote it to other users.

2.3. How to Interact with the Customers?

Of interest next is the overall process of customer interaction. This entails issues such as modes, overall style, and methods of interaction.

2.3.1. *Modes of customer interaction*

A service manager may use one or more of the following modes to interact with potential customers. These modes are presented as options. The actual choice may depend on several factors, such as a firm's innovation culture and its overall relationship with the customers.

2.3.2. *Qualitative techniques*

A service firm may invite customers to help brainstorm for service ideas, conduct focus groups, or conduct in-depth interviews to identify the customers' changing needs. The main objective of a face-to-face interview is to translate the customers' definition of desired value into a service. Choosing the right customer interaction model recognizes that every customer interaction is an opportunity to create customer value. Therefore, a typical one-on-one interview probes a customer's whole situation to discover both general and detailed needs of the customers (Griffin and Hauser, 1993). That is, the focus should be on the customer "problem solving" because successful new services often emerge from a problem that was once unmet in the marketplace. Simple customer feedback can also be the basis for the next innovation. Recently, a major US airline, Delta, re-launched its frequent flyer program based on customer feedback. Jeff Robertson of Delta summarizes their efforts in obtaining customer input (Shermach, 2005, p. 24) as:

> *We frequently request and receive customer feedback and use it to help shape the program as it evolves.*

To get input from a larger customer base, a firm may conduct focus groups or brainstorming. The main advantage of both focus group and brainstorming is that the inherent group dynamics play a key role in generating useful information about the new service. All these modes of interaction — interview, focus group, and brainstorming — can be integrated into another mode of interaction, innovation retreat and summit, which is discussed next.

2.3.3. *Innovation retreats and summits*

A firm may invite key customers to their innovation retreats and summits. Recently, a large financial service firm organized a weekend retreat to identify new service opportunities. They invited two managers from their client firms to attend the retreat, where those customers provided an input for innovative new service ideas and assisted the firm in developing several new service concepts. Specifically, several brainstorming sessions were used to generate new service ideas. In this regard, a manager enthusiastically remarked:

> *In the innovation retreat, one of our customers actively participated in the innovation related activities. He suggested a number of new service ideas and assisted us in converting them into real products. Actually, an open and free discussion in a relaxed and friendly environment did the trick.*

2.3.4. *Customers inducted into an NSD team*

Customers can join a cross-functional NSD team and provide an input on various aspects of the development process. The presence of customers in an NSD team minimizes hidden knowledge and provides a better perspective for NSD decisions. Customers can also help reconcile the interfunctional conflicts by expressing their unique customer perspectives. For example, a multinational banking firm, while developing an investment service for the big emerging international markets, invited representatives from customer firms active in overseas business to join a service development team. The customers actively participated in the team meetings and provided input on the economic, financial, and political environment of various overseas markets. The team environment also facilitated a debate on the risk factors of various markets, which proved rather crucial in an early stage of the service development process particularly in taking go/abandon decisions. The CEO of the firm spoke about the effectiveness of team environment:

> *Our clients have a much better access to overseas markets' information. Obtaining that information was easy and quick via customer interaction. Particularly, a team environment facilitated rather enriching dialogues and critical analysis of the information that are so crucial for NSD.*

2.3.5. *Customer-advisory panel*

A firm may ask selected customers to be part of a customer panel and occasionally provide input at various stages of the NSD process. Customer-advisory programs have long been used for tangible products, but it is slowly evolving for services as well. Levi's had formed a panel of fashion conscious young consumers in major European cities such as Milan, Paris, and London and had asked them to comment on product use situations and the latest trends and provide other input for its highly successful innovation *Engineered Jeans* (Dignam, 2002). Several well-known US service firms www.monster.com (an online firm providing employment/job search services worldwide), Sovereign Bancorp Inc. (financial services), and Harvard Pilgrim Health Care (health insurance) have formed a customer-advisory program for their NSD efforts. These companies actively collaborate with selected customers to keep up with their evolving needs and use this insight for their NSD efforts. Monster.com's senior vice president Marcel Legrand explains that Monster has built this program to stay close to the customers (Dorfman, 2005, p. 23):

> We involve our customers in setting the agenda and we also send them Monster's business review documents to read before the meeting. This way we can spend less time on the past and we can together focus on the future.

2.3.6. *Observation of customers*

A firm may obtain new service ideas and information by simply watching a service delivery process. Customers' needs and choices are often susceptible to a variety of influences, such as the number and features of alternatives and the timing of purchase. For example, customers may be less reliable in suggesting their future needs of new services in an interview or focus group situation (Simonson, 1993), whereas customer observation in a real purchase situation may better identify the needs and choices of customers. For example, a banking firm sent its financial advisers to several importers to generate ideas by examining transactions related to the cross-border payments and receivables. The financial advisers observed that the client firms were dealing with multiple global banks for their cross-border transactions and were generally not happy with the inefficiencies and the costs associated with that arrangement. Based on this observation, the firm got an idea for a new international clearing house. Similarly, a car rental firm sent its managers to different airport locations to observe the cross-selling of collision insurance during the car rental process for business customers. Based on the observation, they developed a new service that included automatic collision coverage for all business rentals.

This technique of customer observation, sometimes referred to as ethnography, can identify "unstated" or "unspoken" customer needs and detect the contradictions between what customers say and what they actually do (Goffin and Lemke, 2004). Wells Fargo, the fifth largest US bank, performs ethnography studies weekly at client sites to obtain new service ideas. Recently, Wells Fargo conducted an ethnography study involving one of their client firms Gary D. Nelson Inc. a staffing company. Wells Fargo staffers interviewed key members of Nelson's management teams for two hours each and observed various financial workflows that employees perform, such as payroll, accounts payable, and accounts receivable (Marlin, 2004). This study uncovered several problem areas, which formed the basis for new service ideas.

2.3.7. *Customer–manufacturer mixers*

Instead of the prolonged retreats or summits, a firm can occasionally organize informal gatherings and engage in dialogs with major customers concerning new services. Examples are occasional innovation lunches and dinners where employees and customers interact informally. The product manager of a large stocks and share firm talked about the role of social interactions between the customers and employees in her firm:

> *We bring our key customers to the headquarters regularly and conduct mini conferences, innovation seminars and idea clinics and even hold picnics and barbeques.*

The newly formed Xerox Global Services division has also developed a similar informal interaction system based on a weekly coffee break where Xerox engineers gather to talk to each other (McCarthy, 2002). Bob Bauer of Xerox Global Services says:

> *The challenge is to allow customers to have our services any way they want.*

2.3.8. *Customer visits*

Service managers may visit their customers regularly to discuss new service opportunities. Wells Fargo has mandated that the managers must schedule regular visits to key business customers to discuss new service possibilities (Marlin, 2004). Wells Fargo's managers literally camp out at customer sites for several days to observe how customers go about their jobs.

Experiments can also be conducted in which the customers may observe a mock service delivery process and provide a feedback on the merits of the service concepts. For instance, while developing a new fire insurance product, a team of product managers of a business insurance firm visited a customer's office and simulated a claim processing process. During this mock session, the firm tested the product, made service design changes, and also added several new attributes to the service. The area manager describes his experience this way:

> *Regular customer visits are compulsory for our staff. In fact, our staffs have described this experience of customer visits as one of the most enriching of their careers because they uncovered a number of unforeseen new service opportunities.*

2.4.   Interaction between Front-Line Employees and Customers

By nature, most services are characterized by an inability to separate production from consumption. Thus, in a service setting, front-line personnel are in a better position to proactively collect, analyze, disseminate, and act on customer information. Tom Kennedy, vice president of Sovereign Bank USA, highly recommends the involvement of other employees of the firm in its customer selection process (Dorfman, 2005, p. 22):

> *Your colleagues may have relationships with customers and by being part of the process, they will have a more vested interest in hearing comments from these customers.*

Kennedy also explains that their line managers even provide names of the customers that would be the best fit for interaction purpose. Similarly, a well-known US stocks and share investment firm regularly uses front-line employees to hunt for the new service ideas. The product manager of that firm describes his experience this way:

Customers know our firm and services so well that they can inspire our firm's next big idea; our stock advisors and analysts (front-line employees) are ideally situated to spot those innovative ideas through their daily contacts with the clients. You only need to create a culture of idea hunting in your firm.

2.4.1. *How to listen to the voice of customers*

To gain maximum benefits, service managers need to adopt "outcome-based approach" to customer interaction. Under this approach, the managers should instruct their customers to suggest benefits and outcomes they expect the new services to offer rather than focusing on ultimate solutions or the make up of a new service (Ulwick, 2002). The main argument is that the customers cannot tell a firm exactly what a service should look like because they are poor reporters of their own needs (Hamel and Prahalad, 1994; Martin, 1995). In contrast, Havener and Thorpe (1994) suggest that the customers can and do identify their problems, but they usually cannot offer solutions to their problems. Therefore, the task of a service manager is to translate the problem into a service that solves it.

Consider this scenario of an outcome-based interaction with a business customer in a financial service firm. A construction firm needs large working capital loans during the high demand period in spring and summer. But the manager of the firm is not happy with the traditional banks imposing conditions on the seasonal requirements of funds, interest rate structure, and other fees and charges.

Customer: "Our business is seasonal, i.e., mainly spring and summer. During this period I need large amounts of cash and I need them fast and at prevailing market rates. But many financial institutions are slack in approving loans, charge higher rates, and impose unnecessary fees and charges".

Outcome: Financial institutions need to offer the loans without much restriction and approve them fast during the peak demand period.

Service: A new working capital product for all the firms in need of funds due to the cyclical changes or market down turns.

The aforementioned comments of this customer prompted the financial service firm to bundle her desired benefits of large amounts of funds, prevailing market rate, and fast approval even in high demand periods in one single service. A marketing manager described this outcome-based approach that had worked in his firm:

> *While talking to the customers we attempt to uncover the actual problems of the customers; their complaints; their dissatisfaction with the competitors' products. We never ask what the customers want. Because if we do, they will ask for free stuff and lower rates. Those kind of things, you know, like unprofitable requests.*

An emphasis on an outcome-based strategy of interaction results in innovative new services because such a strategy is more proficient in discovering customers' latent and unarticulated needs. An outcome-based strategy also stimulates customers to suggest ideas beyond their usual frame of mind. In contrast, the firms that adopt a solution-based interviewing approach may end up developing incremental innovations. For instance, if a firm ask its customers what type of services they need. The customers may suggest incremental modifications to the existing services because they concentrate on existing solutions and make selections from a familiar service category. That is, the customers become pre-sold to certain concepts and think of the existing service before answering the questions.

2.4.2. *Customer interaction as an iterative process*

It is important that the customers' needs are monitored throughout the course of the NSD, as they rarely remain completely static. Moreover, customer voices are diverse, and these diverse voices must be considered, reconciled, and balanced to develop a successful service. Another common criticism is that the customers cannot clearly articulate their requirements and generally ask for things that are unprofitable, such as lower prices and free services (Martin, 1995). Consequently, an iterative problem solving approach to interaction is needed because it provides the opportunity to challenge, question, and clarify customer input and requirements until they make sense. An iterative approach may also be needed to establish the relative importance of customer information, which may assist in prioritizing the customer needs.

The iterative process may work this way: First, service managers draw on customer need information to generate attributes for desired new services. Next, they develop an initial service blueprint and concept that appears responsive to the results desired by the customers. The raw concept in the form of a blueprint is then tested with the same group of customers for the accuracy of the initially stated needs. If the blueprints do not match the customers' initial response, they are modified in search of a closer match. This iterative cycle is repeated several times until an acceptable match is found. A service manager describes this iterative process this way:

For the simple straightforward ideas, one or two contacts with the customers is sufficient; however for more complex ideas, we meet several times, we even visit our customers in their workplace and try to convert the raw ideas into their working shapes acceptable to both customers and our service delivery staff. There are instances where our customers virtually adopted the role of service developers and devoted a substantial time in NSD.

Consider this iterative interaction process used by a fund and investment-banking firm in developing commercial cards for business-to-business payments. A client firm's need for making payments for its employees' recurring travel expenses triggered the innovation process for the electronic payment cards for businesses. The banking firm obtained an input from the same customer repeatedly. First, the client firm's manager requested an easy 24 hours access to account information via the Internet so as to monitor employees' expenses and make changes to the cardholders' accounts electronically. Next, she emphasized the need to transmit data on spending trends and employee compliance. To satisfy these needs, the firm added expense management tools and reporting capabilities to the product. In another meeting, the customer requested the firm to include other small purchases on the card as well. Finally, the customer pointed out the importance of streamlining the process for all small purchases, travel, and even fleet expenses. In the end, the firm came up with a robust new card concept that offered a single payment platform by combining the travel and entertainment expenses, small purchases, and fleet capabilities in a single card.

2.4.3. *Stages of customer interaction*

In which NSD stages should a manager interact with the customers? Overall, customer interaction may occur at all the stages of NSD, although the intensity of interaction may vary across various stages. Seemingly, customer input into the fuzzy front-end stages of idea generation, screening, and concept development is more critical and useful than the other later stages. Philips, for example, while developing an on-line children's game in Europe, interacted with customers more intensely during the fuzzy front-end stages. Philips sent a team of designers and psychologists in mobile vans to various European countries to interact with both adults and children for their proposed new service. First, they hosted a series of dialogs with the selected group of people intensively to help brainstorm for ideas for the new service. After generating a number of ideas, they screened them with the help of those potential customers and finally selected one new on-line interactive game for children. Later, the team of researchers went back to the potential customers and tested the new service concept on the same children (McKenna, 1995).

Although managers need to interact intensely with customers earlier in the development process, they should make an effort to involve them throughout the process because customers can provide a valuable input at other key stages too. Table 1 presents an exhaustive list of activities that a customer may be able to perform at some of the key stages of the NPD process. The details given in this table may be used as a checklist of the customer interaction activities for most innovation projects.

2.5. Selecting Customers for Interaction

What types of customers should be selected for interaction? There are three criteria that should be considered for customer selection. First, a firm may obtain input from the customers with whom they have a *close relationship* because confidentiality can be a major issue. A service manager can trust close customers to keep sensitive information confidential. A close customer may also display his commitment in conducting NSD activities efficiently. A senior manager of an insurance firm stressed the significance of a relationship this way:

> *We selected the customers whom we knew and we could trust. They were enthusiastic about their involvement and came up with some excellent suggestions about various aspects of service development tasks.*

Second, customers themselves can initiate an innovation by (1) informally discussing ideas with the managers, (2) complaining about existing services, (3) discussing the new service ideas with the sales staffs, and (4) providing other unsolicited suggestions. For example, a major transportation and logistics firm carefully examines all the conversations its phone agents have with the customers and uses the results to develop new service ideas.

Table 1:   Customer activities at key stages of the development process.

Development stages	Activities performed by the customers
Idea generation	Describe needs, problems, and possible solutions; suggest desired features, benefits, and preference in a new service via brainstorming or focus group sessions; identify problems not solved by the existing services; evaluate existing services by suggesting likes and dislikes; identify gaps in the market; provide a new service wish list.
Idea screening	Suggest rough sales guide and market size of various new service ideas; rate the liking, preference, and purchase intents of all the new service concepts; critically react to the concepts by analyzing how they would meet customers' needs; compare the concepts with competitor's offerings; examine the overall salability of a new service.
Business analysis	Limited feedback on financial data, including profitability of the concepts, competitors' data.
Formation of cross functional team	Join top management in selecting team members.
Service design and process/system design	Jointly develop initial service blue prints; review and evaluate the initial service blueprints to crystallize the concepts; suggest improvements by identifying fail points in service delivery; observe the service delivery trial by the front-line service personnel. Compare their wish list with the proposed blue prints of the service.
Personnel training	Observe and participate in mock service delivery process by the key contact employees; suggest improvements.
Service testing and pilot run	Participate in a simulated service delivery process as a customer; compare their wish list with the proposed initial service blue prints.
Test marketing	Provide feedback on various aspects of the marketing strategies and suggest desired improvements; give input to sharpen sales arguments and advertising themes; examine the overall salability of the new service.
Commercialization	Adopt the service as a trial; provide feedback about overall performance of the service along with desired improvements, if any; offer word of mouth communications to other potential users.

Third, lead users are a major source of innovative and profitable new product and service opportunities and thus a key selection criterion for interaction (von Hippel, 1986). The lead user concept is based on the assumptions that (a) the lead users have a real world experience with the needs that future profitable innovations must serve and with attributes they must contain, and (b) they expect to benefit substantially by obtaining a solution to their needs. Since the lead users stand to benefit substantially from the innovations, they will be highly motivated to participate in the interaction process. However, one major concern in lead user interaction can be noted. Because they are not average users, lead users may suggest ideas for the highly specialized services that may have only limited appeal. To answer this concern, several case studies have proposed a systematic process for searching and involving lead users in new service/product development (e.g., von Hippel *et al.*, 1999; Urban and von Hippel, 1988). One key step of that process involves further probes into lead user input by discussing the ideas with a large sample of average customers. A part of these probes involves gauging average customers' reaction to the concepts and their willingness to adopt the new services. A manager described the suggestion this way:

> *When we decided to search and involve leading edge customers, we were fully aware of the many challenges and risks involved. For example, we first took note of input from the leading edge customers and later discussed that input with a number of other customers. When those customers showed some interest only then did we decide to move ahead with the service concepts.*

Finally, a firm may consider multiple characteristics for selecting customers. A lead user, for example, with whom a firm has a close relationship, may initiate the innovations. Customers with multiple characteristics could be the best partners for interaction.

2.6.   Problems in Customer Interaction

Despite many advantages, there are problems and impediments that might occur during the customer interaction process. These impediments include the following:

2.6.1. *Over-customization of a new service*

Listening to customers too closely may create a risk of over-customization of new services, as noted by the manager of a well-known insurance firm (Alam, 2005):

> *We have burnt our fingers; recently a new service failed due to its over-customization. Now we have set the rules of the game in advance; take your ideas and concepts to a larger group of customers and rate the merit of each and every concept carefully.*

It can be argued that a customer's positive reactions to a service concept should not be construed as an intention to use or buy that service because no money is changing hands; thus, no real commitment is necessary. Hence, one should probe customers' initial positive reactions to the new service concepts through further market studies.

2.6.2. *Confidentiality*

Customers through the course of interaction might get access to certain confidential information and proprietary skills. There is the potential that these customers might reveal the information intentionally or unintentionally to competitors. An interaction program requires mutual trust and open, collaborative relationships, as well as standards for capturing and exchanging information. This problem can also be resolved by selecting customers with whom the company has a *close relationship*.

2.6.3. *Identification of customers*

Locating appropriate customers for interaction is another major problem because an intimate knowledge of the market and customer contacts is necessary. A firm also needs to consider all different types of customers, end-users, and even customers' customers for interaction.

2.6.4. *Lack of customer cooperation and motivation*

Customers may be disinclined to cooperate because of the conflicting objectives and intents of managers versus customers. For example, many service managers ask this question: "why would customers agree to take time out of their busy schedules to think about your innovation?" The answer is that if the customers feel part of a team and believe that they are influencing a firm's innovation process, they will cooperate. The managers of a US health insurance firm, Harvard Pilgrim Health Care Inc., motivate customers by simply demonstrating that Harvard Pilgrim is listening to them (Dorfman, 2005). Customers may also cooperate in order to exchange feedback with other customers and remain on the cutting edge of new applications and innovations.

To improve the overall process of customer interaction, the experts suggest staying focused on a limited number of somewhat homogeneous service development projects. Moreover, specific goals for the interaction should be set for each stage of the development process, as these remarks of an NSD consultant suggest:

> In my 20 years of consultancy I have seen many managers setting their aims too broadly. They try to cover as much territory as possible when it comes to the customer interaction. The goals quickly become lofty and the managers get lost in airy aimless interaction with the customers. Instead the goals should be to solve the specific problems at hand in the simplest way possible.

2.7. Conclusions

The success of an NSD hinges on a firm's ability to decipher the needs of a demanding, fickle, and volatile marketplace and to respond with superior and differentiated offerings. Firms should therefore adopt the axiom that says "To be successful, firms should know their customers better than their customers know themselves." As a corollary to this axiom, customer interaction should become a key element in a firm's innovation activity. This chapter has proposed several customer interaction strategies to outline a course of action that managers can apply in their quest for successful new services.

References

Alam, I (2006). Removing the fuzziness from the fuzzy front-end of service innovations through customer interactions. *Industrial Marketing Management*, 35(4), 468–480.

Dignam, C (2002). Prosumer power. *Marketing*, March 14, 24–25.

Dorfman, S (2005). Investment in customer advisory programs. *Marketing News*, 39(8), 22–24.

Goffin, K and F Lemke (2004). Uncovering your customers' hidden need. *European Business Forum*, 18, 45.

Griffin, A and JR Hauser (1993). The voice of customer, *Marketing Science*. 12(1), 1–27.

Hamel, G and CK Prahalad (1994). *Competing for the Future*. Boston. MA: Harvard Business School Press.

Havener, C and M Thorpe (1994). Customers can tell you what they want. *Management Review*, 83(12), 42–45.

Marlin, S (2004). Closer to customers. *Information Week*, October 18, 81–84.

Martin, J (1995). Ignore your customers. *Fortune*, May 1, 123–126.

McCarthy, J (2002). Innovative service. *Info World*, 24(31), 40.

McKenna R (1995). Real-time marketing. *Harvard Business Review*, July–August: 87–95.

Shermach, K (2005). Delta uses mileage plan to boost customer satisfaction. *Marketing News*, 39(8): 21 and 24.

Simonson, I (1993). Get closer to your customers by understanding how they make choices. *California Management Review*, Summer: 68–84.

Teresko, J (2003). Interconnecting innovation. *Industry Week*, December, 26–33.

Ulwick, AW (2002). Turn customer input into innovation. *Harvard Business Review*, January, 91–97.

Urban, G and E von Hippel (1988). Lead user analyses for the development of new industrial products. *Management Science*, 5, 569–82.

von Hippel, E (1986). Lead users: A source of novel product concepts. *Management Science*, 32(July), 791–805.

von Hippel, ES Thomke and M Sonnack (1999). Creating breakthroughs at 3M. *Harvard Business Review*, September–October, 3–9.

3

The Role of the Customer in the Development Process

Bodil Sandén, *Anders Gustafsson*[†] *and Lars Witell*[‡]

Service Research Center, Karlstad University, Sweden
*bodil.sanden@kau.se
[†]anders.gustafsson@kau.se
[‡]lars.witell@kau.se

3.1. Introduction

Although the use of customer information has been recognized as a key success factor for new product development, the differences in the use of customer information in different market contexts is mostly unknown. In a recent overview of development practices in the US, Cooper *et al.* (2004) conclude that the use of customer information is a discriminant between companies with high and low product and service development performance. The areas where the largest differences can be found concern information on customer needs, wants, and problems and information on competitors (pricing, products, and strategies). Differences have been found between the consumer market and business market for product development practices. First, concerning product strategy, Hultink *et al.* (1999) conclude that there are differences in product introduction. Successful consumer products take longer to develop and they are introduced into slightly slower growth markets (but still growing faster than GNP). Successful industrial products appear to be slightly faster to develop, introduced to lower cost, and increase penetration in higher growth markets in the maturity phase, but only when there are few competitors. Second, Griffin (2002) concludes in an investigation of lead times in product development that consumer goods always take less time to develop than do business market goods, although the relative difference between the two diminishes as one moves from the more innovative to the less innovative projects. Differences between industrial and consumer markets regarding development of new goods and services have been identified. Our research contributes to deepen the knowledge of possible differences in customer involvement between different markets.

Most of the research on customer involvement is based on case studies and is conducted in a single industry setting. Our knowledge is limited about the extent that customer involvement is practiced, the types of customers involved, how they are involved, and perceived benefits and problems, etc. Consequently, the objective of this chapter is to provide a baseline analysis of the customer's role in the new product and service development process. Drawing on previous research in market orientation and new product and service development, the chapter reports on an empirical investigation of how 366 Swedish organizations involve their customers in the development process. Our results provide evidence that most companies involve their customers in the development process to some extent, but there are large differences between companies and industries concerning how and the extent that customers are involved.

3.2. Research Design

The sample for our investigation of customer involvement practices included Swedish firms from various industries and of various sizes. The survey was distributed via e-mail to R&D and marketing managers in Swedish firms. E-mail addresses for managers were obtained from PAR Affärsregister AB. Telephone interviews were conducted with 100 managers of the non-respondents to find out how many of the companies conduct development projects. Of the 100 managers, 37 said that their company does not conduct any development projects. As a result, the 366 companies that responded constitute an effective response rate of 26.4%.

The responding firms represent both goods and service firms in the following industries: wood, pulp and paper, chemicals, plastic products, fabricated metal products, machinery and equipment, electrical and optical equipment, construction, hotels, transport, renting and real estate, data, construction services, and business services. The major industries represented in our study are construction services (20%), construction (11%), machinery and equipment (7%), fabricated metal products (7%), and wood, pulp, and paper (6%). The firms range in size from only a few employees to several thousand. Forty-five percent are small firms (less than 50 employees), 44% are medium sized firms (51–1000 employees), and 11% are large firms (more than 1001 employees). About 76% of the firms mainly work in a business-to-business market, and 24% are actors in the consumer market.

The final questionnaire used in our survey included 52 questions. Most of the questions were close-ended, although some open-ended questions were included to solicit verbal comment. The questions were first pre-tested with five colleagues, and then a pilot study was conducted with a subset of managers. The questions covered a wide range of areas related to customer involvement, ranging from what type of customers are involved and what methods are used, to what degree customers are involved and supporting and inhibiting factors. Subjective performance measures of the development practices were also collected to enable an analysis of the relationship between customer involvement and business performance.

3.3. Customer Involvement in New Product and Service Development: Previous Research and Results

Through service research, the view of the customer has somewhat changed. Instead of being seen as a receiver of an output, the customer is described as a co-producer who influences the outcome of the service (Normann, 1984; Toffler, 1980). It can easily be argued that since the customer influences the perceived quality of service delivery, the customer should be a natural participant in the development process. This view, however, has not been particularly evident in the literature on new service development or in new product development literature. But there are of course exceptions. Von Hippel has been a pioneer in the field with his research on lead users (von Hippel, 1986, 1989) and later toolkits for user innovation (von Hippel, 2001; Thomke and von Hippel, 2002). More recently, and due to the increased complexity of modern development activities, customer involvement in new product and service development and supporting methods has received greater interest (see e.g., Alam, 2002; Nambisian, 2002; Deszca *et al.*, 1999; Martin and Horne, 1995; Leonard and Rayport, 1997; Thomke, 2003). Customer involvement is defined here as those processes, deeds, and interactions where a product or service provider collaborates with current (or potential) customers at the program, project, and/or stage level of innovation, to anticipate customers' latent needs and develop new product or service accordingly. In this chapter, a lot of work practices concerning the use of customer information are covered. Some of these practices, such as the use of surveys, are not in the core of customer involvement according to our definition. If a number of work practices are put on a continuum, the use of internal information and surveys are considered to be of a low degree of customer involvement, while work practices related to the lead user method are considered to be of a high degree of customer involvement.

Customer involvement entails a different approach to value creation in new product and service development. In a development project where the customer is involved to a high degree, value is created interactively among the parties. This implies a refined role distribution, a longer relationship, and the possibility of acquiring new knowledge (Wikström, 1995). It is different from the traditional value chain that views value creation as linear and transitive (Ramirez, 1999).

The elements of customer involvement that we highlight in this chapter are illustrated in Fig. 1. The two arrows symbolize an on-going, iterative development program where development projects build up the product and service portfolio of a firm. Customer involvement requires making a decision about the following factors: what type of customers to involve, to what extent they should be involved, and how it should be done, for example, what techniques to use. The broken line illustrates the organizational context, in which a firm decides on the strategy of the development organization. The motives to involve customers (referred to here as supporting factors) are also important and will determine how customer involvement is carried out and what results can be achieved. Finally, there might be problems associated with customer involvement (referred to here as inhibiting factors). These issues will be addressed by reviewing previous research and comparing it with our findings.

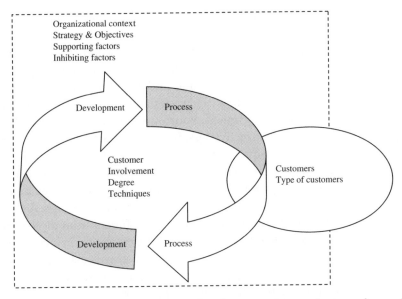

Figure 1: Elements of customer involvement in product and service development.

3.3.1. *Different types of customers*

A traditional approach of product and service development is to obtain information from representative customers at the center of the intended target market. Companies often obtain information about customer needs only, and assign manufacturers with the task of generating ideas for solutions leading to new products (Lilien *et al.*, 2002). Company employees are required to translate needs into solutions that should fit these needs. In customer involvement literature, research suggests that the types of customers who are most conducive may vary according to market characteristics. By studying high technology industrial markets, von Hippel (1986) suggests that average users who are selected to provide input data through market research are limited by their own real-world experience and are therefore unlikely to generate novel ideas or concepts. Lead users, on the other hand, present strong needs that will become general in a market place months or years in the future. As there are no products or services available on the market to fulfill their needs, lead users often develop a solution on their own and can therefore provide design data as well. Consequently, the lead user process takes a different approach from that of traditional methods, collecting information about both needs and solutions from the leading edges of the target market and from markets facing similar problems in a more extreme form. In slow-moving industrial markets, "average users" may provide satisfactory input to the development process (Gales and Mansour-Cole, 1995). Gruner and Homburg (2000) explored the relationship between customer characteristics and new product success in a machine industry context. Four customer characteristics were used, including technical attractiveness, financial attractiveness, closeness of relationship with the customer, and lead user characteristics. They found that financially attractive customers, lead users, and close customers had a positive impact on new product success. Technically attractive customers, on the other hand, had a negative impact on new product success. A possible explanation is that they have needs that are different from those of the market in general and therefore can mislead the company. In a consumer context, Ciccantellli and Magidson (1993) used average customers, claiming that they are often best equipped to design functional products and services for situations with which they are familiar.

Nambisian (2002) lists selection and recruitment of customers as one of the great challenges of customer involvement. In our investigation of customer involvement in the Swedish industry, a majority of the companies that actively involve customers primarily involve customers with some type of expertise, for example, lead users. Some companies choose to primarily work with financially attractive customers, whereas about 30% of the companies do not make any special selection of customers. An overview of the results from the investigated companies is provided in Fig. 2. For some companies, the strategy is to work with the customers who are interested in co-operation or to co-operate with the customers who are available at a specific moment. The literature suggests that the types of customers who are most conducive may vary according to market characteristics. When comparing different types of market characteristics, that is, B2B or B2C, we found that companies on the business market are more likely than companies on the consumer market to use customers with a special expertise (Chi-square $= 23.9$, $p < 0.01$). This is consistent with the findings presented by von Hippel (1986). On the contrary, companies on the consumer market work with financially attractive customers in their development process to a greater extent. This finding is also supported by Gruner and Homburg (2000), although they investigated customer characteristics in a machine industry context. A possible explanation for the selection of financially attractive customers could be that customer involvement is seen as

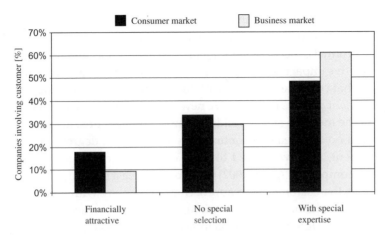

Figure 2:   An overview of the type of customers that are involved in the development process.

an opportunity to build and sustain long-term relationships (Alam, 2000),
since the purpose of any business is to attract and satisfy customers at a
profit (Drucker, 1954).

3.3.2. *Degree of customer involvement*

Another important element in our framework is the intensity or degree of
customer involvement. Alam (2002) argues that the degree of customer
involvement can be described on a continuum ranging from passive
acquisition of customer input, feedback on specific issues, and extensive
consultation with customers to full customer representation in the project.
As we move along the continuum, the sharp distinction between customers
and designers ceases to exist. In such a role, customers become agents of
value transformation rather than objects (Nambisian, 2002). Alam (2002)
found that most companies are in the middle of the continuum or more
toward the higher end of the continuum. The two most preferred levels of
involvement were extensive consultation and feedback on specific issues.
The companies' choices of degree of customer involvement were chosen
because they are less expensive, less time consuming, and are much easier
to manage.

Gruner and Homburg (2000) measured the intensity of customer interaction in the different phases of the product development process, including idea generation, product concept development, project definition,

engineering, prototype testing, and market launch. Their results show that a high degree of customer interaction in certain stages, including prototype testing, product concept development, idea generation, and market launch has a positive impact on new product success. The main implication of their study is that customer involvement during the early and late stages of the development process can improve new product success, whereas involvement in the medium stages yields no impact on new product success.

Based on the idea of a continuum with different degrees of customer involvement, we investigated to what degree customers are involved in Swedish companies. Alam (2002) described the least intense side of the continuum as the customer who approaches a company with a new product or service that he has developed on his own as passive acquisition of customer input. In recent research on toolkits for user innovation (von Hippel, 2001; Thomke and von Hippel, 2002), it is argued that it is costly to transfer sticky information from the customer site to the company site. To minimize these costs, companies should provide customers with special toolkits, that is, user-friendly tools integrated into a package which enable customers to run repeated trial and error experiments rapidly and efficiently. Following this line of reasoning, we argue that the scenario described by Alam (2002) (that a customer approach a company with an already developed product or service) should in fact be placed at the higher end of the continuum.

Figure 3 displays the extent to which customers are involved in the development activities of Swedish companies. We have tried to view customer involvement as a continuum from no involvement to full involvement where customers develop new product or service on their

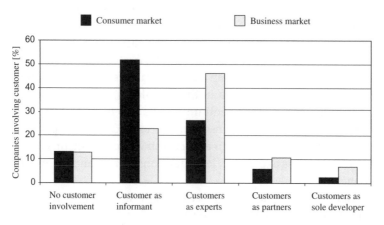

Figure 3:   The degree of customer involvement in Swedish companies.

own. About 13% of the companies do not involve customers in their development processes. Their products are developed based on the company's core competence and/or new technology. About 30% of the companies maintain that customers are involved by means of market research activities such as surveys, focus groups, and interviews. Using customers as experts in part of the process is the most common way they are involved. This finding is supported by Alam (2000). The highest degrees of customer involvement are also the least common ways to use customer information in the development process. About 10% of the companies have customers represented in the project team where they contribute with their knowledge and competence throughout the entire process. An additional 6% of the companies state that a large proportion of their new products and services are actually developed solely by customers. Overall, these findings are different from those of Alam (2000). Although we found that most companies fall in the middle and the least intense end of the continuum, Alam (2000) found that most companies fall in the middle of the continuum and also toward the intense end of the continuum. One possible explanation could be the context. Alam (2000) investigated one particular industry, that is, financial services, while we have studied a variety of industries. Pitta (2001) and Nambisian (2002) states that it is now relatively well established that the usefulness of customers as a resource varies with the maturity of the technology and the alignment of the product line with the current customer base (Christensen, 1997; Leonard-Barton, 1995). When both dimensions are high (continuous innovation), customers are an excellent source of innovation, whereas when both dimensions are low (i.e., evolving technologies and emerging markets), the value of current customers as a resource is limited. The context will therefore influence customer involvement practice.

When investigating differences between companies operating under different market characteristics, that is, B2B and B2C, some differences can be identified (Chi-square $= 27.5$, $p < 0.01$). A majority (51.8%) of the B2C companies involve customers through the use of traditional market research techniques (customers as informants). Twenty-seven percent of the respondents state that they use customers as experts during part of the development process, and 6% work with customers as partners. In a business to business context, most respondents (46%) indicate they use customers first and foremost as experts, whereas 11% work with customers as partners, and 7% state that a majority of their new products and/or services are actually developed by customers. One relevant question to ask is how many of the surveyed companies actually view customer involvement

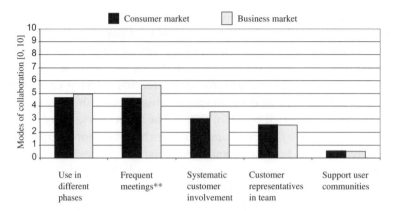

Figure 4:   Modes of collaboration concerning customer involvement (*p < 0.05, **p < 0.01).

in accordance to our definition of the concept. From our perspective, the collaboration between the company and the customer is the key to success. Consequently, only companies that work with customers as experts, partners, or co-developers are using customer involvement in accordance with our definition. This kind of work practice is most common for companies in an industrial market, which is natural because long term relationships with few customers are one of the characteristics of industrial markets.

In addition to investigating the degree of customer involvement on an overall level, we investigated the actual mode of collaboration with customers (see Fig. 4). The respondents were asked to rate to what extent they carried out certain activities related to collaboration with customers. The most common responses were frequent meetings with customers, collaboration with the customer in different phases throughout the development process, and systematic customer involvement. There was not much support of user communities on the Internet. The one aspect where we found statistically significant differences between B2B companies and B2C companies, concerned frequent meetings with customers ($t = 2.63$, $p < 0.01$). An active participation of the customer in project meetings with the development team was more common in companies on the industrial market.

3.3.3. *Techniques*

One important feature of customer involvement is the methods or techniques that are used throughout the development process. A lot of critic has been mentioned that traditional market research techniques do not deliver information about customers' latent needs (e.g., Dahlsten, 2003; Flint, 2002; Leonard, 1995; Slater and Narver, 1998). There are few empirical studies, however, to support this claim. In a study of how project novelty influences the new product development process, Tidd and Bodley (2002) found that focus groups, partnering customers, and lead users are considered to be more effective in the concept development phase for high novelty projects. They also found that for concept development, only about a third of the firms exploit user developers or customer partnerships; those that do rated them as being highly effective.

In his work on customer orientation, Johnson (1998) distinguishes between reactive and proactive techniques of collecting and using customer information. Many of today's traditional data collecting methods aim to chart the customer's relation and attitude toward the current service offer and can be considered to be *reactive*. These methods are very useful when a company would like to get a deep understanding of how the customers view the offer and the service provider (Gustafsson *et al.*, 1999). Another collection of approaches concerns the work of trying to predict what product or services the customer would want to have in the future. A method that aims to fulfill this need is called *proactive*. Proactive methods aim to get a deeper understanding of the customers, that is, the values that lie behind a choice of a product. As implied in the beginning of the section, market-oriented businesses should combine reactive techniques with proactive techniques in order to be better equipped to discover customers' latent needs (Slater and Narver, 1998) and to drive generative learning (Senge, 1990).

One useful technique for identifying latent needs is observing customers' use of products or services in normal routines (Deszca *et al.*, 1999; Slater and Narver, 1998), also called empathic design (Leonard and Rayport, 1997). Empathic design is the creation of new products or services based on an understanding of customer's unarticulated needs. It is a process in which not only the product developers themselves, but also the trained anthropologists and ethnographers, observe potential customers in their own environment. Empathic design has three unique attributes: First, people give non-verbal cues of their feelings as well as spontaneous, unsolicited comments that are stimulated by an actual product, service, or prototype. Second, trained observers with a knowledge of technical possibilities can see solutions to unarticulated needs or problems, which users could not conceive. Third, it occurs in a natural setting and does not interrupt the usual flow of activity. The observation of customers in real situations can access five types of information which traditional market research cannot. First, what trigger is used? What is it that makes people use the product or service? Are they using it in the way that is intended and expected? Second, how does the user interact with the environment? Third, does the user reinvent or redesign the product or service to better suit his/her own purpose? Four, how does intangible attributes of the product or service influence the user? Finally, observation could reveal users encountering a problem which they do not realize can be fixed or may not even view as a problem (Leonard, 1995; Leonard and Rayport, 1997).

Alam (2002) identified the following six modes of customer involvement: face-to-face interviews, user visits and meetings, brainstorming, users' observations and feedback, focus group discussions, as well as phone, faxes, and e-mails. In-depth interviews and user visits were the most common because they were stated to be easy and inexpensive. In contrast, focus group discussions were the least preferred technique because it was considered to be both expensive and time consuming. The brainstorming sessions were conducted only at the idea generation and screening stages, whereas user observation and feedback were used only at personnel training and commercialization stages. Finally, the use of phone/fax and e-mail was another least preferred mode and was used only at strategic planning and business analysis stages. The techniques identified include both formal and informal market research techniques.

We investigated the following techniques: internally collected information and knowledge about customers, surveys, customer interviews, observations, and the lead user method (see Fig. 5). Internally collected information was given the highest ratings or highest frequency of usage, followed by observation. The lead user method was found to be the third most commonly used technique. From previous interviews with Swedish managers, however, we know that the lead user method is not a well known technique, so we defined it as "working with leading customers," which is a more general definition than the one provided by von Hippel (1986). Surveys and interviews were stated as being the least common techniques.

Figure 5 shows the differences in the various techniques used by companies operating under different market characteristics. Companies operating in the consumer market, use surveys ($t = 5.03, p < 0.01$) and internally collected information ($t = 2.20, p < 0.05$) to a greater extent compared to companies at the business market. On the other hand, B2B companies use the lead user method more often compared to B2C companies ($t = 3.02$,

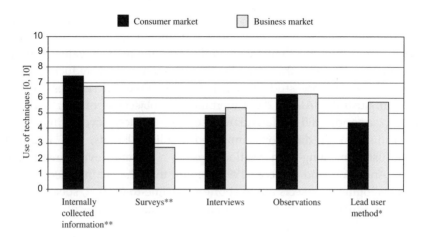

Figure 5:   Use of techniques for customer involvement (*$p < 0.05$, **$p < 0.01$).

$p < 0.01$). This is consistent with the results of previous research on lead users, which has been mainly carried out in an industrial context (e.g., von Hippel, 1986). The differences are also consistent with our results concerning different degrees of customer involvement. B2C companies tend to use their customers more as passive informants compared to B2B companies that more actively engage their customers. We found no significant differences between companies in different markets concerning the use of customer interviews and observations.

3.3.4. *Supporting factors of customer involvement*

One important element of our framework is why companies choose to involve customers in the first place. Research displays multiple objectives in terms of customer involvement. These aspects can be viewed as beliefs and not necessarily as facts about what customer involvement may lead to. The basic idea behind customer involvement is that by spending time with customers and actually taking part in activities with them, deep insights have an opportunity to emerge (Flint, 2002). Tacit, sticky information and insights cannot be detached from the social context in which they are generated. Therefore, the transfer of tacit, sticky information and knowledge requires deeper interactions and processes of communication, for example, customer involvement (von Hippel, 1994; Gales and Mansour-Cole, 1995). Based

on previous research, Magnusson (2003) identified six major objectives
of customer involvement: new ideas and inventions, testing ideas, concepts and prototypes, enhanced understanding of user value, mutual
learning, enhancing the customer's competence, and reducing cycle
time. Based on case study research from 12 financial services companies in Australia, Alam (2002) identified six objectives of user involvement: superior and differentiated service, reduced cycle time, user
education, rapid diffusion, improved public relations, and building
and sustaining long-term relationships. In a system development context, Anderson and Crocca (1993) report that the main objectives of
co-development projects are to shorten the time-to-market, speed up the
learning process about an application domain, and to get feedback from a
real-life testing ground.

In our study, the primary reason why the respondents engage in
customer involvement is that it provides an opportunity to market the
organization and the new products and services (see Fig. 6). The second reason is that the involvement of users leads to more user friendly
products and services. A belief that it saves money, that it can result in
reduced cycle time, and that customers are more innovative were additional
incentives for engaging in customer involvement activities. The fact that
competitors involve customers in the development process was the least
common explanation for engaging in customer involvement activities.
There are two aspects where we find significant differences between companies on the two types of markets: B2C companies seem to feel that when
involving customers in the development, their products become more innovative ($t = 2.45, p < 0.05$) and user friendly ($t = 1.98, p < 0.05$). It is only
possible to speculate as to why these differences occur. One reason may

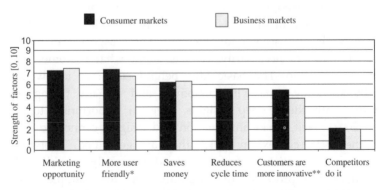

Figure 6:   An overview of the strength of supporting factors (*$p < 0.05$, **$p < 0.01$).

be that B2C companies are further from their customers and their use and misuse of products.

3.3.5. *Inhibiting factors of customer involvement*

The last part of our framework concerns the problems, or inhibiting factors, in adopting customer involvement practices. Martin *et al.* (1999) argue that customer involvement increases input uncertainty due to the diversity of customer demand and customer disposition to participate. Nambisian (2002) notes a long list of challenges in terms of customer involvement: the selection of customer, the creation of appropriate incentives for customers, capturing customer knowledge, increased level of project uncertainty, customers may need to possess higher levels of product/technology knowledge, customer co-creators will need to be well integrated with internal NPD teams, customer contributions can be limited by the high cost of providing facilities of mechanisms to structure and channel customers' inputs, and ensuring the involvement of a diverse set of customers.

In their work on the involvement of lead users in product development, Lilien *et al.* (2002) provide three major implications. First, ideas developed via the lead user process might have low organizational fit with the technical, production, and market environment and hence be less likely to be judged worthy of funding by the management. Second, a process built upon distilling new ideas from lead user needs and prototype solutions would result in ideas that could not be effectively patented by the company. Third, many lead user participants express concerns about the greater time and effort involved in the lead user idea generation method relative to alternative approaches, and the impact of that time and effort on managers' willingness to use the method. Also analyzing the lead user method, Olson and Bakke (2001) offer some suggestions why an IT company that had used the method with successful results, did not continue to use it. The non-technical product concepts generated by lead users were seen as ambiguous and hence overly simplistic and less valuable by the new product development personnel. The technical language spoken by the new product personnel increased the inertia of old technology push by making it more prestigious and comfortable to plan new products with their technology suppliers. There was no pressure from market conditions, the firm's financial status, or management to make permanent changes to established routines. Hsia *et al.* (1993) conclude that there is a wide gap between the state of the art and the state of the practice in terms of user involvement in systems development. They list a number of reasons: requirements are difficult to uncover, requirements change, some methods being used are inappropriate, training is insufficient, project schedule is always unrealistically tight, developers lack confidence in requirements engineering, and communications barriers separate developers and users.

In our empirical investigation of Swedish companies, we found that the increased workload was the primary reason for companies to not engage in customer involvement. In a study of the implementation and use of QFD, Ettlie and Johnson (1994) provide empirical support that firms that actively work to improve their customer focused method, can actually lose customer focus in the short run. Initially, new and different ways of working will lead to more work, but after a period of implementation, a better understanding of the customer will arise. Customer involvement is also found to be difficult and complicated, and available market research techniques are perceived as insufficient. Another perceived problem is organizational factors such as an organizational structure or culture that does not foster customer involvement. The least common inhibiting factors are an increased uncertainty and an anxiety that customers might steal the ideas of new products and services. The level of the inhibiting factors are perceived similarly in both B2B and B2C companies, except for the anxiety that customers might steal the ideas of new products and services that is perceived to be stronger for B2B companies ($t = 2.72, p < 0.01$). One possible explanation is that B2B companies use a different set of techniques compared

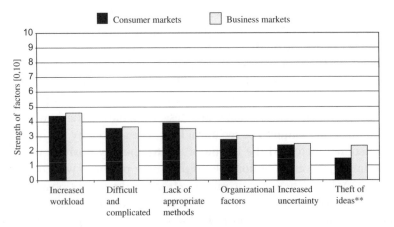

Figure 7:   An overview of the strength of inhibiting factors (*$p < 0.05$, **$p < 0.01$).

to B2C companies, that is, they work much more with the lead user methodology. The closer relationship between the company and its customers on
the industrial market provides the customer with a lot of knowledge about
the company. The higher level of anxiety, about customers stealing the ideas
of the company, makes the choice of customers much more important for
B2B companies (Fig. 7).

3.3.6. *The results of customer involvement*

As the last part of our empirical investigation of customer involvement
in Swedish companies, we investigated whether companies with a higher
degree of customer involvement receive a payoff in their performance. In
this part of our investigation, we defined a company with a high degree
of customer involvement as a company that uses the different modes of
collaboration, that is, that have organizational routines aimed at involving the customer to a large extent. The different facets of organizational
performance that were investigated were changes during the last three
years concerning market share, financial performance, customer satisfaction, customer complaints, and customer loyalty.

All companies have perceived major improvements during the last
three years. This holds for all companies without considering their degree
of customer involvement (see Fig. 8). But a comparison of companies with

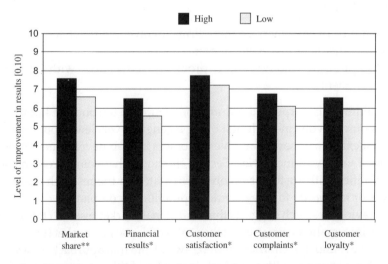

Figure 8:   A comparison of improvements of performance measures between companies with different degrees of customer involvement (*$p < 0.05$, **$p < 0.01$).

a high degree of customer involvement (collaboration > 4.6) and a low degree of customer involvement (collaboration < 4.6) shows that companies that collaborate heavily with their customers have perceived much larger improvements in results. There are statistically significant differences concerning all results: market share ($t = 3.0$, $p < 0.01$), financial results ($t = 2.44$, $p < 0.01$), customer satisfaction ($t = 2.15$, $p < 0.05$), customer complaints ($t = 2.24$, $p < 0.01$), and customer loyalty ($t = 2.17$, $p < 0.01$). We can conclude that companies utilizing a higher degree of customer involvement in their development process perceived a larger improvement in their performance during the last three years. An analysis reveals that these differences between companies with different degrees of customer involvement are larger for B2B companies when compared to B2C companies. This could be attributed to a higher degree of use of techniques such as the lead user method in B2B companies, but it could also be attributed to the lower sample size for B2C companies.

3.4.   Discussion

The objective of this chapter is to analyze the role of the customer, given by the organization, in the new product and service development process. Based on an e-survey to 366 Swedish organizations, the following issues were addressed:

- What type of customers do these firms involve and to what extent?
- How is customer involvement carried out?
- What are the motives and problems associated with customer involvement?

By fulfilling this purpose, the study contributes to the body of knowledge of customer involvement. It first offers a general overview about how and to what extent companies involve customers in their development process across a variety of industries. Second, it shows that some problems and possibilities with customer involvement stated in the research are not so severe or important for the general population of companies.

   Previous research suggests that traditional market research techniques collect information from users at the center of the target market (Lilien et al., 2002). We found that 60% have moved away from that approach to carefully selecting customers with a particular expertise. Still, it is surprising to find that as many as 27% do not make any special selection of customers. This may indicate a non-structured, informal customer involvement approach. We could ask these companies about the effectiveness of their approach and whether or not it could be more effective to select customers more carefully.

Customer involvement researchers have different views on what constitutes customer involvement. Some researchers believe that customer involvement involves all types of market research (e.g., Alam, 2002). Others argue that customer involvement is different from traditional market research because it is a proactive approach of learning from and with customers to uncover latent needs (Matthing *et al.*, 2004). Also, from an empirical perspective, customer involvement is a complex notion. When interviewing managers, almost all claim that they involve customers in their development process. When describing how they involve customers, however, it appears that many view and use the customer as a passive informant. The results from this empirical investigation of Swedish companies show that the perspective on the customer may be changing from a passive informant to an active participant. Still, 30% maintain that customers are involved by means of market research activities such as surveys, focus groups, and interviews. However, 50% use customers as experts or partners in the development process. It is interesting to find that the majority of these companies are B2B companies. Thomke and von Hippel (2002) maintain that it can sometimes be costly to transfer information from the customer to the company and suggests that companies can delegate large parts of the development activities to the customers. Our results show that in 6% of the investigated companies, a large proportion of their products are actually developed solely by customers.

In terms of market research techniques, we found that companies rely on internally collected information, such as information from sales personnel or customer complaints. The second most popular technique is observations. In our empirical investigation, we did not define observation, so we can assume that the respondents' answers cover everything from informal observations by, for example, sales personnel and management, to formal ethnographical studies using video cameras to document data and behaviorists to interpret data. As formal ethnographical studies are highly expensive, we can also assume that a large proportion of these observations are of an informal character. The lead user method was found to be the third most commonly used technique. From previous interviews with Swedish managers, however, we know that the lead user method is not familiar, so we defined it as "working with leading customers", which is a more general definition than the one provided by von Hippel (1986).

Surveys and interviews were stated as being the least common techniques. We can only speculate that these results could be due to the fact that the traditional market research techniques do not deliver the level of detail needed to develop new products and services, and therefore, only minor improvements are the result (Harari, 1994). "Lack of appropriate techniques" was also stated as one of the main concerns in terms of customer involvement.

We were surprised to find that the primary reason why the respondents engaged in customer involvement was that it provided an opportunity to market the organization. According to the literature, the main advantage of customer involvement is the possibility of developing deep customer insights in terms of customers' expressed and unexpressed needs, preferences, and behavior, that is, knowledge that is vital if development efforts are to be successful (de Brentani and Cooper, 1992). Literature studies reveal a number of perceived problems with customer involvement. We found that the respondents' primary reasons to avoid engaging in customer involvement was increased workload, followed by the perception of customer involvement as being difficult and complicated.

In terms of companies operating under different market conditions, that is, B2B or B2C, we found some important differences. About a third of the companies on the consumer market involve customers who have a special expertise. About a fourth of the companies do not make a special selection of customers, and about 14% choose to involve financially attractive customers. About half of the B2C companies involve customers through the use of traditional market research techniques (customers as informants). About a fourth of the companies use customers as experts during parts of the development process, and 6% of the companies work with customers as partners during the development process. B2C companies use internally collected information, observations, and interviews most frequently. They also use surveys to a greater extent than companies operating in a business market do. Companies in the business market, on the other hand, are more likely than companies in the consumer market to use customers with a special expertise. They involve customers as experts, and are more likely to involve customers as partners. Seven percent state that a majority of their new products and/or services are actually developed by customers. B2B companies use internally collected information, observation, and the lead user method. It is not difficult to imagine that B2B companies have closer relationships with their customers and to a lesser extent deliver their product to a mass market. It is also easy to imagine that B2B customers have more incentives, at least monetary ones, and time to participate in different types of product development projects. Improved products may lead to considerable cost savings for a B2B company.

The managerial implications of our research can guide marketing and R&D managers in their search for new products and services. First, customer involvement is not for everyone, for example, if a competitive advantage primarily originates from the development of new technology. In our study, 13% of the companies do not involve customers in the development process as their products are developed based on the company's core competence and/or new technology. If a competitive advantage is built on developing new products and services from new technology based on deep customer insights, however, a customer involvement approach should be considered. In order to succeed, it requires a truly proactive market-oriented organization. Second, customer involvement potentially offers a number of important benefits besides a marketing opportunity, for example, uncovering customer latent and expressed needs, superior and differentiated products and services, generation and test of new ideas, reduced cycle time, and enhanced customer competence (Alam, 2002). Managers should carefully decide what the objectives are and work accordingly. Third, the techniques are the means by which customer information and knowledge are created. To achieve the previously stated objectives, the ways of working should be designed to facilitate customer knowledge development (Nambisian, 2002). Finally, a customer involvement approach integrates market research and R&D. Consequently, different knowledge and skills are needed to collect, interpret, and learn from customer knowledge. The R&D function should be developed to a multi-functional site including marketers, engineers, and behaviorists, etc. (Griffin, 1997).

Our findings also raise new issues to be addressed in future research. In particular, empirical research is needed to discover the depth of customer involvement in the product and service development process and to investigate the empirical relationship between customer involvement and performance measures such as new service success, degree of innovation, and financial results. More research is also needed to determine where in the development process customer involvement is most effective. Also, under what circumstances (contextual factors) is customer involvement appropriate and when should it be avoided? Finally, the matter of how to organize customer involvement projects needs to be further explored.

References

Alam, I (2002). An exploratory investigation of user involvement in new service development. *Journal of the Academy of Marketing Science*, 30(3), 250–261.

Anderson, WL and WT Crocca (1993). Engineering practice and co development of product prototypes. *Communications of the ACM*, 36(6), 49–56.

Ciccantelli, S and J Magidson (1993). From experience: Consumer idealized design: involving consumers in the product development process. *Journal of Product Innovation Management*, 10(4), 341–347.

Cooper, RG and EJ Kleinschmidt (1987). New products: What separates winners from losers? *Journal of Product Innovation Management*, 4, 169–184.

Dahlsten, F (2003). Avoiding the customer satisfaction rut. *Sloan Management Review*, 44(4), 73–77.

Dahlsten, F (2004). Hollywood wives revisited: A study of customer-involvement in the XC90 project at Volvo Cars. *European Journal of Innovation Management*, 7(2), 141–149.

de Brentani, U and RG Cooper (1992). Developing successful new financial services for businesses. *Industrial Marketing Management*, 21, 321–241.

Deszca, G, H Munro and H Noori (1999). Developing breakthrough products: Challenged and options for market assessment. *Journal of Operations Management*, 17(6), 613–630.

Drucker, P (1954). *The Practice of Management*. New York: Harper and Row.

Ettlie, JE and MD Johnson (1994). Product development benchmarking versus customer focus in application of quality function deployment. *Marketing Letters*, 5(2), 107–116.

Flint, DJ (2002). Compressing new product success-to-success cycle time: Deep customer value understanding and idea generation. *Industrial Marketing Management*, 31(4), 305–316.

Gales, L and D Mansour-Cole (1991). User involvement in innovation projects: A reassessment using information processing. *Academy of Management Proceedings*.

Griffin, A and JR Hauser (1996). Integrating R&D and marketing: A review and analysis of the literature. *Journal of Product Innovation Management*, 13 191–215.

Gruner, KE and C Homburg (2000). Does customer interaction enhance new product success? *Journal of Business Research*, 49(1), 1–14.

Gustafsson, A, F Ekdahl *et al.* (1999). Customer focused service development in practice: A case study at Scandinavian Airlines System. *International Journal of Service Industry Management*, 10(4), 344–358.

Harari, O (1994). The tar pits of market research. *Management Review*, 83(3), 42–44.

Hsia, P, A Davis *et al.* (1993). Status report: Requirements engineering. *IEEE Software*, November.

Johnson, MD (1998). *Customer Orientation and Market Action.* Upper Saddle River, NJ: Prentice-Hall.

Kaulio, MA (1998). Customer, consumer and user involvement in product development: A framework and a review of selected methods. *Total Quality Management*, 9(1), 141–149.

Leonard, D (1995). *Wellsprings of Knowledge — Building and Sustaining the Sources of Innovation.* Boston, MA: Harvard Business School Press.

Leonard, D and JF Rayport (1997). Spark innovation through empathic design. *Harvard Business Review*, 75(6), 102–113.

Lilien, GL, PD Morrison *et al.* (2002). Performance assessment of the lead user idea-generation process for new product development. *Management Science*, 48(8), 1042–1059.

Magnusson, PR (2003). Benefits of involving users in service innovation. *European Journal of Innovation Management*, 4(4), 228–238.

Martin, CR and DA Horne (1993). Services innovation: Successful versus unsuccessful firms. *International Journal of Service Industry Management*, 4(1), 49–65.

Martin, CR and DA Horne (1995). Level of success inputs for service innovations in the same firm. *International Journal of Service Industry Management*, 6(4), 40–56.

Martin, CR, DA Horne *et al.* (1999). The business-to-business customer in the service innovation process. *European Journal of Innovation Management*, 2(2), 55–62.

Nambisian, S (2002). Designing virtual customer environments for new product development: Toward a theory. *Academy of Management Review*, 27(3), 392–413.

Normann, R (1984). *Service Management: Strategy and Leadership in Service Businesses.* New York: John Wiley & Sons.

Olson, EL and G Bakke (2001). Implementing the lead user method in a high technology firm: A longitudinal study of intentions versus actions. *The Journal of Product Innovation Management*, 18(6), 388–395.

Parkinson, ST (1985). Factors influencing buyer–seller relationships in the market for high-technology products. *Journal of Business Research*, (13), 49–60.

Ramirez, R (1999). Value co-production: Intellectual origins and implications for practice and research. *Strategic Management Journal*, 20, 49–65.

Reinertsen, DG (1999). Taking the fuzziness out of the fuzzy front end. *Research Technology Management*, November–December: 25–31.

Rothwell, R, C Freeman, A Horlesy, VTP Jervis, AB Robertson and J Townsend (1974). SAPPHO update — Project SAPPHO Phase II. Research Policy, 3, 258–291.

Senge, P (1990). The leader's New Work: Building learning organizations. *Sloan Management Review*, 32(1), 7–24.

Slater, SF and JC Narver (1998). Customer-led and market-oriented: Lets not confuse the two. *Strategic Management Journal*, 19, 1001–1006.

Thomke, S (2003). R&D comes to services: Bank of America's path breaking experiments. *Harvard Business Review*, 81(4), 71–79.

Thomke, S and E von Hippel (2002). Customers as innovators: A new way to create value. *Harvard Business Review*, 80 (April), 74–81.

Toffler, A (1980). *The Third Wave*. London: Pan Books Ltd.

Veryzer, RW (1998). Key factors affecting customer evaluation of discontinuous new products. *Journal of Product Innovation Management*, 15(2), 136–150.

von Hippel (1989).

von Hippel, E (2001). User toolkits for innovation. *The Journal of Product Innovation Management*, 18(3), 247–257.

von Hippel, E (1986). Lead users: A source of novel product concepts. *Management Science*, 32(7), 791–805.

Wikström, S (1996). The customer as co-producer. *European Journal of Marketing*, 3(4), 6–19.

Woodruff, RB (1997). Customer value: The next source for competitive advantage. *Journal of the Academy of Marketing Science*, 25(2), 139–153.

Zirger, BJ and MA Maidique (1990). A model of new product development: An empirical test". *Management Science*, 36(7), 867–883.

4

Customers as Co-Innovators: An Initial Exploration of Its Strategic Importance

Ulf Mannervik and Rafael Ramirez

NormannPartners, Sweden, and Oxford University, UK
ulf.mannervik@normannpartners.com
rafael.ramirez@sbs.ox.ac.uk

4.1. Introduction

A billboard advertisement by Nokia in the Stockholm subway, in mid-2005, asks people to create the next Nokia ad for that billboard: "Like to put something on this billboard? Just send an SMS, MMS, or a picture that you would like to see here."

The fact that customers and potential customers are invited to take a role in co-producing the marketing content of an advertisement no longer surprises us. This chapter explores reasons for this involvement as well as how customers can play a vital role in designing the offering as such, and calls for a strategic and systemic view on this opportunity.

Whole businesses have flourished on the notion of co-production. EBay is perhaps the best known example at the time of this writing (mid-2005). It has taken for itself the role of electronic gardener — harvester of small fees in extremely large volumes of customer-driven, customer-generated, and customer-validated advertising. Users of eBay who are both suppliers and customers as well as producers, all in one integrated set of roles enabled by eBay, take on the roles of describing and listing items, storing goods, stating acceptable prices, arranging payment, carrying transaction risks, and ensuring delivery of the goods.

Nokia and eBay exemplify how customers take part in the value creating activities of an offering, which they help to "invent" in the sense of adding critical information about the offering, or even making it come to the market. Offerings are information, service (meaning work and risk sharing between co-producing "supplier" and "customer"), and product combinations (for a further theoretical discussion of offerings, see Normann and Ramirez, 1994).

Re-distribution of roles in the offering is an old phenomenon, but the possibility to disentangle information and to move it around as messages has made it easier to spot its significance. IKEA is an example of a company that succeeded by re-distributing its industry's traditional roles. The IKEA customer finds the item in a catalog (which they typically share with customers in at least 10 other families, who tell one another about these items), picks it from the storage in an IKEA facility, transports it to his home, assembles the item, and checks the quality at assembly. IKEA defines the roles and organizes the value creating system, getting the customer to perform some of the key activities in the offering that enable the offering to be of value. As phrased by Normann and Ramirez (1993), IKEA has designed an interactive strategy in which customer co-creation of value is a key dimension.

What is new is the extent to which this kind of role redistribution or value co-creation takes place, and the broadening of co-production to earlier phases extending to co-innovation. In co-innovation, customers are becoming increasingly involved in the very definition, development, and shaping of offerings, not just in carrying out activities pre-defined by the interactive strategist or taking on competences pre-defined in the interactive architecture that this strategist has set in advance. This chapter is about the need to understand customer involvement in innovation in a systemic and strategic manner, rather than reducing the involvement to a functional service or product development issue.

We first look at how customers participate in value co-creation and how an understanding of this is crucial to stay ahead of the competition. Second, we look at how the logic of value co-creation is extended into the innovation of offerings. We then turn to historical origins and examples of customer co-innovation — some successful and others not so. We then call for a strategic view of customer co-innovation, beyond perspectives limited to New Product Development processes. We propose a strategic typology of customer co-innovation along two dimensions that categorize customer co-innovation which focus on the role of the customer. After providing cases illustrating the typology, we suggest a draft model of strategic management of customer co-innovation. The chapter ends with conclusions.

4.2. Customer Value Co-Creation As a Path to "Prime Mover-Ship"

New technology, foremost information technology, and advanced users have enabled the extensive re-distribution of traditional company roles that the Nokia and eBay examples illustrate.

Normann (2001) argued that the most crucial competence of business today is to organize systems of value creation, redistributing capabilities to increase value creation. Ramirez and Wallin (2000) and Normann (2001) call such re-definers of systems of value creation Prime Movers.

Prime Movers are entrepreneurial companies or organizations which, like IKEA, imagine and realize that un-tapped or under-utilized resources and capabilities can be released to co-create far more value if they are better organized. Prime Movers enhance value creation through re-allocating capabilities, getting them to work together more effectively. In doing so, they can change the playing field and the rules of the game in a strategic and profound way, just as IKEA or eBay have done.

Prime Movers recognize that customers create value in using what they buy, and mobilize capabilities and resources to help customers do that better. Customers may destroy what they buy (e.g., milk is drunk), but the focus of Prime Movers such as Tetra Pak is not on the destruction of what they sell (milk) but in the value creation (growing healthy kids) that involves the customer.

In a sense, value co-creation and co-production with customers have always happened. No one would buy anything if it did not help them create value. What is new is the extent to which this is now understood, and the technological possibilities that now exist to re-arrange resources.

In this chapter, we take these insights one step further, for customers not only play a vital role in the value creation that the offering itself affords them, but also in designing the offering as such.

4.3. Welcoming Customers into Co-Innovation

Customer co-innovation is today becoming a key concern in New Product Development. A Booz Allen survey (2005) of European senior executives found that executives ranked "understanding their customers better" as the most important step to increase the value of innovation created in the product development process.

In an Oxford University research program (2004–2005) on how innovation and strategic renewal are related, in which we have been involved in, customer co-innovation was identified as an important issue in a wider context for R&D, innovation, and strategy professionals in large companies.

One of the companies we studied, a large European IT services company, considered 99% of the ideas for future innovation to be found outside their own company, particularly among their customers. The company itself has a strong track record within innovation, so rather than saying they themselves lack innovation capabilities, they point to customers and other external parties as an enormous creative resource.

So far, in our exploratory research, we have tentatively identified an initial set of driving forces that contribute to explaining an apparent increase in customer co-innovation activity.

4.3.1. *Differentiation*

First and foremost, as companies strive to avoid commoditization even in how innovation takes place (e.g., using wind tunnels to improve aerodynamic performance in cars, rendering their shapes ever more similar), they seek a wider set of ideas — including those of their customers — to secure differentiation, and thus allow themselves to charge for a premium.

4.3.2. *Customer empowerment*

Customers are better educated and have greater access to information. They are thus increasingly demanding. This demand can be re-interpreted from a passive-critical stance to a more active-constructive one. For example, many years ago, Charles Schwabb changed the name of the "complaints department" (which no one really wanted to work in) to "office of the chairman", giving those employed there who could convert a complaint into repeat business a substantial bonus (which made it an "elite" place within the company). With innovation, these drives from customers who already care enough to complain are taken to the next logical step — developing the next generation of offerings.

4.3.3. *Information access*

Customer co-innovation can help managers to access valuable information that customers would not otherwise express and which cannot be attained by means of traditional marketing research such as surveys or focus groups. Empathic design where developers study users in their natural habitat is one method to access such information. Another more direct customer co-innovation is to by-pass the interpretation of customer information and ask the customer to suggest new offerings instead. Ikea, for example, ran workshops with children who drew furniture ideas, which were then further developed into prototypes by Ikea designers.

4.3.4. *Customer loyalty*

Customer co-innovation can enhance customer loyalty. Being able to influence your service or product can strengthen your emotional ties to a company or organization. In some cases, the customer even co-creates a company's brand, as it becomes embedded and enacted in the customer's context. The motorcycle company Ducati only use their "tribe" of devoted customers, the "Ducatisti", in their ads and arrange large racing events with them all enacting the Ducati brand. Another example is how the global Linux community uses a "credit file" to acknowledge members — Linux users — who contribute to new programing, which is a continuous and real-time branding of what Linux is about.

In spite of the growing importance of these driving forces and the current increased attention to customer co-innovation, it should be noted that co-innovation has existed for a long time. SKF, the Swedish ball-bearing company, created Volvo not only to find a market for its products, but also to understand its customers' innovation better. Ryder, which leases trucks and other elements to trucking companies, is active in trucking as well. Although its trucking operations are profitable, its interest in being active in trucking also helps its main operation (supplying trucking companies) to co-innovate with customers in ways which being entirely outside that game would disallow.

4.4. Historical Examples of Customer Co-Innovation

Customer co-innovation has been a natural aspect of the business models of large industrial business-to-business companies although they may not phrase this aspect of their work as such. Unique solutions in large scale projects such as Terminal 5 in London's Heathrow or oil pipelines crossing specific territories such as the Alaskan tundra are co-developed in close dialog with clients.

Customer co-innovation has also been embedded for a long time in management consulting and related professional services such as law firms and IT service suppliers. The practice of strategy and management undergoes constant changes. New methodologies in management consulting emerge in engagements with advanced and demanding clients, typically in new territories of practice where methodology is yet to be defined. When these methods are applied to a wider target group of clients with similar needs, they generate "scale" profitability for such firms. The same can apply for other professional service companies.

Development of business systems software has often followed a similar pattern, with a new generation of software being tailored with key customers' staff to their specific situation. These customers are on steering committees during the development, host pilots for early versions of the software, and more or less directly co-fund and influence development of the next generation of the software.

Yet another example of customer co-innovation in business-to-business activity is present in consortia where, for example, various vendors team up to deliver a new jet fighter for a government whose own experts co-design the offering. This is a version of what Chesbrough (2003) called "Open" innovation. This approach to co-innovation speeds up innovation by tapping into each member's specialized capabilities, including those of small creative players, and allowing each in the constellation to focus on what it does best.

Yet, history has shown that customer co-innovation is no panacea for all, as we see in the next sub-section of the chapter.

4.5. Co-Innovation is Not Always a Good Idea

Ford's flop with the Edsel car shows that customer co-innovation is neither new nor is it always a success formula. The development of the car model was led by extensive market research on customer preferences — a passive form of customer involvement in offering development. The designers tried to make a car that with new and innovative solutions met the identified needs of all the mid-market target groups that had been consulted through market research. By trying to be everything to everybody, the Edsel did not really meet anyone's preferences. The Edsel included a marketing hype that could not be fulfilled, particularly as it was launched during a recession.

More targeted customer co-innovation is also hazardous, as Christensen and Raynor (2003) show. In their research, some established market leaders undermine the sustainability of their own business by focusing innovation efforts on expressed desires of their most profitable and advanced customers. In responding to their increasing demands for advanced performance, these market leaders underestimate the offerings of new entrants that initially offer less performance — but whose products will increase their performance faster and at better prices and lower costs than that offered by the leader. Gradually, the new entrants may build up economies of scales around their less performing offerings, extending them into higher performance and larger market shares, and eventually eroding the market leaders' position from beneath.

The fact that customer co-innovation can be the wrong strategic approach implies that companies need a strategic view on their use of customer co-innovation.

4.6. A Strategic View of Customer Co-Innovation

Customers, and in particular lead users, are often recognized as an important source for new product ideas in the management of product development, but other elements of user-centered innovation are rare in the management literature (von Hippel, 2005). It would appear that today customer co-innovation is foremost centered on new product development (NPD), where it is treated as a concern of the NPD processes and more or less as a "bolt-on" option.

Some research studies oppose the idea that innovation should be driven by manufacturers in response to their understanding of customers' demand, but instead should be driven by the so-called lead users and enabled by manufacturers (i.e., von Hippel, 2005).

We suggest that one can also look upon customer co-innovation in a strategic perspective of business innovation. Here we attempt to develop this perspective by offering a strategic typology that provides the beginnings of a systemic approach to the managing of customer co-innovation.

4.7. Toward a Typology

A strategic and critical understanding of various customer co-innovation approaches includes, but is not limited to, NPD approaches. NPD research tends to categorize innovation activities into linear phases of product and service development processes (i.e., Wheelwright and Clark, 1992).

To understand customer co-innovation from a strategic perspective, we propose two dimensions that categorize customer co-innovation that — we believe for the first time — focus on the strategic role of the customer.

The two dimensions we propose concern how active the customer is, and if that role is linked to inventing a new offering or developing the existing offering. There are no explicit a priori values for these dimensions — the active or passive role can be appropriate in given settings, as can the inventing of new offerings or development of those that exist.

The passive or active role dimension concerns aspects such as the following:

- insight into the field of usage,
- literacy with concerned technology,
- role of the customer in marshalling capabilities and other resources,
- proportion of overall risk taken on by the customer,
- proportion of overall work taken on by the customer, and
- type of role (e.g., master contractor) taken on by the customer.

A passive customer has a more indirect influence on the ultimate design of the offering than an active one, reacting to a proposed design, or having preferences interpreted by some kind of "priesthood" such as market researchers, industrial designers, or engineers.

The second dimension concerns whether or not the customer participates in inventing a new offering, or in developing the existing offering. A role with the intention to invent a new offering tends to be more remotely linked to the existing offering and something of a bolt-on to the company as, for example, customers involved in a free-standing focus group informing R&D innovation which functionally is separated from the "live" offering. A role aimed at developing an existing offering, on the other hand, tends to be integrated with the offering; customer co-innovation has been built

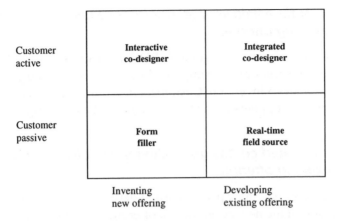

Figure 1:   Evolving archetypes for customer involvement in innovation.

into the offering and the business model where the customer's capability is engaged in co-innovation on an ongoing basis. This is the case of the coach of a soccer team, for example.

Combined, these dimensions produce four archetypes for customer co-innovation: form filler, interactive co-designer, real-time field source, and integrated co-designer (Fig. 1).

4.7.1.   *Form filler: Customer passive — inventing new offering*

In this archetype, the customer's role is separated from the offering, as in an R&D unit, where development is separated from the normal operations of the business. The customer is mainly listened to (fills survey forms) or is observed (focus groups).

4.7.2.   *Interactive co-designer: Customer active — inventing new offering*

Here the customer takes on a role that has been pre-determined by the supplier. Customers in this category engage in dialogs and interactions that aim at creating new offering ideas. Customers may even suggest new forms of interaction, but these are "options" for the core offering and not integral to it.

4.7.3.   *Real-time field source: Customer passive — developing existing offering*

Companies using bar codes (and now RFIDs) to capture buying habits or credit card companies monitoring spending patterns are examples of this type of customer co-invention. Customers unwittingly co-design patterns of behavior that suppliers use in better targeting their offerings.

4.7.4.   *Integrated co-designer: Customer active — developing existing offering*

Here customers knowingly play a role and deploy their own specific capabilities to design the next generation of offerings, and it is part of how the offering itself works. An example is how e-based development forums are inhabited by users, sharing practice or using provided tools to modify and develop the existing software.

4.8.   Cases Illustrating the Typology

The four archetypes can be illustrated with cases, which also show co-innovation activities or methods that are used in each archetype (Fig. 2). Some cases and methods appear in intersections between archetypes; the

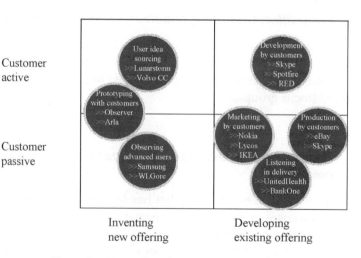

Figure 2:   Examples of co-innovation activities.

archetypes are not stale boxes into which reality neatly allows itself to be sorted. Instead, they are more like Weberian "ideal types."

4.8.1. *Observing advanced users*

The consumer electronics company Samsung, is a recent success case of a company that is deploying traditional design methodologies of user observance in its product development. With mock-ups of user environments, product developers observe how different target groups tend to use specific goods. Product developers are also relocated temporarily to various representative or cutting edge geographical markets, to develop an understanding of their tastes and preferences.

Another company that takes great care in studying advanced users is the innovative materials and technology company WL Gore & Associates, Inc. most known for its GORE-TEX® fabrics. Although many of their customers are manufacturers, WL Gore pays great attention to end users. The Associates spend a lot of time with military Special Forces in environments where textile fabrics are truly put to the test. They spend time in operation rooms, to observe surgeons using WL Gore's medical products. These encounters develop a deeper understanding of the use and the users, and can result in concrete and sometimes unexpected ideas for new offerings. The dental floss Glide was developed by Gore after observing a surgeon using suture material as dental floss.

4.8.2. *Prototyping with customers*

The global market leader in media monitoring and communication intelligence, the Observer Group, involves customers in an active role that is nevertheless somewhat separated from its main offering. When the company developed new service concepts, it tested prototypes of the concepts — and various sales and support tools enabling them — with selected clients on key markets. Some clients were aware of the "prototype-mode", whereas others were not. Using occasional client interactions as "wind-tunnels" enabled the Observer Group to test and fine tune the concepts, and to detect further systems, support, and internal training needs.

The Scandinavian diary group Arla, provides another example of prototyping with customers. When developing a new low-fat cream for cooking, at the time, something new to the market, it used various customer interactions to test and develop both the product and its marketing concept. Prototyping with real customers helped Arla reduce some of the risks that inevitably accompany the introduction of a new category of products in a fairly conservative market.

4.8.3. *User idea sourcing*

Inviting its customers into a more active co-innovation role, the Swedish youth web-community Lunarstorm asks its large community of users to give concrete suggestions on new services and features, or improvements on existing ones. The site's community is fairly familiar with the technology and its possibilities and is aware of recent developments of similar sites. The community also seems to enjoy taking an active role in shaping its virtual hometown.

Another example of user idea sourcing comes from Volvo Car Corporation (VCC). Striving to tap into the trend sensitivity of devoted fans, Volvo created the Concept Lab Volvo. It is a website where people are informed of the design principles behind Volvo and emerging car design concepts. People are invited to view feedback on future concept cars, which informs them about ongoing design work on other car concepts and market readiness for new concepts. Visitors are also invited to chat with Volvo developers. What visitors do not know is that these developers are senior designers, who also listen for new ideas and may test some hot ideas from ongoing development work. In addition to this, Volvo applies other methods for user idea sourcing, such as workshops where target groups — often in trend-sensitive lead markets and global design hot spots — are invited to design textiles or other car interior surfaces and solutions or whole cars, as in the case of the Your Concept Car, designed by eight invited women. Like the Concept Lab, a "priesthood" of designers and developers monitor the workshops and they seek, filter, interpret, and refine ideas that emerge for these occasional customer or target group interactions.

4.8.4. *Listening in delivery*

The fastest growing and most profitable health management organization in the US, the UnitedHealth Group, has built in listening to customers into its very delivery process. Deploying a variety of tools for involving or learning from customers in the company's innovation efforts, its command center approach deserves specific attention. All call centers interact with managers of corporate health benefit plans and are coordinated by one command center located at the UnitedHealth Group headquarters. The command center tracks flows of calls on big screens. If calls take too long to answer, they flash red, are captured, and the command center can tap into them and try to understand how the question can be resolved. A department located right next to the command center picks out the top 25 questions and seeks patterns by root cause analysis looking for items such as "Are there any commonalities?" "Are the questions from a specific customer or category of customers?" and, most importantly, "How can we stop them from calling?" The findings are made actionable and brought to a task force which can act anywhere in the business model, as long as it is within certain budget limits. To use a phrase from Richard Normann, United Health Group has built real-time learning into their "moments of truth" (Normann, 2002) which are the service interactions where the perceived quality is realized.

4.8.5. *Marketing by customers*

The Nokia case that opened this chapter is an example of customers and potential customers taking on an active role in shaping the marketing. Mobile phone and terminal users send in their own suggestions for individual billboard ads. It is not the marketing concept that is co-innovated by the customers, but the content.

In some cases like IKEA, customers or potential customers take on an active role in carrying out marketing activities (as by sharing the catalog), although they may not change the offering itself.

The internet company Lycos enabled people to download the screensaver "Make love not spam" which connected with and made spam advertising sites overloaded and slow. It was intended to promote Lyco's efficient anti-spam filter in their email services. During its campaign, the cultish screensaver was downloaded and marketed by internet communities through blogs, forums, news sites, and homepages, and generated a 10-fold increase of new e-mail customers. Internet users took on active roles in the marketing, but not in innovating its concept or its direct content. Internet users arguably co-innovated the marketing content indirectly by making it a conversation piece for various purposes in communities throughout the Internet.

4.8.6. *Production by customers*

The eBay case, in the beginning of this chapter, tells of customers taking on production roles by carrying out activities such as listing items, storage of goods, stating acceptable prices, arranging payment, carrying transaction risks, and delivering the goods. Of these in particular, the listing of items implies co-innovation of the production at eBay, since it shapes new categories. Some user groups are also linked directly into eBay's corporate email system and can communicate feedback directly to category managers. EBay is a platform and enabler of millions of small web businesses which in turn indirectly co-innovates the virtual bazaar and its production capability by innovation of their own businesses.

Another example of production by customers is the rapidly expanding free global telephony company Skype, which enables peer-to-peer communication over the Internet. Its customers co-produce the directory by downloading the Skype software and registering as users. They expand the directory by recommending it to friends and colleagues. Furthermore, the helpdesk is run by customers; users helping other users. Skype does not need mainframes, for it "borrows" unused capacity in its users' PCs. This implies that the users facilitate the value creation of other users, sharing and developing Skype practices, and by that co-innovating the production. In all of these examples, Skype has linked customer co-innovation to its offering.

4.8.7. *Development by customers*

Some companies directly involve customers in the innovation of their existing offerings. This is part of what the offering is, on an ongoing basis. Skype, like many IT software intensive organizations such as Microsoft, runs a number of forums which give users access to, that is, feedback on existing Skype software and its use, BETA versions of new software, ideas for new software or new usages, or allows them to simply share experiences. These forums are regularly visited by Skype developers, and marketing and business people. More tightly linked to the offering are forums for developers, who are provided with guidance on programing interfaces. They are assisted in their application of Skype into other software and hardware.

A similar case is Spotfire, the analytics application and service company, which visualizes and helps clients see new patterns and trends in massive and complex data to inform business decisions. Spotfire stages a developer central with blog, network, and webcasts. Developers get assistance from other developers who have integrated Spotfire's applications into their own infrastructure. Jointly they share and co-innovate the applied practice of Spotfire.

Within a broad campaign on co-creation of healthcare services (Cottam and Leadbeater, 2004), the British Design Council's research unit advocates a similar approach in health of expert patients and care givers who can mentor others with similar problems.

4.9. Toward a Strategic Management of Customer Co-Innovation

The archetypes and their examples we have introduced are tentative and exploratory, but they show that there are choices to be made in deciding to enter, and to deploy, customer co-innovation. We note that the cases with active roles that are integrated into the development of the existing offering tend to operate in fast moving IT-intensive business environments. The cases with passive roles that are more separated from the offering and focus on inventing new offerings tend to operate in arguably slower business environments.

If customer co-innovation is to be treated strategically, it is important to recognize the differences between the archetypes, and reflect on what mode of customer co-innovation may suit a company, a situation, an environment, a technology, and a relationship best.

The four categories we have introduced show that there are contingencies to be taken into account when deciding to deploy customer co-innovation. We offer four considerations that we suggest will help managers to strategically determine what forms of customer co-innovation help them the most. At this point, we do not provide guidance on how to apply the systemic approach on a detailed level. Instead, we suggest the four considerations to be taken into account, and systemic solutions to be developed on a contingency basis, recognizing specific challenges of unique customer co-innovation opportunities and challenges at hand.

First of all, companies need to be clear about what purpose co-innovation should serve. No technology or approach is an end in itself, and we suggest that setting a strategic intent and mission that is meaningful to both suppliers and concerned stakeholders can help channel their energy toward mutual value creation. IKEA's mission *to create a better everyday life for the many people* sets the stage for and defines the role of customer co-innovation. Such missions explain why it makes sense to mobilize under-utilized customer capabilities to enable innovation. Commenting on current innovation challenges of business, Newton (2004), dean of UC

Berkley, means that what is missing today is "inspired leadership that has a lofty enough vision to spur great things along the way" (Business Week, 11 October 2004). We believe this is relevant for customer co-innovation too, if a supplier is to mobilize and channel its customers' creativity in a desired direction.

Second, a definition for a co-innovation arena is needed. The arena consists of the context and tools that enable co-innovation. When the intention is to invent new offerings, the arenas can be supplier owned laboratories (such as Concept Lab Volvo), customer development settings (such as WL Gore's weekends with elite forces), or commercial projects (such as the development of new service concepts at the Observer Group). When the supplier is striving to develop an existing offering, the arena can be the offering itself (such as UnitedHealth Group's root cause analysis), extensions of the offering (such as eBay's platform for small web businesses) or support in offerings (such as Spotfire's developer central). Arenas need to support the required role distribution, and be equipped with suitable tools, systems, and processes. These will differ depending on the archetype and customers' and the company's capabilities, as the cases have indicated.

The third component is target customers' own capabilities. Suitable customer capabilities depend on the purpose of customer co-innovation and on the customer role archetype. Thus, for example, if developers observe users in action, users do not have to be very knowledgeable about the technology in the offering. A more active role for the customer will require more understanding of the technology and the application field. It will also require leadership and clear semantics, with tasks and tools enabling and empowering the customer in his co-innovation role. Suppliers will also need to ensure that customers are motivated and remunerated appropriately. The choice of customers will be based on the purpose and arenas of co-innovation, as well as on the suppliers' own capabilities of enabling co-innovation. Co-innovation with active customers will require fairly advanced customer capabilities of both technologies and the field of application, in particular in development of existing offerings, where the innovation role is integrated into the offering and the emergence of the customer's practice. Linux is a clear example.

Co-innovation where the customer is more passive will require less advanced customer capabilities of technologies or the field of application.

In particular, the customer capabilities of technologies and its limitations and possibilities are of less relevance, since it is the supplier who takes on the active co-innovation role in the relation.

We want to stress again that there is no *a priori* value in more or less active customer roles in co-innovation. Also, passive customer roles can be powerful and purposeful, as shown in the cases with the WL Gore (passive customer, invention of new offering) and the UnitedHealth Group (passive customer, development of existing offering). Furthermore, we believe it is important to recognize the impact enabling technologies and interaction tools can have for unlocking and unleashing the power and potential of more active customer co-innovation.

The fourth and final component of the strategic system for co-innovation concerns the supplier's own capabilities. It is important that the supplier's organization itself is tuned into innovation. We advocate that suppliers need to ensure that concerned parts of its organization understand why it embarks on customer co-innovation, and that it ensures capabilities for the relevant kind of customer co-innovation. We also believe it is crucial to align, transform, or in other ways deal with existing incentives for managers and other professionals. Our research and experience indicate that innovations that go against the grains of a business' current remuneration criteria will face difficulties which Christensen and Raynor (2003) also observed.

When customer co-innovation is geared at inventing new offerings, the required supplier capabilities will concern foremost that part of the organization that is directly involved in innovation-related customer observing or interacting. However, outcomes risk ending up in the "valley of death" — between proven ideas and their successful implementation — if there is a lack of co-authorship by the rest of the organization, or if it is motivated to favor a preserving of existing offerings.

When customer co-innovation aims at developing existing offerings, and is linked to it directly, or its support extension, the supplier's capabilities for co-innovation will need to be aligned and integrated with the organization's other capabilities enabling the offering. Openness to change will become an ongoing and continuous concern.

We advocate that suppliers who invite customers to become co-innovators should ensure that the organization embraces them as such, or they may risk customer co-innovation not being realized, or even back-firing, if created expectations cannot be met (Fig. 3).

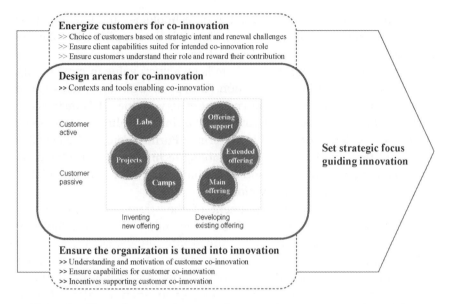

Figure 3:   Toward a strategic system for managing customer co-innovation.

4.10.   Conclusions

We have seen customer co-innovation as an old practice that has gained renewed attention. We have proposed a strategic and systemic approach for the managing of customer co-innovation which is, as far as we know, a first attempt in the literature in this direction. Our purpose is modest — to show that developing such a model is promising and timely, and to also indicate conditions where each of the possibilities we have identified makes sense. Our framework is thus contingent on the purposes, types of capability in customers and firms, and IT- intensity and speed of the market in which the decision makers are located.

We have shown that involvement of customers in offering development and innovation can take many shapes, and advocate a strategic view to reflect and decide on what kind of customer co-innovation a company could take initiative to establish, to gain Prime Movership in its business context — including its relation to its customers.

Co-innovation is a natural further role that increasing acceptance of value as co-production holds for customers. Paradoxically, when companies see themselves as buyers, they accept customer co-innovation much more than when they see themselves as suppliers. Over the last decade, companies have been actively re-defining their supply chains, outsourcing non-core activities, off-shoring some of these to other continents, and determining conditions of collaboration and openness (including access to financial statements) of THEIR own suppliers that put them — as co-producers — very much in the co-innovation of relationships mode. This chapter suggests that their own customers, who consider them as suppliers, are going to be doing the same (and not only in B2B relationships), and that it is better for them to proactively think of how to enable their customers to become co-innovators — before it is the co-innovating customer that dictates what will happen to that relationship.

References

Booz, AH (2005). How companies turn customers' big ideas into innovations. *Strategy + Business and Knowledge @ Wharton*, January 12.

Chesbrough, H (2003). Open innovation: *The New Imperative for Creating and Profiting from Technology*. Boston: Harvard Business School Press.

Christensen, CM and ME Raynor (2003). *The Innovator's Solution*. MA: Harvard Business School Publishing.

Cottam, H and C Leadbeater (2004). Health: Co-creating services. RED paper 1, Design Council, London.

Newton, R (2004). *Business Week*, October 11.

Normann, R (2002). *Service Management — Strategy and Leadership in Service Business*. 3rd Ed. Chichster: Wiley.

Normann, R (2001). Reframing Business — When the Map Changes the Landscape. John Wiley & Sons, Chichester.

Normann, R and R Ramirez (1993). Designing interactive strategy: From value chain to value constellation. *Harvard Business Review*, July–August: 65–77.

Normann, R and R Ramirez (1994). *Designing Interactive Strategy*. Chichester: John Wiley & Sons.

Ramirez, R and J Wallin (2000). *Prime Movers — Define Your Business or Have Someone Define It Against You*. Chichester: Wiley.

von Hippel, E (2005). *Democratising Innovation*. Cambridge: The MIT Press.

Wheelwright, SC and KB Clark (1992). Revolutionizing product development: Quantum leaps in speed, efficiency and quality. *Free Press*.

5

Customer-to-Customer Interaction in Service Development: A Many-to-Many Approach

Evert Gummesson

Stockholm University School of Business, Sweden
eg@fek.su.se

5.1. Introduction

The expression "many-to-many" represents a network approach to marketing, encompassing all those who enter into relationships and interaction with one another during a marketing process. The chapter is an adaptation from my book *Many-to-Many Marketing* (Gummesson, 2004, 2006) but here many-to-many thinking is applied to service development and a special case of customer involvement, namely, customer-to-customer interaction, C2C.

The now established concepts of relationship marketing, CRM (Customer Relationship Management), and one-to-one marketing are almost exclusively focused on the pair relationship, that is, the dyad of a single customer and a single supplier. They all convey the message that the most profitable business strategy is to build long term relationships with loyal customers.

Many-to-many marketing goes a step further. It claims that a broader set of stakeholders and relationships have to be considered. To underscore the network aspect, the two expressions one-to-one and many-to-many are used as contrasts. In many-to-many, the customer's network meets the supplier's network, that is, many meet many. Apart from suppliers and customers, the networks can include intermediaries, competitors, investors, government agencies, the media, family members, school mates, or whoever influences a selling and buying situation, be the influence direct or indirect, of a short term or of a long term. By wearing the many-to-many eyeglasses, we see marketing from a different angle.

My proposed definition is the following: "Many-to-many marketing describes, analyzes, and utilizes the network properties of marketing." So far, network models of marketing have almost exclusively emerged within business-to-business marketing, B2B. Many-to-many is a general marketing theory which also brings on board business-to-consumer marketing, B2C, and C2C.

Many-to-many draws on network theory which is rapidly developing in both social and natural sciences. The basic concepts of network theory are *nodes* and *links*, for example, the consumer's (node 1) relationship (link 1) to a supplier (node 2). If there are more than two nodes and more than one link, a network is in the making. The nodes interact through the links and influence and are influenced by each other.

Network theory is applied as a means of highlighting four aspects of marketing and management that are decidedly relevant and realistic but are sadly neglected in theory. Business activities are characterized by the following:

- being *complex*,
- appearing in a *context*,
- undergoing constant *change*,
- being a mix of technology and human input, expressed as *high tech/high touch*.

In live management and marketing situations, there is no limit to the number of variables and links that appear. In an effort to make reality manageable, however, research makes simplified assumptions and reduces the number of factors and their connections. The risk is that the validity and relevance becomes severely impaired.

Network theory is a powerful tool to describe and analyze marketing. There are no other restraints than our own intellectual capacity, creativity, and stamina. Network theory is flexible and can be employed with various degrees of depth and sophistication. It can not only be systematic and well structured, but it can also be a reflection of how we think in practical life using experience, common sense, intuition, insights, wisdom, and our judgment, that is, our tacit knowledge.

Networks are most often presented as graphs, but they can be treated verbally or mathematically as well. A series of properties of networks adding life and process to the basic structure of nodes and links have emerged. To mention a few central properties, networks can have powerful hubs (nodes with many links) and close clusters of nodes and hubs. They can be random or planned, scale-free, exposed to contingency or law-controlled behavior, error tolerant or sensitive to small changes, and dependent on transition phases, tipping points, and critical thresholds.

To understand networks, we can draw on many sources. Araujo and Easton (1996) identified pertinent network approaches originating not only from marketing but also from entrepreneurship, organization theory, sociology, political science, economic geography, and economics. Network theory has been used to some extent in B2B marketing (Håkansson and Snehota, 1995; Iacobucci, 1996; Möller and Wilson, 1996), but limited attention has been given to its application to general management and marketing theory (exceptions are Lipnack and Stamps, 1994; Iacobucci, 1996; Achrol and Kotler, 1999; Christopher *et al.*, 2002; Gummesson, 2002, 2006).

Network theory has a long history in social sciences; on social network analysis (see Scott, 1991; Degenne and Forsé, 1999; Kilduff and Tsai, 2003), and applications of networks and relational thinking (see Granovetter, 1973, 1978, 1985; Schluter and Lee, 1993, 2003; Castells, 1996; Rosen, 2002; Tanner, 2003). Modern natural sciences show a growing interest in networks. The Internet offers new opportunities for scientists to study universal properties of networks on a large scale. It has contributed through its complex and still not very well understood structure and its capricious behavior. There is also dissolution of boundaries between natural and social sciences (Barrow, 1992; Zohar, 1997; Capra, 1997, 2002; Gladwell, 2000; Barabási, 2002; Buchanan, 2003).

Those interested in research and network theory in marketing are advised to read about network basics in both social and natural sciences.

5.2.   Dissolving Established Categories and Roles

To see how contributions to service development through customer involvement emerge, it is necessary to rethink established categories and roles in marketing and accept interdependency and fuzziness. The dichotomies of goods and services, B2B and B2C, customer and supplier, and high tech/high touch will be discussed.

5.2.1.   *Goods and services*

Many-to-many embraces both goods and services because all offerings or "products" are a combination of things (goods) and activities (services). To further generalize the service concept, it was previously established that "goods are wanted because they are capable of performing services" (Norris, 1941). This is in line with Grönroos' (2000) view of a service perspective on all business and the "service-dominant logic" championed by Vargo and Lusch (2004a). In this sense, we can talk about service development and view the goods element as an integral part of an offering, rather than view goods and services as two separate categories with distinctly different properties requiring separate types of marketing. Their alleged differences, as presented in the service literature, have recently been under heavy fire (Lovelock and Gummesson, 2004; Vargo and Lusch, 2004b). For a review of different perceptions of the service concept, see Edvardsson *et al.* (2005).

Abandoning the production-oriented notion of goods and services as two categories and accepting a user-oriented notion of the output of economic activity as being of service or value. Value is an accepted term in marketing, and it avoids confusion of the two concepts of service, either as input to consumption or as output. Whether the value is rendered by goods or services in the traditional sense becomes immaterial.

The value economy, however, is incomplete as a concept; it needs an accompanying platform of how and where value emerges. Network theory provides such a platform. Combining value and networks leads to defining today's economy as a *value-creating network economy*; its output is value, and its emergence is network based.

5.2.2.   *B2B and B2C*

In a landmark article, von Hippel (1978) explained that the development of new products in B2B is often initiated and managed by the buyer rather than the seller. On the difference between B2B and B2C, he noted that "The generation of consumer product ideas is usually manufacturer-active . . . " and continued " . . . the role of the customer is essentially that of respondent, 'speaking only when spoken to'. It is the role of the manufacturer to select and survey a group of customers to obtain information on needs for new products or modification of existing products; analyze the data; develop a responsive product idea; and test the idea against customer perceptions and purchase decisions" (pp. 39–40). He further claimed that this strategy has been extremely successful for standardized, packaged consumer goods and added that the experiences from B2C can work in certain B2B situations.

Although von Hippel concludes that customer involvement is common in B2B and uncommon in B2C, in many-to-many I venture the generalization to all goods and services and to B2C. A major reason is that the B2B and B2C categories are not clear and have already been stretched far too far in marketing. They are relativistic and arbitrary constructs based on superficial observation and not on substantive data and comparison between cases.

A major criticism is that there are hardly any pure B2B or B2C companies; most include both. In B2B, one firm sells to another firm which in turn sells to another firm and so on. The chain can be shorter or longer, but eventually a B2C relationship appears. Examples are Nokia and Ericsson who deliver both the cell phones and systems for mobile telephony. Telephone systems are B2B selling to telecom operating companies and never to consumers. The systems must be designed in a way that they can produce services for telecom operators, who in turn are providers to those who use the phone either professionally or as private consumers. The phone itself should therefore be designed to be attractive for individual buyers and users. Nokia and Ericsson do not sell their telephones to users but to retailers who are involved in both B2B and B2C. Even if the relationship is indirect, the customer's customer must be considered by the manufacturers. The initiative to development can come from a series of stakeholders: suppliers, telecom operating companies, subscribers of telecom services, and users of the cell phone hardware and software.

5.2.3. *Customer and supplier*

Re-thinking B2B and B2C requires an examination of the relevance of the customer/supplier categories. Suppliers are said to add value in a value chain and customers "consume", that is, "destroy" the value in the process of usage. With services, it is common that production, marketing, and consumption are simultaneous, although it may not be as universally valid as is claimed in the mainstream service literature (Lovelock and Gummesson, 2004).

The strict distinction between production and consumption and between producer and user cannot be upheld. It is perhaps more common for mass manufactured and mass distributed packaged consumer goods, but this instance has become the standard for marketing concepts and theories. It keeps underpinning the marketing literature and claims to be general. The attitude of companies, as expressed in consumer contacts, is still all too often "speak only when spoken to." Telephone interviews and postal questionnaires directed to statistical samples of consumers and discussions in focus groups are often considered sufficient to "understand" consumers.

The role of the customer in services marketing becomes evident in the service encounter. In this encounter — face-to-face, ear-to-ear, letter-to-letter, email-to-email, customer-to-website, and customer-to-machine — a service may be developed, produced, and delivered with input from several sources:

- independent contributions from the service provider,
- independent contributions from the customer,
- contributions through provider–customer interaction, and
- contributions through customer-to-customer interaction.

An obstacle for genuine understanding of value creation is even if suppliers confess to a "customer in focus" paradigm, they keep watching the customer from a skewed lookout. The reality in the valley does not appear the same as when you stand on top of the mountain. My experience of marketing in practice is that companies are better at rhetoric than at customer-centric and empathic implementation.

5.2.4. *High tech/High touch*

A reason why forecasts about new products, services, and markets come out wrong — often *very* wrong — is that we do not pay proper attention to the high tech/high touch balance. In the book *Megatrends*, Naisbitt (1982) discusses high tech/high touch based on the notion " ... to balance the material wonders of technology with the spiritual demands of our human nature" (p. 42). His conclusion was "The more high technology around us, the more the need for human touch" (p. 52). That was before the arrival of the personal computer, before e-mail, before the Internet, before the cell phone, and even before the fax. His observation is even truer today and is boosted by IT development.

High tech/high touch is evident in many ways. The more comfortable our lives become with the assistance of technology, the more people indulge in adventure travel, sailing, and hiking in the mountains. They go to their cottage where they have physical contact with nature. Television technology does not only give us an opportunity to watch our favorite sports around the clock, but also the interest to run the marathon and even the triathlon is on the increase. At the same time as Internet trade was launched, huge supermarkets and malls kept growing, offering experiences through theme parks, cinemas, hotels, and even churches. According to personal observations, the number of international conferences and participants increased during the second half of the 1990s, at the same time as the Internet and e-mail became an integral part of both professional and private life. And why — in the name of economic rationality — do delegates not convene in Internet conferences? They need not even leave their homes or offices and do not have to pay for air travel and hotels. But cost effectiveness in a rational, technological sense may not be sufficient.

A possible explanation why high tech and high touch grow in tandem is that e-relationships and the swift global communication stimulate the need for human relationships instead of replacing human contact. We encounter the principle of yin and yang where the dynamic tension between two extremes never quite finds equilibrium but keeps trying forever.

Yet another observation underscores the interdependence between technology and human beings. High tech may be felt as cold and less human, but high touch is not always warm and human either. For example, there is often a lack of knowledge and social skills in front-line interactions with customers, which gives rise to customer dissatisfaction. Not everyone wants personal contact with others; some prefer to be impersonal and anonymous.

High tech can also add human dimensions that are in short supply in the physical world; we can call it IT-mediated high touch. The computer becomes an extension of mental abilities and can satisfy needs and wants. The Internet and e-mail allow for chat groups to deal with the quality of goods, services, and suppliers. A search on the Web can help the sick to find medical information and be better prepared for their high touch meeting with the doctor. IT can offer social interaction among groups with common lifestyles, which was previously associated only with physical presence.

5.2.5. *Synthesis*

In the acronym B2B, it is not clean as to which B represents the supplier and which represents the customer. For a specific situation, it can be determined depending on whose role one wants to stress. The acronym B2C clearly puts the supplier first and the consumer second. But we could just as well turn B2C into C2B and note that consumers can take the initiative and set the agenda. Customer complaints and suggestions for improvements from consumers, however, are often treated in a counterproductive way. Usually, consumers do not get beyond the company's customer service department or call center and have difficulty finding someone who is empowered to make a decision. However unsatisfactory from a customer point of view, the harsh reality of decision makers often entangles them in pressing operative issues, and they cannot simply absorb deviant or annoying information. When customers do not get a response, they may give up or turn somewhere else.

The conclusions from studying networks in organizations and contemporary society are that the customer input could be more properly handled in business practice and marketing theory. It does not matter whether it is B2B, B2C/C2B, or C2C, or goods, or services.

Figure 1 illustrates how the Bs and Cs relate to each other in an environment of offerings of goods and services, high tech/high touch, and value creation.

With network theory applied as many-to-many marketing, the chapter proceeds to discuss elements for inclusion in service development. The focus will be on customer involvement through C2C interaction and its role in development demonstrated in examples, cases, and comments. The chapter ends with conclusions and recommendations.

5.3.   On Development, Innovation, and Being New

Based on an earlier model, Gummesson (1993) has supplemented the traditional disconfirmation paradigm of service quality — balancing expectations against experiences — with the two concepts of *design and engineering quality* and *production and delivery quality* (Fig. 2). The figure is generalized

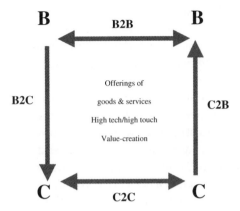

Figure 1:   B and C are linked together. Source: Gummesson (2006). Reproduced with permission.

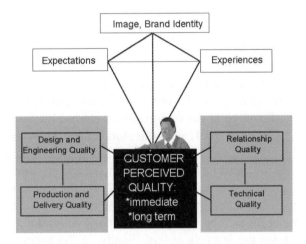

Figure 2:   A quality model. Modified from Gummesson (1993). Reproduced with permission.

to encompass goods and services and their joint contribution to *customer perceived quality*, which is another word for value.

Only the lower left part of the figure will be explained here as it specifically relates to service development (for background and further discussion, see Grönroos, 2000, pp. 67–72). The model says that the quality of the design and engineering of a service is an antecedent to production and delivery. For example, low design/engineering quality of the software for service delivery will persistently lower both the ability of service personal to perform the services and the ability of customers to contribute. This means that design/engineering is dependent on feedback from staff and customers; design/engineering influences production/delivery and vice versa.

What is development and what is a new service? This chapter includes both incremental improvements and quantum leaps. Development follows many paths. It can be a straightforward R&D process, but this is not often a true description of what really happens. We tend to have an unrealistic belief in our ability to innovate in a systematic way according to some rational, sequential model. In a network spirit, these steps are rather nodes in a network of events that develops in iterations back and forth. At a later stage, service development may be the object of tighter planning and implementation. For an overview of service development concepts and models, see Edvardsson (1997).

5.4. C2C Interaction

How do C2C networks influence marketing and specifically the development of new services? With some exceptions, companies do not yet seem to take advantage of the opportunities offered by customer power in marketing. Gatarski (2001) tells the story of the Volvo chat community www.classicvolvo.com. Ford, who had bought Volvo passenger cars, sued the enthusiast Hans Rekestad who admired and celebrated the Volvo car and bought and sold car parts. "This is brand intrusion!" said the Ford lawyers. "Shut down the website!" With economic support from his network, among them "The Electronic Frontier Foundation," the accused managed to keep the lawyers at bay. Finally, in the spring of 2002, the court dismissed the case. Instead of seeing opportunities, Ford stamped the customers as intruders. One could argue about who "owns" a car brand. Is it the car owner who drives around exposing the manufacturer's logotype for free year after year, or the one who manufactures the car in a day? Volvo has since initiated a website which invites enthusiasts to become part of the Classic Volvo Car Club.

In services marketing, it has long been noted that customers interact with one another. This is so trivial and obvious that marketers should understand it intuitively. If you operate a ballroom, you know that the service is built on the fact that guests dance with one another and intermingle.

The interaction even starts in the waiting line outside where customers speak with one another, compare impressions and views, and offer tips.

IT has expanded the opportunities for business customers and consumers to communicate with companies and with other customers. Sometimes, I hear that the Internet is the enabler of C2C interaction. But C2C interaction occurs in a physical encounter in the marketplace as well as in the virtual, IT-mediated encounter in market space. The chapter will consider both high tech and high touch aspects of customer involvement. Some results from C2C research will be accounted for subsequently.

Nicholls (2003) has classified physical C2C interaction by studying critical incidents of both positive and negative customer involvement in several services in Poland. He finds a great variety of events that can be related to time, place, conversation, need for information, and need for help or turning down help. Most concern one-to-one, but some occur in a public environment and involve all those present. A context of many-to-many is created.

This is also the case in a study by Harris and Baron (2004) who examined conversations between strangers on trains in England. In a model for C2C, they expose the consequences for consumers and providers. Among other things, the results show that conversations among passengers on trains have a stabilizing effect on the mood of the passengers when, for example, delays occur, and they reduce dissatisfaction. Results also show that when employees are not available, passengers perform employee tasks. This can be information about the timetable or where to change trains. From the railway company's perspective, the passenger is an unsalaried part-time employee. The interaction can also be seen as a purely social act, the joy of helping somebody or telling something you know. Customers enhance the value of the service to the benefit of themselves and the service provider. Unfortunately, the providers may not see the contribution of this involvement and fail to support it.

Gatarski and Lundkvist (1998) have analyzed actors and interaction on the Internet. Conversation, dialog and interaction — or more colloquially chatting — has become part of the social life on the Internet. It can be chatting between a customer and a supplier, B2C/C2B, or between customers, C2C, but there are also new actors, "artificial consumers." One example is Pricerunner, which is an agent helping consumers to search, select, and report price information. The agents can sometimes even make decisions. When it comes to C2C, the authors define three types of relationships and interactions in the network of the customer and the producer. On the left

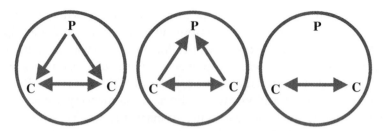

Figure 3:   Three types of relationships and interactions in the network of customers and a producer. Source: Gatarski and Lundkvist (1998, pp. 50–51). Reproduced with permission.

side of Fig. 3, it is the producer (P) who controls and supports C2C; in the middle, the initiative rests with customers C2B or C2C; and to the right, C2C interaction occurs without producer involvement. An example of the latter is medical patient associations whose members want to exchange information without being controlled. This may be because of discontentment with doctors, the health-care system, governments, the pharmaceutical industry, and insensitive and stereotypical handling of the patient's situation. The association develops its own services to its members.

Hair and Clark (2004) show how C2C interaction on the Internet can occur in a football fan club. Their research method is based on ethnography in electronic communities, sometimes called "netnography", as opposed to classic ethnography applications used in physical societies. Interaction takes place through written text, and messages are posted in an electronic community forum. The messages can be addressed both to individuals and groups, and they are eventually put in an archive. The researchers find great differences in the contents, quality, frequency and personal proximity and commitment of the interaction. We do not yet know how this should be applied in marketing and service development. This requires basic research to enhance our understanding of customer behavior in a new type of networks.

Conversation can be more than just chatting. It can be an interactive relationship where customers exchange knowledge and information, involve themselves in creating new knowledge, and define and solve problems. Two cases will form the core of the remainder of the chapter. They highlight certain aspects but are only a beginning; they will only cover part of the customer's involvement in service design and engineering. The first case is a modern — or perhaps postmodern, but true — success story. It is about the Linux operative system and about C2C interaction that develops the system in a network context, and customers who constitute an informal but highly efficient R&D department.

5.5. Case: e-mail from Linus

5.5.1. *First episode: How it all started*

Linus Torvalds from Helsinki, Finland, has been a star on the international IT sky for a long time. He had his first "hit" when he was barely 20, which is hardly possible for anyone but a hacker or rock star. In 2003, he was number 3 on *Fortune's* list of the most influential people under 40 in the US.

It began in 1991 with an e-mail to other hackers (Fig. 4). You do not need to understand the technical jargon to note the effort to develop something. It was a hobby, nothing big or professional, with no promises. But something big happened. The Linux operative system was born. Linux is developed on cheap hardware through interaction between users, C2C. An operative system is a kind of infrastructure for the digital world. Bill Gates became the world's richest man on Microsoft's operative system, which in practice has had a monopoly and exists in every computer. Linus went another way. Through an open source code, free to anyone to enter into the

---

Message-ID: 1991Aug25.205708.9541@klaava.helsinki.fi
From: torvalds@klaava.helsinki.fi (Linus Benedict
Torvalds)
To: Newsgroups: comp.os.inix
Subject: What would you like to see most in minix?
Summary: Small poll for my new operating system

Hello everybody out there using minix-I'm doing a (free) operating system
(just a hobby, won't be big and professional like gnu) for 386 (486)
AT clones. This has been brewing since April, and is starting
to get ready. I'd like any feedback on things people like/dislike
in minix, as my OS resembles it somewhat

Any suggestions are welcome, but I won't promise I'll implement them
   Linus

Figure 4:   Linus Torvalds' e-mail to other computer freaks, 25 August, 1991.

system and try it out, a distributed cooperation quickly emerged between all those interested to further develop Linux. Linus did not earn money on the system; his curiosity drove him.

The original community consisted of a cluster of some hundred enthusiasts. The development occurred in a self-organizing system. Linus has been the hub and kept the network of contributors together. Despite the fact that the system is free and anyone can improve it in cooperation with others, Darwin's law of survival of the fittest is valid: the best improvement wins in competition. Linux adapts more quickly than anyone else in the IT business. In terms of security, for example, when the virus "Ping of Death" crashed operative systems around the world, Linux stopped the attack within a few hours. "Somebody posted a report of the ping", recalls Alan Cox, the author of the fix, "so I just sat down, fixed it, and posted the fix straight back."

Linus has not just become a marginal and short lived event. Its distribution is not restricted to hackers. It is difficult to know exactly how many users there are, but the system's market share in servers rose from 6.8% in 1997 to 24% in 2003 and is still increasing. Linux began to be adopted by such diverse organizations as Boeing, Disney, NASA, the NASDAQ stock exchange, the tax authority in the US (IRS), and universities. In 2005, it was almost everywhere, for example, Google, Motorola, and Volvo use it in some of their products and services, and Dell, HP, and IBM run it in their servers and PCs. In the wake of Linux, companies have developed facilitating products and services, and a commercial market has emerged.

At age 29, Linus was the youngest recipient of an honorary doctorate from the University of Stockholm. In the motivation for the doctorate, it states that "From an academic point of view software projects of these types are especially interesting as they show that the rhetoric of 'free exchange of information' and 'transparency' is useful even outside of academic research." At the age of 34, he could list three honorary doctorates in his résumé.

This is an excellent example of service development through C2C interaction. But what might happen when such a network grows?

5.5.2. *Second episode: How it proceeds*

Linux grew from its inherent strengths, but in 1999, the informal organization was approaching a critical tipping point. There were thousands of contributors to the system, and Linus could not handle it all without great delays. He was urged to delegate work. After some hesitation, he complied. The result was that contributions could be processed five times faster. How did they do it?

The former network captain now has a team of lieutenants. In 2005, IBM, HP, Intel, and others contributed thousands of programmers. IBM alone had assigned 600 programmers to Linux as compared to two in 1999. But Linux is still a network with no official headquarters, no CEO, and no employees. Companies in the network profit from selling Linux packages, user manuals, updates and other services, and manufacturers preload Linux in servers and PCs.

To get a glimpse of the organization at work, we can follow the development of the new Linux version which was released in December 2003. It is an iterative process in which Linus first sets the goals together with contributors. Engineers in cooperating companies write codes and pass them on to "maintainers" who review the contributions. Then individual programmers, who work in their spare time, add their suggestions and submit them to the maintainers. When after interaction with contributors, the maintainers are satisfied, they pass the software on to Linus and his top aide Andrew Morton. They review the code and add it to the central piece of the operative system. New updates are posted for thousands of people to test, and finally, the system is released. The next step is for distributors to put together a package, and within roughly one year, customers begin installing the new version.

In the development process, we have met a series of hubs and nodes in the Linux network that in turn have their own networks: Linus, contributors from IT companies, spare time contributors, maintainers, Andrew Morton, distributors, and customers. The network culture is highly cooperative but also highly competitive. The ultimate decisions will be made by Linus — but only as long as the network trusts him. (The second episode is primarily based on Hamm, *BusinessWeek* 2005.)

5.5.3. *Comments*

Suppliers can be in charge and control a service to some extent, but networks are also self-organizing and emerge seemingly at random or as planned by somebody else such as a customer. The Volvo Internet network was run by an enthusiastic customer. The Linux case is a remarkable instance of C2C interaction creating a new computer service, performed in a way that defies all traditional theories of innovation processes and management. There is no plan but rather a direction — or rather an obsession — in the minds of one or several customers. Service design/engineering and service production/delivery work hand in hand, and it is difficult to tell them apart. The Linux case is not just high tech, but it is equally Internet-mediated high touch.

We can also learn that when a network grows it may have to modify its structure and processes. This happened with Linux, but it was not because of his initiative, but of the customers. It is noteworthy that the considerable size of Linux today has not forced it into a traditional corporate structure. It stays a C2C network supplemented by alliances with different clusters of suppliers.

The next case is different. It is about Scandinavian Airlines, SAS, and the Star Alliance to which it belongs together with some 25 airlines. The case represents spontaneous and ad hoc C2C service development. The service providers offer arenas, but what then happens is largely beyond their control. The service is developed by the passengers, C2C.

5.6.   Case: How SAS and the Star Alliance Brought Me and Elvis Together

5.6.1.   *First episode: Miss Sweden*

I was on my way to Nashville via Chicago, non-stop Stockholm–Chicago with SAS, to proceed with its partner in the Star Alliance, United Airlines. This was my lucky day. I was upgraded to business class! They had given me a window seat, but I asked if it was possible to change to an aisle seat. "We can do that", they said.

When I found my seat, the neighboring seat was already taken by an elegant woman. Blond, not young, but younger than me. She looked Swedish. We said hello.

The bad habit of glancing at what the neighbor is reading paid off. I saw that she was reading an article about complimentary health care, an interest of mine. So I started to talk. She conversed intelligently with a sense of humor. It turned out that she lived in Beverly Hills and was a real-estate agent. Before that she had been Miss Sweden, and she was number 3 in the Miss Universe contest. For 10 years, she was a starlet in Hollywood and had taken part in many movies, television sitcoms, and soap operas, and had made some 50 TV commercials. She had worked with many of the great ones, among them being the legend, Elvis Presley.

We spent eight hours together. We were offered drinks, a luncheon, and snacks. It was almost like a date. We were stuck with each other. I did not object. She had played in one of the 32 movies that Elvis made. "And you know what", she said, "in the movie Elvis and I kiss."

Wow, I had met somebody who had kissed Elvis! And she told me about the original Elvis as he was before fame became a burden to him. He was nice and gentle, paid attention to everyone and gave them small presents. And I was on my way to Nashville, the capital of country music, and not far from the Elvis' own Memphis.

When we had disembarked at O'Hare Airport, we stood there talking and waiting for our connecting flights. We had a good time. SAS had arranged a blind date. Before we left each other, we kissed on the cheek, the European way.

So now I've kissed a woman who has kissed Elvis, be it on the cheek, but still. So I must have some kind of relationship with Elvis.

5.6.2. *Second episode: Mr. XXL*

A couple of months later, I flew from Copenhagen to Beijing, economy class and no upgrade. The airplane was packed. The guy next to me turned out to be the CEO of a large enterprise. He was friendly and liked to discuss politics. A recurrent theme was his distrust in politicians. A Danish government minister was on the plane, and he noted that she traveled business class. "It's a waste of taxpayers' money", he said.

I wanted to sleep and read, even if I agreed with what my fellow passenger said about politicians. It did not help that I closed my eyes. He touched my arm lightly to get my attention and continued the political discussions.

The size of the man was XXL, Extra Extra Large. It meant that his body partly spilled over into my chair, which was size S, Small, as is common in economy class. His breath was not peppermint, and he was a virgin market for deodorants.

We spent nine hours together. We had drinks, dinner, and breakfast. We were stuck with each other. I had silent objections.

5.6.3. *Third episode: The circle closes with "Miss Brazil"*

Relationships grow to networks and they cross borders globally. On a flight to Brazil — Star Alliance, operated by Lufthansa — I sat next to a woman who could not have been Miss Sweden but very well Miss Brazil. She turned out to be the sales manager of a publishing company and had been to an advertising festival in Cannes, France. She told me she had been a fashion model, which I had no reason to doubt.

I told her the story about me and Elvis. She laughed and joked about it.

When we departed at the Sao Paulo Airport after 11 hours, she said to me in Latino inspired English and with committed gestures: "Now you must kiss me on my cheeks and I must kiss you and your cheeks so I can tell my friends that I had been kissed and have kissed a guy who has kissed a girl who kissed Elvis."

5.6.4. *Comments*

Airlines are high tech, but passengers are exposed to high touch in B2C/C2B and C2C interaction. In the Elvis case, this is particularly true. It epitomizes Jensen's (1999) concept of the "dream society", where dreams, experiences, emotions, and storytelling are the central factors in value creation. The service is not developed by the provider but by passengers; their perception and storytelling constitute the sustaining outcome in the mind of the passenger.

What is important when you choose an airline? The price of course, especially if you pay out of your own pocket. Other factors are the timetable, how well the departure and arrival times suit your needs, the possibilities to make changes, punctuality, safety, leg space, food, free drinks, pleasant flight attendants, and so on. All this exerts an influence on the passengers' evaluation of the service.

But this is not what I remember from the three trips. I remember Miss Sweden, Mr. XXL, and "Miss Brazil" — three new relationships that determined my perceived quality of each flight. I link the experiences to SAS, Lufthansa, and the Star Alliance. When I remember the C2C interaction, everything else about the flights is forgotten.

To what extent can an airline control service quality, especially relationship quality? Should airlines hire Miss Sweden, Miss Brazil, Miss Universe, and others to travel with the most preferred customers to turn the long flight into an event? This might be too difficult or going too far. Will these C2C relationships develop further and create new stories? It depends on the traveler. I got the telephone number of two of them, but not of Mr. XXL.

Note the unexpected. I happened to fly those days. Miss Sweden, Mr. XXL, and "Miss Brazil" happened to fly those days too, and they happened to be seated next to me. The Star Alliance did not organize this, but it offered an arena where I could engage in C2C interaction.

What are the consequences of the networks? Occasionally, I discuss my flying experiences with friends and others in my networks. I use the experiences when I make presentations or, as here, contribute to a book. I become a part-time marketer. To what avail? Will the Star Alliance sell more tickets? Probably not as a measurable consequence of these events. But the events can contribute to loading the brand with images. The provider's "objective" design/engineering and production/delivery of the service is beaten by the customer's "subjective" involvement and perception.

5.7. Conclusions and Recommendations

The chapter has presented customer networks and customer *involvement* as positive forces in service development. C2C interaction is neither prominent in marketing theory nor in practice, even if there are successful exceptions.

The cases show how companies can design an arena for customer networks and customer interaction and consciously apply a C2C strategy. But the Elvis event is largely out of the airline's control. It shows how coincidences and storytelling can become more important for the customer than the core service itself.

C2C interaction in the physical environment is important. Then the Internet, e-mail, and the mobile phone have been added. They create totally new social behavior, where C2C interaction can grow in unpredictable directions. C2C can offer an alternative to service development which has primarily relied on a company's own specialist resources.

Practitioners can develop C2C interaction in many ways:

- use C2C networks as a lever to reach competitive advantages,
- add C2C networks to the marketing plan and discuss how interaction between customers can become a creative force,
- support the customers' interaction with each other,
- utilize the knowledge of customer networks in service development and in improvement programs.

Both as scholars and practitioners, we need comparison between hundreds of cases in our pursuit of more general and valid knowledge of customer involvement in service development.

References

Achrol, RS and P Kotler (1999). Marketing in the network economy. *Journal of Marketing*, 63(Special Issue), 146–163.

Araujo, L and G Easton (1996). Networks in socioeconomic systems. In *Networks in Marketing*, ID Iacobucci, (ed.), Thousand Oaks, CA: Sage.

Barabási, A-L (2002). *Linked: The New Science of Networks*. Cambridge, MA: Perseus.

Barrow, JD (1992). *Theories of Everything*. London: Vintage.

Buchanan, M (2003). *Small World*. London: Phoenix.

Capra, F (1997). *The Web of Life*. London: Flamingo/HarperCollins.

Capra, F (2002). *The Hidden Connections*. London: HarperCollins.

Castells, M (1996). *The Rise of the Network Society*. Oxford, UK: Blackwells.

Christopher, M, A Payne and D Ballantyne (2002). *Relationship Marketing*, 2nd Ed. Oxford: Butterworth-Heinemann.

Degenne, A and M Forsé (1999). *Introducing Social Networks*. London: Sage.

Edvardsson, B (1997). Quality in new service development — key concepts and a frame of reference. *International Journal of Production Economics*, 52(1/2).

Edvardsson, B, A Gustafsson and I Roos (2005). Service portraits in service research: A critical review. *International Journal of Service Industry Management*, 16(1), 107–121.

Fukuyama, F (1995). *Trust*. New York: The Free Press.

Gatarski, R (2001). *Artificial Market Actors: Explorations of Automated Business Interactions*. Stockholm: Stockholm University.

Gatarski, R and A Lundkvist (1998). Interactive media face artificial consumers and must re-think. *Journal of Marketing Communications*, (4), 45–59.

Gladwell, M (2000). *The Tipping Point*. London: Abacus.

Granovetter, MS (1973). The strength of weak ties. *American Journal of Sociology*, 78, 3–30.

Granovetter, MS (1978). Threshold models of collective behavior. *American Journal of Sociology*, 83, 1420–1443.

Granovetter, MS (1985). Economic action and social structure: The problem of embeddedness. *American Journal of Sociology*, 91, 481–510.

Grönroos, C (2000). *Service Management and Marketing, Chichester*. UK: Wiley.

Gummesson, E (1993). *Quality Management in Service Organizations*. New York: ISQA.

Gummesson, E (2002). *Total Relationship Marketing*. 2nd Ed. Oxford, UK: Butterworth–Heinemann/Elsevier.

Gummesson, E (2004). From one-to-one to many-to-many marketing. Plenary Session Presentation at the *QUIS 9 Symposium*. Sweden: Karlstad University, 15–18 June. Published in B Edvardsson, *et al.*, (eds.) Service Excellence in Management: Interdisciplinary Contributions, *Proceedings from the QUIS 9 Symposium*, Karlstad, Sweden: Karlstad University: 16–25.

Gummesson, E (2006), Many-to-many marketing (forthcoming).

Hair, N and M Clark (2004). When all hell breaks loose: A 'digital' exploration of consumer relationships in electronic communities. In *Workshop on Relationship Marketing*, EIASM, Bryssel, January 27–28.

Hamm, S (2005). Linux Inc. *BusinessWeek*, January 31, 50–57.

Harris, K and St Baron (2004). Consumer-to-consumer conversations in service settings. *Journal of Service Research*, 6(3), 287–303.

Håkansson, H and I Snehota (1995). *Developing Relationships in Business Marketing*. London: Routledge.

Håkansson, H and I Snehota (2000). The IMP perspective. In *Handbook of Relationship Marketing*, I Sheth, N Jagdish and A Parvatiyar (eds.), Thousand Oaks, CA: Sage.

Iacobucci, D (ed.) (1996). *Networks in Marketing*. Thousand Oaks, CA: Sage.

Jackson, BB (1985). *Winning and Keeping Industrial Customers*. Lexington, MA: Lexington Books.

Jensen, R (1999). *The Dream Society*, New York: McGraw-Hill.

Kilduff, M and W Tsai (2003). *Social Networks and Organizations*. London: Sage.

Lipnack, J and J Stamps (1994). *The Age of the Network*. New York: Wiley.

Lovelock, CH and E Gummesson (2004). Whither services marketing? In search of a new paradigm and fresh perspectives. *Journal of Service Research*, 6(5), 20–41.

Möller, K and D Wilson (eds.) (1996). *Business Marketing: Interaction and Network Approach*. Boston, MA: Kluwer.

Naisbitt, J (1982). *Megatrends*. New York: Warner Books.

Nicholls, R (2003). On-site customer-to-customer interaction: A classification system. Paper presented at the *AMA Servsig Services Research Conference*, Reims: Reims Management School.

Norris, RT (1941). *The Theory of Consumer Demand*. New Haven, CT: Yale University Press.

Rosen, E (2002). *The Anatomy of Buzz*. New York: Currency.

Schluter, M and D Lee (1993). *The R Factor*. London: Hodder & Stoughton.

Schluter, M and DJ Lee (2003). *The R Option*. Cambridge, UK: The Relationship Foundation.

Scott, J (1991). *Social Network Analysis*. London: Sage.

Tanner, L (2003). *Crowded Lives*. North Melbourne, Australia: Pluto Press.

Vargo, SL and RF Lusch (2004a). Evolving to a new dominant logic for marketing. *Journal of Marketing*, 68(1), January: 1–21.

Vargo, SL and RF Lusch (2004b). The four service marketing myths. *Journal of Service Research*, 6(4), 324–335.

6

New Service Development: Learning from and with Customers

Bodil Sandén*, Jonas Matthing† and Bo Edvardsson‡

Service Research Center, Karlstad University, Sweden
*bodil.sanden@kau.se
†jonas.matthing@kau.se
‡bo.edvardsson@kau.se

6.1. Introduction

Market-oriented companies have mainly focused on satisfying the expressed needs of the customer, typically by using verbal techniques such as focus groups and customer surveys, to gain an understanding of the use of current products and services (Narver *et al.*, 2004). The problem is, however, that those techniques tend to result in minor improvements rather than innovative thinking and breakthrough products (Harari, 1994). This problem arises because customers have trouble imagining and providing feedback about something that they have not experienced (e.g., Leonard and Rayport, 1997; Ulwick, 2002; Veryzer, 1998; von Hippel, 1986). Organizations simply cannot access, understand, and meet the latent needs of the customers by only using surveys and interviews. Latent needs can be referred to as what customers really value or the products and services they need but have never experienced or would never think of requesting (Senge, 1990).

Recently, it has been assumed that "a market-oriented and learning organization is compatible with, if not implied by, the service-centered model" (Vargo and Lusch, 2002, p. 6). The service-centered view of marketing is customer centric (Sheth *et al.*, 2000) and market driven (Day, 1999). This means being more than simply consumer oriented; it means continually collaborating and learning with customers in order to respond to their individual and dynamic needs. Service-centered logic implies that value is defined by and co-created with the consumer and determined by the customer on the basis of value in use, rather than being embedded in a predefined output (Vargo and Lusch, 2002). Thus, from a new service development perspective, the customers become not only a necessity but also an opportunity.

Most scholars argue that services are activities, deeds or processes, and interactions (Solomon *et al.*, 1985; Lovelock, 1991; Zeithaml and Bitner, 2000; Edvardsson *et al.*, 2005) where the customer plays the complex role of both contemporary consumer and producer (Normann, 1984; Toffler, 1980). Because this process of customer–company interaction often occurs at the same time as the customer experiences the service, it is problematic to obtain relevant feedback from customers in advance. Adding to the complexity is the fact that many services today are interactive, technology intensive, and embedded in relationships. Altogether, new service development relies on the difficult task of understanding and anticipating changing customer needs, with little help from traditional market research. In addition, the nature of services clearly adds to the complexity.

To facilitate proactive learning about the customer in order to uncover latent needs, recent findings stress customer participation in the development process or observations of customers in real action (Deszca *et al.*, 1999; Martin and Horne, 1995; Leonard and Rayport, 1997; Prahalad and Ramaswamy, 2000; Thomke, 2003). Only a limited number of articles are available in the literature, however, on the involvement of customers in new service development (Alam, 2002). The aim of this study is threefold: First we carry out a review of the previous literature on the involvement of customers in new service development. Second, we offer a definition of approaches that facilitate learning from and with the customer in new service development. And finally, based on the review, we design, test, and analyze a field experiment that captures the concept of learning from customers by actively involving them in the creation of new services ideas. In the experiment, we compare customers' and professionals' contributions to innovative services. The results of the experiment, together with the learning process it provides, are analyzed, and the final section is devoted to a discussion on the theoretical and managerial aspects of the study.

6.2. Theoretical Framework

6.2.1. *Market and learning orientation in innovation*

The service-centered model (Vargo and Lusch, 2004) describes an active customer that interacts with personnel, the service script, and/or supporting tangibles. This implies the need to develop close and trusting relationships to increase customer perceived value. Such relationships are fostered by a market orientation. Market orientation, as an implementation of the marketing concept, entails learning about customer needs, the influence of technology, competition, other environmental forces, and acting upon that knowledge in order to become competitive (Slater and Narver, 1995). The perspective on market orientation as mainly a business philosophy (Kohli and Jaworski, 1990; Narver and Slater, 1990) has gradually shifted toward including a behavioral element of organizational learning. Accordingly, market orientation is viewed as an organizational learning capability consisting of cognitive associations (e.g., shared beliefs, values, and norms) and behavioral outcomes reflecting these cognitions (Kok *et al.*, 2003). Day (1994a,b, 2002) maintains that organizations continuously learn about their markets through an the linked processes of market sensing and sense making, which follow the usual sequence of information processing activities. Market sensing includes the collection and distribution of information about the needs, expectations, and requirements of customers through an open minded inquiry. Sense making includes the interpretation and utilization of the collected information. Further learning is achieved when an evaluation of the outcomes is completed. The overall learning process generates a context for market information, and converts it into knowledge about the customer (Kok *et al.*, 2003).

Morgan *et al.*, (1998) showed that firms with a high market orientation possess a greater organizational learning capability. Furthermore, Hurley and Hunt (1998) proposed that market and learning orientation are antecedents to innovativeness. They argue that learning facilitates behavioral change, which leads to an improved performance. This is supported by Han *et al.*, (1998) who showed that market orientation facilitates organizations' innovativeness, which in turn positively influences performance. Organizational learning is valuable to a firm and its customers because it supports the understanding and satisfying of customers' expressed and latent needs through new products, services, and ways of doing business (Day, 1994a; Sinkula, 1994). Organizational learning makes it possible to not only create products ahead of competitors, but also to create products before the recognition of an explicit customer need (Hamel and Prahalad, 1991; Slater, 2001).

According to Senge (1990), organizational learning involves two distinct types of behavior: adaptive and generative learning. Adaptive learning focuses the organization on adjusting to serve the present market. With a continued focus on the present market, it is possible that companies present core capabilities can dominate the direction and development of the firm, and thus constrain it. They would become core rigidities that inhibit innovation (Dahlsten, 2003; Hamel and Prahalad, 1991; Slater and Narver, 1995). In contrast, generative learning requires an organization to challenge its own assumptions about its mission, customers, competitors, and strategy (Slater and Narver, 1995). If a company can look at its environment beyond its familiar assumptions, it may be able to discover new directions and new possibilities and may thus be able to create new innovative services.

Most companies still focus on satisfying expressed needs of the customer by using focus groups and customer surveys (Dahlsten, 2003; Flint, 2002; Slater, 2001). Vast criticism has been aimed at such traditional market research techniques that cannot deliver information about customer latent needs (Griffin and Hauser, 1993; Leonard, 1995). New approaches and techniques are now evolving to elaborate on customer latent needs to foster organizational innovativeness. But, even though research supports the significance of market-oriented innovation and its implementation, there is little research about how to operationalize and implement market-oriented innovation, that is, what needs to be changed and completed in new approaches (Kok *et al.*, 2003; Day, 1994b).

6.2.2. *The involvement of customers in new service development*

User involvement is suggested to result in important benefits such as reduced cycle times, superior services, and user education (e.g., Alam, 2002). However, how companies achieve these benefits is less known. We conducted an extensive literature search (in the databases Business Elite Source, EBSCO HOST, and Emerald) on the involvement of customers in new service development, as well as related notions and research areas.

The search showed that involvement of customers in innovation in order to learn from and with them involves many disciplines such as cognitive psychology, design theory, engineering design, human–computer interaction, marketing, organizational theory, product development management, and quality management (Alam, 2002; Kaulio, 1997). Consequently, reviewing previous research is difficult. Our strategy involves a problem-based approach. We build first and foremost on the marketing aspects of service and product development. This approach allows us to build a more comprehensive framework of customer involvement in new service development. Previous marketing research about service development is limited; therefore, the number of references to build on and the conceptual variety is drastically reduced. Articles were selected based on two criteria: the main focus of the article is on activities or processes of involvement of the customer, and the main focus of the article is on market research techniques that support learning from and with customers.

Many articles highlight "customer involvement" as a secondary subject relating to other issues meaning there is a lot of fuzz but not much solid work. The review of the literature, however, reveals a limited number of studies focusing primarily on involvement of customers in the new product and service development process. Table 1 provides an outline of this research. As previously stated, the majority of these studies is founded on research about new product development (e.g., Anderson and Crocca, 1993; Ciccantelli and Magidson, 1993; Durgee *et al.*, 1998; Leonard and Rayport, 1997; von Hippel, 1986, 2001). Only few studies have a primary focus on the involvement of customers in new service development (Alam, 2002; Martin and Horne, 1995; Martin *et al.*, 1999; Thomke, 2003). This finding is supported by Alam (2002) and Kaulio (1998).

The following parameters are used to describe the involvement of customers: degree or intensity of user involvement (Alam, 2002; Gruner and Homburg, 2000; Foxall *et al.*, 1985; Kaulio, 1998; Martin and Horne, 1995; Voss, 1985), antecedents to customer involvement (Lin and Germain, 2004), customer characteristics (Gruner and Homburg, 2000; von Hippel, 1986; Lüthje, 2004), objectives and benefits of customer involvement (Alam, 2002; Anderson and Crocca, 1993; Dahlsten, 2003; Magnusson, 2003; Magnusson *et al.*, 2003), phases of the innovation process (Alam, 2002; von Hippel, 1986; Mullern *et al.*, 1993), customer role in the innovation process (Mullern *et al.*, 1993; Wikström, 1996), modes and supporting methods of customer involvement (Alam, 2002; Ciccantelli and Magidson, 1993; Durgree *et al.*, 1998; von Hippel, 1986, 2001; Gustafsson *et al.*, 1999;

Table 1:   Studies on customer involvement in new product or service development.

Authors	Primary focus	Type of study	Sample/data	Context	Definition of customer involvement & summary of comments/findings
Alam (2002)	Objectives, stages, intensity and modes of user involvement	Review of the literature and case study research	12 case programs, 48 new service projects and 36 in-depth interviews	B2B, financial services industry, Australia	User involvement is more intense at initial stages of idea generation and screening and the later stages of testing and commercialization. six objectives were reported, including rapid diffusion and decreased t-2-m.
Anderson and Crocca (1993)	Learning from a joint co-development project	Anecdotal evidence	NA	B2B, software development, US	Co-development is when a company, together with its customer users, evaluates a new technology together with established work practice. Direct collaboration around the use of technology in actual work settings enlarges and enriches the work practice of both parties.
Ciccantelli and Magidson (1993)	Consumer idealized design	Empirical: case study research	NA	B2C, multiple industries, US	Consumer idealized design is a supporting method of customer involvement. Customer involvement has often not produced the expected results. Six principles have come out of examination of successful and failed efforts, including, e.g., probe for the reasons why consumers want what they want.

(Continued)

Table 1: (*Continued*)

Authors	Primary focus	Type of study	Sample/data	Context	Definition of customer involvement & summary of comments/findings
Dahlsten (2003)	Experiences and benefits of customer involvement in the XC90 project at Volvo Cars	Empirical: case study research	NA	B2C, automobile industry, US	Customer involvement is a process where the technology originator and the customer become intimately involved in an integrated development project, where both parties contribute their expertise to the development project. Customer involvement lead to reduced uncertainty, increase customer understanding, and influenced product design.
Durgee *et al.* (1998)	Mini-concepts	Empirical: interviews	Thirty mothers	B2C, food processing technologies US	Mini-concepts are found to be a supporting method of customer involvement. Given the diversity of the target consumers, it might be better to expose them to many functions than to expose a short list and try to find a function that gets a high rating across most of the sample.
Foxall, *et al.* (1985)	User-initiated or customer dominated product innovation	Empirical: Case study research	NA	B2B, Aerospace, Great Britain	CAP2 is an extension of the MAP and CAP conceptualization introduced by von Hippel (1978). CAP2 ascribes entrepreneurship to the user and recognizes his role in product innovation.

(*Continued*)

Table 1:   (*Continued*)

Authors	Primary focus	Type of study	Sample/data	Context	Definition of customer involvement & summary of comments/findings
Gruner and Homburg (2000)	Impact of customer interaction. (A) Intensity, (B) customer characteristics.	Empirical: interviews and survey	$n = 1219$ 310 (25.4%)	B2B, machinery industry, germany	Indicate that customer interaction in certain stages has a positive impact on new product success. Financially attractive customers or lead users have also a significant effect on new product success.
Gustafsson *et al.* (1999)	Observation of customers in their real environment	Anecdotal evidence	NA	B2C, Airline industry, scandinavia	Observation is a supporting technique of customer involvement. This approach helped SAS in developing a series of innovations complementing each other to form a holistic travel experience, based on the individual needs of the customers during the travel process.
Kaulio (1998)	Intensity of customer interaction	Conceptual: review of literature	NA	NA	Customer involvement is defined as the interaction between customers and the design process. Three types of involvement are identified: design for customers, design with customers and design by customers.
Leonard and Rayport (1997)	Empathic Design, based on observation	Anecdotal evidence	NA	B2B and B2C, multiple industries	Empathic design is a supporting technique of customer involvement; (1). Observe your customers, (2). Capture data, (3). Analyze and reflect, (4). Brainstorm for solutions, and (5). Develop prototypes.

(*Continued*)

Table 1: *(Continued)*

Authors	Primary focus	Type of study	Sample/data	Context	Definition of customer involvement & summary of comments/findings
Lin and Germain (2004)	Antecedents to customer involvement: for example, tech. turbulence, product complexity, formalization	Empirical: Survey	$n = 480$ (227) $n = 2000$ (289)	B2B, multiple industries, US and China	The greater product complexity, the greater the degree of customer involvement in innovation. Formalization has a positive association, but decentralization has a negative association with the customer involvement in innovation.
Lüthje (2004)	Characteristics of innovating users	Empirical: Interviews and survey	Five key informants, $n = 609$ 153 (25.9%)	B2C, outdoor sports industry, Germany	37.3% of respondents generated ideas for improved or new products. Nine percent of the users build prototypes. High expected benefit in combination with high commitment to the product field lead to user innovations.
Magnusson *et al.* (2003)	User innovation in comparison with professional developers	Empirical: Field experiment	Twelve professionals 19 users, 20 consulting users	B2C, mobile communication, Sweden	In comparison with professional service developers, end users came up with ideas that were more original, offer greater user value but are less producible.
Martin and Horne (1995)	Examination of successful innovations	Empirical: Interviews, group	Eighty senior executives, 25 groups	B2B and B2C, multiple industries, US	Customer participation is defined as the direct, overt participation by the customer, their overall involvement. There is more direct customer

(Continued)

Table 1: (Continued)

Authors	Primary focus	Type of study	Sample/data	Context	Definition of customer involvement & summary of comments/findings
	within the same firm	discussions and survey	with 378 executives and 470 (88, 18.5%)		participation for more successful service innovations.
Martin et al. (1999)	Customer-input uncertainty	Empirical: Case study	NA	B2B, Consultant Services, US	Input uncertainty in terms of diversity of customer demand and customer disposition to participate has the potential to interfere with the success of reciprocal B2B service innovation.
Mullern et al. (1993)	Taxonomy of participatory design	Conceptual	NA	NA	Participatory design is a process at early stages of a joint development project where the customer is highly involved as a member of a team.
Neale and Corkindale (1998)	Co-development	Review of literature and anecdotal evidence	NA	B2B, Electronics industry, Australia	Co-development is the process where the technology originator and the customer become intimately involved in an integrated or joint development project.
Olson and Bakke (2001)	Implementation and follow-up on the lead user method	Empirical: Longitudinal case study	NA	B2B, IT industry, Norway	Lead user method resulted in profitable products and services, however, e.g., time pressure, personnel turnover, limited pressure to continue due to already excellent performance, and that engineers saw it as not prestigious enough to work with customer, led to implementation failure.

(Continued)

Table 1: *(Continued)*

Authors	Primary focus	Type of study	Sample/data	Context	Definition of customer involvement & summary of comments/findings
Pitta and Franzak (1996)	Organizational learning and techniques for consumer involvement	Conceptual and anecdotal	NA	B2C	The presented methods offer the potential of learning consumer wants and needs in detail. The best method is to involve the consumer in each step. Early and ongoing consumer input distinguishes successful from unsuccessful products.
Prahalad and Ramaswamy (2000)	Co-opting customer competence	Anecdotal evidence	NA	B2B and B2C, multiple industries	Customer competence is a function of the knowledge and skills they possess, their willingness to learn and experiment, and their ability to engage in an active dialog. Co-opting concerns e.g., engage customers in an active dialog, manage customer diversity.
Thomke (2003)	Experiments conducted live with real customers	Empirical: Case study	NA	B2C, Financial services industry, US	Experiments with new services are most useful when they are conducted live with real customers engaged in real transactions.
Ulwick (2002)	A methodology that focus outcomes, not solutions	Conceptual and anecdotal	NA	B2C, B2B, multiple industries, US	Provide a supporting technique. Presents a five-step process to outcome based interviews.
von Hippel (1986)	Launch the concept of lead users and a method	Conceptual and anecdotal	NA	B2B and B2C	Lead users are users whose present strong needs will become general in a marketplace in the future and are positioned to benefit significantly by obtaining a solution to those needs.

(Continued)

Table 1: (Continued)

Authors	Primary focus	Type of study	Sample/data	Context	Definition of customer involvement & summary of comments/findings
von Hippel (2001)	Toolkits for user innovation	Conceptual and anecdotal	NA	B2B, B2C, multiple industries	A toolkit for user innovation is a supporting technique of customer involvement. As toolkits are more generally adopted, users will increasingly be able to get *exactly* the products and services they want.
Voss (1985)	The role played by users based on their degree of participation in the innovation process	Empirical: interviews and survey	Interviews: 18 innovations, Survey: $n = 115$ 46 (40%)	B2B, Application software industry, UK	If the user formulates an idea distinguish between *user active* from *supplier active*. Innovative solutions can be developed by users even if they do not have a computer department, providing they can maintain at least a modest familiarity with new technology.
Wikström (1996)	Customer as co-producer	Empirical: Case study research	NA	B2C, multiple industries, Sweden	Given the programmed procedures for interacting with customers in the service process, very little learning — adaptive or generative — is likely to accompany the interaction.

Leonard and Rayport, 1997; Pitta and Franzak, 1996; Thomke, 2003; Ulwick, 2002), contributions (Neale and Corkindale, 1998; Prahalad and Ramaswamy, 2000), and inhibiting factors of customer involvement (Martin *et al.*, 1999; Olson and Bakke, 2001).

Second, in terms of research methodologies and types of studies, we found that findings have been based mainly on case study research and anecdotal evidence. A few studies are also based on interviews, surveys, or a combination of the two. Five articles are conceptual, and three provide a review of the literature. Recently, field experiments have been used to investigate the benefits of customer involvement (Kristensson *et al.*, 2002; Magnusson *et al.*, 2003).

Third, in terms of research context, the distribution between B2B and B2C is equal. Seven articles report data from multiple industries. The specific industries that have been studied span from airline services, financial services, and systems development to aerospace, machinery, and automobiles.

Fourth, we find that there has been no attempt to examine the empirical relationships between customer involvement in innovation, innovativeness, and business results such as new product and service success.

Also, in terms of research on supporting techniques, for example, lead user method (von Hipple, 1986) and toolkits for user innovation (von Hippel, 2001), we found that these are first and foremost developed and tested in a product context.

6.2.3. *Conceptualization of the involvement of customers*

We also found that explicit definitions of these concepts are often absent. There are, however, a few exceptions. Neale and Corkindale (1998, p. 419) define co-development as

> *a process where the technology originator and the customer become intimately involved in an integrated or joint development project, where both parties contribute their expertise to the development project.*

Anderson and Crocca (1993), state that co-development is when a company, together with its customer users, evaluates a new technology together with established work practice. Kaulio (1998, p. 148) defined user involvement as "the interaction between customers and the design process." Prahalad and Ramaswamy (2000, p. 80) argue that customer competence is a function of "the knowledge and skills [customers] possess, their willingness to learn and experiment, and their ability to engage in an active dialog." Martin and Horne (1995, pp. 44–45) defined customer participation "as the direct, overt participation by the customer, their overall involvement."

In analyzing these definitions, we notice three important details: First, none of the definitions states the purpose of the involvement of customers (and related concepts). Second, none of the definitions highlights the different levels of innovation, for example, program, project, or stages level of innovation. Finally, even though several studies implicitly report on learning from and with the customer (e.g., Anderson and Crocca, 1993; von Hippel, 2001, which builds on "learning by doing" from von Hippel, 1994; Tyre and von Hippel, 1997), no definition makes an explicit connection between the involvement of customers and learning.

Drawing on research in new product and service development (Cooper 1993; Fitzsimmons and Fitzsimmons, 2000; Leonard 1995; Tidd *et al.*, 1997), market orientation (e.g., Day 1994a, b, 2002; Sinkula 1994), and exploratory field interviews with marketing and R&D managers, we define learning from and with the customers as the processes, deeds, and interactions where a service provider collaborates with current (or potential) customers to anticipate and learn customers' latent needs and develop new services accordingly. The definition emphasizes activities and behavior as the involvement of customers' aims to facilitate the process of market sensing (Day 1994b, 2002), that is, the generation and dissemination of market intelligence and the organizationwide responsiveness to it (Kohli and Jaworski, 1990).

From an output perspective, that is, the purpose of user involvement, the literature states that involvement of users is suggested to result in important benefits such as reduced cycle times, superior services, and user education (e.g., Alam, 2002). Our definition asserts that the main purpose of learning from and with customers is to develop a comprehensive understanding of what creates value for the customer in general and anticipate customers' latent needs in particular. Latent needs are here defined as "opportunities for customer value of which the customer is unaware" (Narver *et al.*, 2004). These are needs that the customers really value but have never experienced or would never think to request (Senge, 1990). These needs are "evident but not yet obvious" (Day, 2002, p. 243). Focusing on latent needs (and expressed needs) offers a high potential in terms of differentiation and competitiveness. The problem is that organizations have difficulty accessing, understanding, and meeting latent needs of the customers by only using structured research methods. They "impose fixed attribute descriptions and scaled response categories to obtain standardized and comparable responses from large samples" (Day, 2002, pp. 243–244). According to our definition, the use of reactive market research techniques to anticipate customers' expressed needs is not considered learning from and with the customers.

In summary, extant literature provides important insights into customer involvement in product and service development. The literature is scattered, and there are few attempts to present a profound picture of how knowledge is created and learning is achieved with real (or potential) customers and then transferred within the organization.

6.3. An Empirical Experiment of Involvement of Customers

The basis for the design of our field experiment is the idea of market and learning orientation manifested by the involvement of customers. We have used previous research (both empirical studies and conceptual work) to direct the design of the experiment.

6.3.1. *Experiments with users for new ideas*

Together with TeliaSonera, a large Swedish telecom operator, we arranged a field experiment to examine processes for enhanced learning, and the basic principle was to emulate authentic conditions and a real world test (cf. Prahalad and Hamel, 1990; Narver *et al.*, 2004; Senge, 1990; Thomke, 2003). The study was designed as a classical experiment including a control group, treatments, and independent judges to evaluate the outcome of where customer involvement was compared to the normal working routines (e.g., getting customer information from the marketing department). The experiment trials were followed by interviews with all the participants where we could probe the ideas and prototypes created (cf. Lynn *et al.*, 1996) in order to understand in more detail how learning may occur (cf. Tyre and von Hippel, 1997). A number of group meetings with the R&D department from the telecom company were held to discuss the study, its results, and the insights from a learning perspective (cf. Olson and Bakke, 2001).

We focused the study on information processing activities (Day, 1994a) in the initial phase of the innovation process, as this has been emphasized as perhaps the most important (e.g., Alam and Perry, 2002; Cooper, 1993;

Martin and Horne, 1993), and also a determinant of future market success (Goldenberg *et al.*, 2001; Lilien *et al.*, 2002). Services are mainly perceived as ideas or concepts (rather than a tangible entity). The more ideas a firm can generate, the greater is the probability of pursuing an idea to success (Alam, 2002). Services are unique in that they cannot be tested in advance. They are abstract, like an idea, until they are realized (Thomke, 2003).

6.3.2. *The context*

The context chosen was an end-user service for mobile telecommunications known as SMS. We assumed that this new type of technology based service (Bitner *et al.*, 2000) was not only of general interest for service research, but also we could test the inherent problems of market research on consumers, where lack of experience is central (cf. Leonard and Rayport, 1997; Ulwick, 2002). An R&D department provided a technical platform called Unified Services™ (US), which enabled access to information on the Internet from the mobile phone through sending and receiving SMSs. A mobile phone can also be employed as a "remote control" via the service, for example switching on and off home lighting or a radiator in a building, or checking whether or not a door is securely locked.

6.3.3. *The sample*

Altogether 86 persons, 57 men and 29 women, participated in the experiment. The mean participant age was 26.4, with a range of 19–54, and 57% were between 21 and 24 years of age. We sought for participants that were current or potential customers of the company and frequent users of mobile phone communication. A majority of the people that voluntarily participated in the experiment were university students. In Sweden, students represent a frequent user group of advanced GSM services other than voice, and therefore were familiar with the context (cf. von Hippel, 1986). Hence, the sample of consumers was expected to incorporate plausible customers of future applications.

6.3.4. *Involvement of customer — The learning process*

The field experiment included three phases: initiation, idea generation, and completion. At the initial meeting, we aimed to motivate the participants by establishing a creative tension (cf. Senge, 1990). The requirement for creative tension was an introduction to the scope of the study and a basic lecture on the US platform. A "user toolkit for innovation" that included mobile phones that carried a special account giving access to the US platform, was demonstrated and distributed (cf. "can be applied to both physical goods as well as information goods and associated services such as custom telephony software and the services it generates", von Hippel, 2001 p. 254). To increase the creative tension, all user participants were given the task of inventing new service ideas that would provide them with added value, and the professional service developers were instructed to design services that they thought would bring value to the customers. To expand the participants' vision of the future and range of possibilities, they were given access to a sample of 10 services on US that the R&D department had used for experimentation. They also received hands-on training on how to use them. Hence, the participants had access not only to the current reality, but also to the vision and tools that would enable them to come up with innovative ideas (cf. Senge, 1990).

Similar to someone involved in consumer idealized design, the participants were encouraged to imagine that the existing services with which they were familiar were not the limitations, but that they had the opportunity to create something new (cf. Ciccantelli and Magidson, 1993 p. 343). All participants were informed that high-quality contributions would be rewarded with a cash prize of €125 and cinema tickets. We hoped, however, that the participants' intrinsic motivation to try out futuristic services would prevail (cf. Olson and Bakke, 2001; Prahalad and Ramaswamy, 2000).

The idea generation phase lasted for 12 days. The task did not focus on any special problem, but instead sought to capture how people could imagine the use of technology to create services that would help them achieve goals in their private and professional lives (cf. Ulwick, 2002). During this time a help-desk was at their service (cf. Anderson and Crocca, 1993), and after six days, we checked how work was proceeding via the mobile phones. To acquire information about the idea creation process, the participants were given a diary and instructed to describe their processes, and whether or not problems had interfered with the processes. We were interested in what the customers were doing and how they were thinking, in order to learn more about how this process could be effectively designed (cf. sticky information, von Hippel, 1994).

A meeting initiated the third and final phase. All equipment was returned, and the participants were asked to write down descriptions of their generated service ideas in a pre-defined service description format. Due to the nature of mobile phones and limited resources, the service developer or we did not have the opportunity to learn from customers' behavior by direct observation. This left us with a relative black box of the customers' world. To compensate for the lack of observations and to get indirect access into real customer environments, information was acquired through the use of interviews and diaries. During the interview, we discussed all of their created services, as well as their documentation of the idea creation processes and service descriptions. Based on the acquired information, we attempted to form a shared interpretation of what happened when the participant used the toolkit in his or her own environment. Even though observation was impossible in this case, it could be included in other contexts and situations. The important question is not whether observation should be used, but rather to make sure to create prerequisites for the service interaction (i.e., value in use), and then perform complementary techniques in order to learn from that interaction.

6.3.5. *The evaluation process*

To objectively determine the performance, the evaluation process was based on the Consensual Assessment Technique (CAT) (Amabile, 1996). This technique makes it possible to compare different designs, independently judging and ranking them relative to each other. Independent judges evaluated the innovative outcomes in terms of ideas for future mobile phone services. The first panel included internal service developers at the R&D department involved in the study, while the second panel could be referred to as external technology consultants who were very knowledgeable in telecommunications. The third panel consisted of internal sales and marketing people, and a fourth panel was composed of customers. The panels thus covered the various aspects within a company, as well as the voice of the customer. Panels 1–3 were composed of three judges each, while the customer panel comprised six persons who were not experts within the given domain (Amabile, 1996). Im and Workman (2004) have suggested that creativity is a mediator between market orientation and new product success. Creativity has also been viewed as a construct that precedes innovation. Besides the dimension of uniqueness, an idea needs to be useful and actionable in order to be creative. Thus, in accordance with creativity research (e.g., Amabile, 1998; Besemer and O'Quin, 1987; Im and Workman, 2004), the dimensions of originality and user value were used to measure the innovative performance of the participants in the experiment. Before evaluating the created ideas, the scoring system was described verbally supported by a description in print. A 10-point scale was used for rating the services. Using the service description, every judge had to score at least one idea as a one point service and one idea as a 10-point service, and then rank the rest comparatively on the scale, both for originality and user value.

6.4. Results: Customer Ideas are More Innovative

In Table 2, the measure of innovativeness (mean of originality and user value) is presented for the professional service developers and the customers from the four panels, respectively. The data show that the panels, in general, assign a higher score to the customers' ideas, which in all cases but one are statistically significant. Hence, in terms of innovativeness, the learning process of customer involvement seems to clearly benefit services ideas with a greater potential, compared to the professional service developer's normal working routines. The process of involving the customer thus creates a situation for learning about a customer's latent needs.

Table 2:   The four panels' evaluation of service ideas in terms of innovativeness.

Panel	Group	N	M	S D	Significance
R&D	Service developers (12)	55	3,254	1,392	
	Customers (74)	374	3,818	1,588	
	Total	429	3,745	1,574	0.013
Techn. consult.	Service developers (12)	55	4,141	1,135	
	Customers (74)	374	4,590	1,429	
	Total	429	4,533	1,401	0.026
Marketing	Service developers (12)	55	4,606	9,525	
	Customers (74)	374	4,859	9,931	
	Total	429	4,826	9,905	0.105
Customers	Service developers (12)	55	4,750	1,032	
	Customers (74)	374	5,165	1,133	
	Total	429	5,112	1,128	0.011

6.5. Analysis: The Enhanced Learning Process

A deeper and better understanding (Sinkula, 1994; Day, 1994a) of attitudes, needs, and behaviors could further be obtained by asking the customer to assist in interpreting information and/or situations resulting in shared interpretations. For example, the participants were asked to explain what triggered an idea, that is, in what type of situation the idea occurred. We also discussed why the idea was relevant to a person's life, in order for us to discover a latent need.

The service descriptions showed that unique ideas (with high scores) were produced at unexpected times. The participants were often triggered by a sudden experience, and they then understood how they could use their toolkits to solve a problem or utilize a possibility. The idea that emerged would have been impossible to imagine in an interview, or while answering a survey. This shows that customers can access latent needs under certain circumstances. Activities and processes designed to facilitate learning thus have a chance to guide users toward innovative thinking. The data showed that the professional service developers normally do not have access to customers' environments and latent needs. Their suggestions simply do not match the customers' suggestions in quality, because they do not match the customers' needs.

One example is a service named "Verdict of the day." In this case, the customer was a person with no clear insight into his financial status and was therefore stressed. The idea occurred as he was walking toward an ATM to get, as he felt it, his "verdict of the day." He passed McDonalds, and he heard someone's phone beep on receiving an SMS. He then realized that it would be very handy to get the balance of one's account through the mobile phone once a day, and that the beep could be replaced by a McDonalds' jingle. In this way, he would be in better control of his money situation, and McDonalds could sponsor and pay for the service as they would receive more advertisements. The interview with the customer showed that this idea was an expression of the latent need of getting information in real time. The "situation" added the feature of a service free of charge by matching his need with an opportunity for a company. This example shows that the experimental method used in the field (Thomke, 2003), together with the design of active involvement of the customer, offers possibilities for new insights because the customers were put in a new set of conditions (Ciccantelli and Magidson, 1993).

Our insights from the service descriptions and interviews were discussed during a few informal meetings with the engineers from the R&D department. These meetings had the original intention of distributing the acquired results and feedback (Day, 1994a; Sinkula, 1994) to those who were involved in the study. We thus made an effort to avoid a traditional market research report. These meetings revealed some interesting experiences. At first, the engineers were opposed to ideas that had received high innovative scores (even though they themselves participated as judges). After a brief discussion about what they at first perceived as outlandish ideas, the discussion triggered an increased understanding of what actually caused the idea — a latent need. At first glance, a mediocre idea could, by the help of need-related information in service descriptions and interviews, capture information about the interaction with the technology and a person's environment that was interesting. If there was a sound reason behind the idea, it could be potentially developed into a service. Hence, the engineers reached a deeper customer understanding and shared customer interpretation, and then could use their knowledge of expertise to leverage the idea into a service that encompassed a latent need (Lynn *et al.*, 1997; Sinkula, 1994). The engineers were surprised, but they also became seriously engaged. The discussions with the R&D department showed that the idea previously mentioned provided a new market, and it could be applied to other situations, for example, "if you use Britney Spears' latest hit on the phone as a ring signal — you could get a discount on her album, which by the way you download and pay for via the phone...." We must remember that this experiment took place two years ago, at a time when these types of services were not available in Sweden. In summary, the only limit for using the customer's creative imagination is the imagination of the professional service developers. The involvement of a customer and creative tension had facilitated generative learning (Senge, 1990). For this to happen, a continuous customer input is required which goes beyond traditional questions and answers (Pitta and Franzak, 1996).

The experience of the experiment tells us that there must be incentives for company staff to involve and work together with the customer. Although the experiment yielded over 400 new service ideas, some of which were found highly innovative and even producible, the utilization and evaluation of market information (Day, 1994a) was limited within the company and among the professional service developers.

6.6. Discussion, Implications, and Future Research

A service-centered view on new service development and a focus on value in use can be captured by the involvement of customers in order to facilitate a learning process. We argue that the inseparable nature of customers as both producer and consumer and the tendency of service development to fall back on informal and ad hoc efforts (Kelly and Storey, 2000; Thomke, 2003), makes it natural and vital to include the customer in the innovation process. By adopting a proactive approach and involving customers early and intensively, service firms can facilitate learning and reduce the risk of being imitated and surpassed by competing organizations.

In this article, we argue that interaction is not only the focal point of services, but it is also the essence of learning from and with the customer. Emphasis is placed on supporting techniques as these are the means by which customer information and knowledge are created. The techniques and ways of working must be prerequisites for customer interaction and be designed to facilitate the systematic learning required to support and strengthen service innovation over time. The field experiment helped increase our understanding of the learning process, and how knowledge is created from and with potential customers and then transferred within the organization for new service development. The role of the customer in service innovation should be "contributing knowledge, skills and experiences, his or her willingness to share frustrations, requirements, problems and expectations, and his or her readiness to experiment and learn" (Prahalad and Ramaswamy, 2000, p. 80).

From the case study and previous research, however, we have learned that there are several problems associated with the involvement of customers. Even though results displayed 429 service ideas and the customers' ideas were found to be more innovative, TeliaSonera did not implement this way of working. One reason could be that the company's current structures, processes, and culture prevented them from continuing with involvement of customers in its current form. In a follow-up study of a successful lead-user project, Olson and Bakke (2001) make some suggestions as to why the company did not continue to use the method. Management explained that product concepts, generated by lead users, were seen as ambiguous and overly simplistic and therefore as less valuable by the new product development personnel. The technical language spoken by the new product personnel increased the inertia of old technology push by making it more prestigious and comfortable to plan new products with their technology suppliers. Furthermore, there was no pressure from market conditions, the firm's financial status, or management to make permanent changes to established routines. Anderson and Crocca (1993) learned from their co-development project, that there were communication barriers between users and developers and that the attitude of product developers made customer involvement difficult. Additional problems with involvement of customers reported in the literature are time consumption and increased efforts, low organizational fit (Lilien *et al.*, 2002), and increased uncertainty (Larsson and Bowens, 1989; Lengnick-Hall, 1996; Martin *et al.*, 1999; Nambisian, 2002). In addition, Nambisian (2002) identifies three important challenges of user involvement: the difficulty in identifying an appropriate set of customers, the difficulty in creating appropriate incitements for participation, and the difficulty of capturing the customers' knowledge.

Perhaps due to the problems and uncertainties associated with customer involvement in practice, traditional market research still dominates. Slater (2001) argues that the pursuit of customer satisfaction involves a set of difficult problems. The first concern is the development of a valid measure. A second problem is that these measures might overwhelm other strategic performance indicators such as those concerned with new product success or organizational learning and this might lead to only a short-term focus. Christensen (1997) reported that lead firms with a strong customer focus can allow strategically important innovation to languish because customers initially reject them due to lack of knowledge about how to use the products or services. Dahlsten (2003) reports that Volvo has historically focused on fixing what has gone wrong, that is, avoiding dissatisfaction, rather than developing what will go right by focusing on the actual customer experience.

Our study makes significant contributions to several important and interrelated research fields such as product and service innovation, market research and adherent techniques, market orientation, and organizational learning. First, it offers one way to operationalize and implement market orientation and organizational learning in a technology-intense service innovation context. Second, current research on learning from customers by involvement of customers in product and service innovation was reviewed and summarized. Based on this and conclusions from research on market orientation and organizational learning, a definition of learning from and with customers in service innovation was proposed. Third, based on previous research on customer involvement, we designed and tested a customer involvement procedure, using experiment, diaries, and interviews that strive to capture latent customer needs. Finally, we also displayed results to support the belief that the involvement of customers in service innovation, if properly managed, obtains valuable customer information and has a positive effect on the innovativeness of the created service ideas. Overall, this study provides a convincing understanding of the contribution made by end users in the generation of new ideas for technology based self services.

The findings of this research should assist the managers of service firms in their search for breakthrough services. First, managers are advised to adopt a proactive approach and involve customers early in the innovation process. A service is generally perceived as an idea and a continual flow of service ideas is necessary in order to succeed. Second, focus should be put on capturing latent needs. Customer solutions, however, should not be dismissed as too original or unrealizable. Behind the solution, there might be an interesting yet unfulfilled need. Third, although service firms can obtain customer input using several other means, they should consider the techniques and ways of working highlighted in this research as they strive to uncover customer latent needs. Finally, innovation should not be left solely to engineers. The R&D function should be developed for a cross-functional site including marketers, engineers, behaviorists, etc. Different knowledge and skills are needed to identify latent needs and to learn from customer behavior, experiences, and preferences.

References

Alam, I (2002). An exploratory investigation of user involvement in new service development. *Journal of the Academy of Marketing Science*, 30(3), 250–261.

Alam, I and C Perry (2002). A customer-oriented new service development process. *Journal of Services Marketing*, 16(6), 515–534.

Amabile, TM (1996). *Creativity in Context*. Colorado: Westview Press.

Anderson, WL and WT Crocca (1993). Engineering practice and co development of product prototypes. *Communications of the ACM*, 36(6), 49–56.

Atuahene-Gima, K (1996). Market orientation and innovation. *Journal of Business Research*, 35(2), 93–103.

Besemer, SP and K O Quin (1987). Creative product analysis: Testing a model by developing judging instruments. In *Frontiers of Creativity Research*, SG. Isaksen (ed.). Buffalo: Bearly Limited.

Bitner, MJ, SW Brown and ML Meuter (2000). Technology infusion in service encounters. *Journal of the Academy of Marketing Science*, 28(1), 138–149.

Christensen, CM (1997). *The Innovators Dilemma: When New Technologies Cause Great Firms to Fail.* Cambridge, MA: HBS Press.

Ciccantelli, S and J Magidson (1993). From experience: Consumer idealized design: Involving consumers in the product development process. *Journal of Product Innovation Management,* 10(4), 341–347.

Cooper, RG (1993). *Winning at New Products: Accelerating the Process from Idea to Launch.* Reading, MA: Perseus Books.

Dahlsten, F (2003). Avoiding the customer satisfaction rut. *Sloan Management Review,* 44(4), 73–77.

Day, G (1994a). Continuous learning about markets. *California Management Review,* 36(4), 9–31.

Day, G (1999). Creating a market-driven organization. *Sloan Management Review,* 41(1), 11–22.

Day, G (2002). Managing the market learning process. *Journal of Business and Industrial Marketing,* 17(4), 240–252.

Day, GS (1994b). The capabilities of market-driven organizations. *Journal of Marketing,* 58(4), 37–52.

Deszca, G, H Munro and H Noori (1999). Developing breakthrough products: Challenged and options for market assessment. *Journal of Operations Management,* 17(6), 613–630.

Durgee, JF, G Colarelli O' Connor and RW Veryzer (1998). Using mini-concepts to identify opportunities for really new product functions. *Journal of Consumer Marketing,* 16(6), 525–543.

Edvardsson, B, A Gustafsson and I Roos (2005). Service portraits in service research — A critical review. *International Journal of Service Industry Management,* 16(1), 107–121.

Flint, DJ (2002). Compressing new product success-to-success cycle time: Deep customer value understanding and idea generation. *Industrial Marketing Management,* 31(4), 305–316.

Goldenberg, J, DR Lehmann and D Mazursky (2001). The idea itself and the circumstances of its emergence as predictors of new product success. *Management Science,* 47(1), 69–84.

Griffin, A and JR Hauser (1993). The voice of the customer. *Marketing Science,* 12(1), 1–27.

Gruner, KE and C Homburg (2000). Does customer interaction enhance new product success? *Journal of Business Research,* 49(1), 1–14.

Gustafsson, A, F Ekdahl and B Edvardsson (1999). Customer focused service development in practice: A case study at Scandinavian Airlines System. *International Journal of Service Industry Management,* 10(4), 344–358.

Hamel, G and CK Prahalad (1991). Corporate imagination and expeditionary marketing. *Harvard Business Review,* 69(4), 81–92.

Han, JK, K Namwoon and RK Srivastava (1998). Market orientation and organizational performance: Is innovation a missing link? *Journal of Marketing*, 62(4), 30–45.

Harari, O (1994). The tar pits of market research. *Management Review*, 83(3), 42–44.

Hurley, R and T Hunt (1998). Innovation, market orientation, and organizational learning: An integration and empirical examination. *Journal of Marketing*, 62(4), 42–54.

Im, S and JP Workman (2004). Market orientation, creativity, and new product performance in high-technology firms. *Journal of Marketing*, 68(4), 114–132.

Johne, A and C Storey (1998). New service development: A review of the literature and annotated bibliography. *European Journal of Marketing*, 32(3/4), 184–251.

Kaulio, M (1997). Customer-focused product development — A practice-centered perspective. PhD Thesis, Chalmers University of Technology, Göteborg.

Kaulio, MA (1998). Customer, consumer and user involvement in product development: A framework and a review of selected methods. *Total Quality Management*, 9(1), 141–149.

Kelly, D and C Storey (2000). New service development: Initiation strategies. *International Journal of Service Industry Management*, 11(1), 45–62.

Kohli, AK and BJ Jaworsky (1990). Market orientation: The construct, research propositions, and managerial implications. *Journal of Marketing*, 54(2), 1–18.

Kok, RA, WB Hillebrand and WG Biemans (2003). What makes product development market-oriented? Toward a conceptual framework. *International Journal of Innovation Management*, 7(2), 137–163.

Kristensson, P, P Magnusson and J Matthing (2002). Users as a hidden resource for creativity: Findings from an experimental study on user involvement. *Journal of Creativity and Innovation Management*, 11(1), 55–61.

Langeard, E, P Reffiat and P Eigler (1986). Developing new services. In *Creativity in Services Marketing: What is New, What Works, What is Developing?* M Venkatesan, DM Schmalennee and CE Marshall (eds.). Chicago: American Marketing Association.

Larsson, R and DE Bowen (1989). Organization and customer: Managing design and coordination of services. *Academy of Management Review*, 14(2), 213–233.

Lengnick-Hall, CA (1996). Customer contributions to quality: A different view of the customer-oriented firm. *Academy of Management Review*, 21(3), 791–824.

Leonard, D (1995). *Wellsprings of Knowledge — Building and Sustaining the Sources of Innovation*. Boston: Harvard Business School Press.

Leonard, D and JF Rayport (1997). Spark innovation through empathic design. *Harvard Business Review*, 75(6), 102–113.

Lilien, GL, PD Morrison, K Searls, M Sonnack and E von Hippel (2002). Performance assessment of the lead user idea-generation process for new product development. *Management Science*, 48(8), 1042–1059.

Lovelock, CH (1991). *Services Marketing*. London: Prentice-Hall International.

Lynn, GS, JG Morone and AS Paulson (1997). Marketing and discontinuous innovation: The probe and learn process. *California Management Review*, 38(3), 8–37.

Magnusson, P, J Matthing and P Kristensson (2003). Managing user involvement in service innovation: Experiments with innovating end-users. *Journal of Service Research*, 6(2), 111–124.

Martin, CR and DA Horne (1993). Services innovation: Successful versus unsuccessful firms. *International Journal of Service Industry Management*, 4(1), 49–65.

Martin, CR and DA Horne (1995). Level of success inputs for service innovations in the same firm. *International Journal of Service Industry Management*, 6(4), 40–56.

Martin, CR, DA Horne and AM Schultz (1999). The business-to-business customer in the service innovation process. *European Journal of Innovation Management*, 2(2), 55–62.

Montoya-Weiss, MM and R Calantone (1994). Determinants of new product performance: A review and meta-analysis. *Journal of Product Innovation Management*, 11(5), 397–417.

Morgan, RE, CS Katsikeas and K Appiah-Adu (1998). Market orientation and organizational learning capabilities. *Journal of Marketing Management*, 14(4/5), 353–381.

Mullern, MJ, DM Wildeman and EA White (1993). Taxonomy of PD practices: A brief practitioner's guide. *Communications of the ACM*, 36(4), 26–27.

Nambisian, S (2002). Designing virtual customer environments for new product development: Toward a theory. *Academy of Management Review*, 27(3): 392–413.

Narver, JC and SF Slater (1990). The effect of a market orientation on business profitability. *Journal of Marketing*, 54(4), 20–35.

Narver, JC, SF Slater and DL MacLachlan (2004). Responsive and proactive market orientation and new product success. *Journal of Product Innovation Management*, 21, 334–347.

Neale, MR and DR Corkindale (1998). Co-developing products: Involving customer earlier and more deeply. *Long Range Planning*, 31(3), 418–425.

Normann, R (1984). *Service Management: Strategy and Leadership in Service Businesses*. New York: Wiley.

Olson, EL and G Bakke (2001). Implementing the lead user method in a high technology firm: A longitudinal study of intentions versus actions. *The Journal of Product Innovation Management*, 18(6), 388–395.

Pitta, D and F Franzak (1996). Boundary spanning product development in consumer markets: Learning organization insights. *Journal of Consumer Marketing*, 13(5), 66–81.

Prahalad, CK and G Hamel (1990). The core competence of the corporation. *Harvard Business Review*, 68(3), 79–91.

Prahalad, CK and V Ramaswamy (2000). Co-opting customer competence. *Harvard Business Review*, 78(1), 79–87.

Senge, P (1990). The leader's new work: Building learning organizations. *Sloan Management Review*, 32(1), 7–24.

Shaw, B (1985). The role of the interaction between the user and the manufacturer in medical equipment innovation. *R&D Management*, 15(4), 283–292.

Sheth, J, RS Sisodia and A Sharma (2000). The antecedents and consequences of customer-centric marketing. *Journal of Academy of Marketing Science*, 28, 55–66.

Sinkula, J (1994). Market information processing and organizational learning. *Journal of Marketing*, 58(1), 35–45.

Slater, SF and JC Narver (1995). Market orientation and the learning organization. *Journal of Marketing*, 59(3), 63–74.

Slater, SF (2001). Market orientation at the beginning of a new millennium. *Managing Service Quality*, 11(4), 230–232.

Solomon, MR, C Suprenant, JA Czepiel and EG Gutman (1985). A role theory perspective on dyadic interactions. *Journal of Marketing*, 49(1), 99–111.

Thomke, S (2003). R&D comes to services: Bank of America's path breaking experiments. *Harvard Business Review*, 81(4), 71–79.

Toffler, A (1980). *The Third Wave*. London: Pan Books Ltd.

Tyre, MJ and E von Hippel (1997). The situated nature of adaptive learning in organizations. *Organization Science*, 8(1), 71–83.

Ulwick, AW (2002). Turn customer input into innovation. *Harvard Business Review*, 80(1), 91–97.

Vargo, SL and RF Lusch (2004). Evolving to a new dominant logic for marketing. *Journal of Marketing*, 68(1), 1–17.

Veryzer, RW (1998). Discontinuous innovation and the new product development process. *Journal of Product Innovation Management*, 15(4), 304–321.

von Hippel, E (1986). Lead users: A source of novel product concepts. *Management Science*, 32(7), 791–805.

von Hippel, E (1994). Sticky information and the locus of problem solving: Implications for innovation. *Management Science*, 40(4), 429–439.

von Hippel, E (2001). User toolkits for innovation. *The Journal of Product Innovation Management*, 18(3), 247–257.

Voss, CA (1985). The role of users in the development of applications software. *The Journal of Product Innovation Management*, 2(2), 113–121.

Wikström, S (1996). The customer as co-producer. *European Journal of Marketing*, 3(4), 6–19.

Zaltman, G and RA Higie (1993). *Seeing the Voice of the Customer: The Zaltman Metaphor Elicitation Technique*. Cambridge: MSI.

Zeithaml, VA and MJ Bitner (2000). *Services Marketing: Integrating Customer Focus Across the Firm*, 2nd ed. Boston: Irwin/McGraw-Hill.

7

Managing Ideas That Are Unthinkable in Advance: A Matter of How and Where You Ask

Per Kristensson

Service Research Center, Karlstad University, Sweden
per.kristensson@kau.se

7.1. Introduction

A common perception one often meet is that the best way to find new innovative ideas outside the company is to conduct a focus group or to invite customers to the user lab and listen to what they have to say about the latest prototype.

Focus groups and user lab testing are important and necessary ways of understanding customer needs and thereby finding new ideas to future products. User lab testing, for example, enables companies to make fine-tune adjustments to their prototypes ahead of full scale market introduction. During focus groups, new ideas of how to tailor market communication might emerge and/or an understanding of how customers experience a certain product can lead to ideas for future innovation projects. Unfortunately, focus groups tend to rely heavily on what the customer says and individuals' thoughts are not stimulated by words but by images (Zaltman, 1997). Likewise, in user lab testing it is only possible to see how a customer uses the prototype in a general situation but not to conceive an authentic situation where the customer would actually need the forthcoming product. Accordingly, different types of market research techniques may affect how a customer thinks in different ways, which have implications for the resulting knowledge that is being created or collected.

Therefore, as this article argues, the traditional way of having customers uttering their thoughts may not always be the optimal way of finding innovative ideas that meet customer needs (Zaltman, 1997). In fact, with the technological content that many products and services consist of today, the traditional methods of getting close to the customer may be too blunt and inefficient and simply not leading to any new knowledge about how to create value for potential and existing customers. As a result, companies may want to reconsider how they choose market research techniques and instead look to new improved methods of getting close to the customer and finding innovative ideas — especially if they are dealing with new technology.

In a research project carried out at Telia, the largest service provider and telecom operator in northern Europe, it was shown that customer input might actually be of more interest to the company if it is captured in the beginning of the development cycle rather than in the middle or at the end of it (Khurana and Rosenthal, 1998). This means that companies should ask their customer what they should produce, instead of how an almost ready prototype should be modified.

In this chapter, some basic but often neglected principles will be offered for companies that seek to cooperate with customers in order to market orient themselves in a technology based consumer market. The aim of the chapter is to discuss the conditions of market research where companies are likely to find highly original and very valuable ideas (for the user). The context is technology based products which is a field where companies often state that it is meaningless to ask customers what they need — the belief is that customers only want what they already have (Zaltman, 2003). The theoretical base of the chapter is constituted by psychological theories that underlie different types of market research techniques and creative ideas. In the conclusion, the Telia case shows how customers generate creative ideas that stretch beyond what in-house product developers are able to achieve — ideas that are unthinkable in advance.

7.2. The Difficulties of Listening to Customers — Conceptualizations of Market Research

Although the idea of having potential or existing customers as idea generators for new innovations appears sound, companies do not seem to agree since research shows that companies seldom turn this idea into practice (Kelly and Storey, 2000). If customer input is being requested, it usually takes place, as previously mentioned, before commercialization and constitutes an important step in the post development review phase (Flint, 2002).

One important reason why companies do not use customers' input, early in the development cycle as a starting point or in the initial screening phase, has to do with a limited understanding of how customers think and, more specifically, how they perceive that different market research techniques are functioning. More precisely, one particular thing that for example managers would benefit from is to understand how various market research techniques actually affect participants' way of thinking, thus, different market research techniques affects how people think and leads to qualitatively different types of result. Having such knowledge will explain why customer ideas are sometimes perceived as unoriginal and during what circumstances they may, on the contrary, come up with ideas that are both original and valuable.

Different methods of collecting customer knowledge can be conceptualized broadly into three types (Sanders and Williams, 2001): First, there are *say* methods which are made up of verbal communication uttered by the user. Second, there are *see* methods which consists of methods where a researcher observes what a consumer is doing and then learns from that, and third, there are *make* methods where consumers are provided with key need-related tools that enable users to create what they need in a given situation (see Table 1).

Each of these three types of methods has their own way of functioning and thus results in different kinds of output. For example, a say method ought to be ideal whenever it is important to understand how a customer perceives a market campaign and likes or dislikes the esthetic appeal of a certain product or other kind of information that is consciously manifested

Table 1:   Conceptualization of different market research methods.

	Say	See	Make
Core characteristic	(e.g., focus groups, interviews) Verbal communication from customer	(e.g., observation, ethnography) Observation of customer	(e.g., customers produce ideas on their own) Customer makes something that creates value for themselves
Benefits (besides providing with input of ideas)	Easy to execute, methods are well known	Takes place in the customer's own environment (setting of use)	May result in ideas that are "unthinkable in advance" and that are highly customized
Risks	Information gathered is known since before	Time consuming and costly, difficult and inconvenient to execute	Unique ideas may be difficult to protect from circulation. Methods are relatively unknown
Expediency	Product/service is well-known to customer. Example: a new soda	Usage is possible to observe, preferably in natural setting. Example: use of vacuum cleaner	Product/service is complex. Technical content makes future usage difficult to foresee. Example: a cell phone and its services
Cognitive locus	Backward — consumer cognition starts out from what is already known, for example, a product that they are familiar with	Present — observation of what is happening during usage	Forward — creation of value is oriented toward solving the user's problem and takes place in customer's own setting of use

for the customer. In addition, the less complicated a product is the more appropriate a say method will be (Zaltman, 2003). Also, say methods should be chosen whenever the aim is to collect information about how something *was* experienced as say methods *make people relate backwards in time* (Trott, 2001).

See methods are suitable whenever the aim is to understand how a customer *uses* a product. Here, the focus is on the *present*, ongoing behaviors (that can be seen) and thoughts (that must be conjectured) that occur. A see method, as a user laboratory test, will be the ideal method to use if a household appliance manufacturer wants to see how users are handling their latest version of vacuum cleaner.

Both *say* and *see* methods are appropriate when market research is carried out in the prototype phase of new product development, that is, in the end of the product development process. It should be noted that none of these two first types of methods is optimal when the aim is to understand latent needs and/or to find novel ideas about hitherto unexploited opportunities of creating customer value, that is, early in the product development phase. In a focus group, the cognitive locus is directed backwards in time; invited users are often unconsciously using their previous experience with existing products as the guiding principle when thinking about new ideas (see Table 1). Consequently, when the ideas produced have originated from what is already existing and well known for the user, the results will seldom be original. If a *say* method is used to find new innovative ideas, these ideas will likely be already envisioned by members of the product development team who are also familiar with the existing products. Hence, it is no wonder that there is a widely held belief among people involved in product and service development that customers are not creative and are seldom believed to conceive creative ideas for future products (Sanders and Williams, 2001).

If the goal is to find ideas of the future, make methods are more appropriate. Make methods are directed forward in time as users are constructing something in their own environment that is intended to help them in a specific situation.

In summary, one reason why companies do not always get the kind of information they need is because the market technique they use does not corresponded to the information they seek, that is, the means and the end do not match. Before routinely using the same methods, companies need to realize that different techniques provide different results. If the aim of the company is to find ideas that might lead to new innovations, then make methods would be beneficial, and if the aim is to make alterations to an almost developed product or understand how users might use a certain product, then *say* and *see* methods are more appropriate.

7.3. Why All Market Research Techniques Do Not Result in Innovative Ideas — The Difficulties of Thinking Outside the Box

The dilemma of having the ability to imagine possible innovations is accounted for by research in cognitive psychology. Psychologists have shown that the more familiarity an individual has with a particular domain, the more difficult it may be to generate creative solutions that lie outside this domain. Previous knowledge within a domain, that is, familiarity with a certain product, acts as a mental set that restricts creative problem-solving attempts outside the domain (Wiley, 1998). If you have developed a certain skill in solving a problem in a successful manner, for example, you may have more difficulty noticing new options of tackling the problem in a smoother way. Thus, the more knowledge one has within a domain, the more difficult it will be to think outside this set of knowledge. This implies a problem for both product developers, who are well acquainted with the products of their company, and for users who are invited to participate in focus groups and trigger their imagination by thinking of their past experiences with a product (Leonard-Barton, 1992). Thus, if customers are asked to find new ideas for mobile phone services, previous experiences with mobile phone services will restrict their ability to identify new and valuable ideas.

Another difficulty that inhibits creativity, also caused by previous experience and knowledge, has to do with priming. Priming is a phenomenon that is illustrated pertinently in the fairy tale about "The Emperor's new Clothes" (by the Danish author HC Andersen). People only see what they expect to see, that is, it is difficult to observe something that lies outside what we expect (as the new clothing that the emperor has bought). If, for example, we are conducting observations of how customers use a product, we are likely to detect only such behaviors that we (more or less consciously) expect to see. Priming is a difficult restriction because it is automatic and requires no intention (Bargh *et al.*, 1996). As in the fairy tale by Andersen, it is those who have no or only little previous knowledge that most easily discovers what other people may not think of. Certain involuntary thought processes may occur which, unfortunately, reduce the chance of discovering interesting aspects in users' behavior that can lead to new innovation opportunities.

Accordingly, customers' ability to guide the development of new products and services are affected by their previous experience. In order for customers to be able to break free and think outside the box (beyond their previous experiences), two things need to happen.

First, it is easier to be creative if one is given a set of tools or pieces of information that represent an opportunity to construct something. This means that a user should be equipped with key need-related information and tools that may be combined into a new product (i.e., make) instead of being provided with their latest product (i.e., see/say). These pieces of information, or tools, should consist of components that are essential in order to produce a solution that could be valuable to a user (von Hippel, 2001). In terms of mobile phone services, for example, key need-related tools and information could include the mobile phone itself, information about possibilities of mobile phone technology in the future, some examples of new ideas for services that do not yet exist on the market, or any other components that are essential in order to make mobile telephony function. The solution-enabling equipment empowers the user to identify a wide variety of different kinds of value-creating opportunities that are important for the user. By combining the solution-enabling equipment in different ways the user will get insights into different kinds of products and services that do not yet exist while actually providing opportunities for the user to solve problems that he thought were hopeless. A motivated user will therefore be able to combine the equipment into a product or service which is 100% personalized and creates surplus value for them (Amabile, 1996). Thus, this procedure facilitates a more unrestricted manner of thinking in a way that is forward looking instead of backward. Another beneficial aspect of this procedure is that the user is "playing" with key components that are essential in the product portfolio of the company, which is why the company is likely to have little problem implementing any ideas or half-finished prototypes that the user has discovered.

Second, problem solving should be carried out in the same environment in which a new innovation (i.e., solution) is likely to play an important role. This means that the user should elaborate with the provided tools in their own setting of use, not in a formal focus group room with people they do not know. The interesting aspect of this scenario is that the user can elaborate on how the solution-enabling equipment can be put together in order to meet their own needs (Tyre and von Hippel, 1997). Ideas that a user thinks of are likely to be about situations that the user him/herself has not previously thought about — these situations are often embedded deeply in the user's own environment. The following true story will illustrate this point.

Jane would really like to go on a vacation but can only afford a non-expensive, last minute trip. However, as she wants to make use of her present holiday as much as possibe, she is not keen on being at the airport or travel agency all day waiting for something that might not happen. She then thinks of the idea that the agency could give her a call whenever a non-occupied trip is available, but soon understands that this service would be too time consuming and costly for the agency as more people are likely to be in the same situation as her. However, as she would really value a trip abroad, she starts to realize that the web site of an agency can fill the function of sending short text messages (SMSs). Motivated by her insight, she creates a service idea where a computerized SMS will be sent to her mobile phone whenever a trip below a certain cost and to a certain destination becomes available. Jane realizes all this after she visits the travel agency to look for the latest incoming offerings on the fourth day in a row. The result is a user-driven service idea that, if implemented, would add surplus value for herself (and the travel organizer, the service provider, and other customers with the same interests).

In the previous example, the personal needs of Jane are coupled with the recently acquired knowledge about mobile phone services and its technology. The knowledge about mobile phones was more or less unconscious to the user but activated when the user unexpectedly realized a situation where this information did indeed fit. The result was an idea for a mobile phone that builds heavily on information that is more or less impossible for an R&D member to gather. The information is so embedded within the user's own environment that it might even be difficult for the user him/herself to communicate about it. This also explains why such valuable ideas rarely show up in a focus group. Focus group interviews are almost never held in the user's own setting, sooner in a nice office room with comfortable chairs along with coffee and a cinnamon roll. Therefore, these kinds of insights where tacit knowledge is detected are unlikely to be communicated to the company. Still, this type of information is important in ensuring that customer value is met or exceeded and the company is likely to miss this information. To illustrate the problem metaphorically, not conducting market research where the need is present (or very close to the need) is like asking someone who is not disabled about what kinds of functions or benefits that are critical and needs to be considered when you are designing a new wheelchair. The feelings, thoughts, and behavior about why you need certain functions/benefits and the circumstances surrounding a certain product are likely to never be the same as when you actually are experiencing the need (which a non-disabled never do). Another illustration would be when you have forgotten to bring a towel in your sport bag, intended for the shower after working out at the gym. When are you most likely to discover that you have neglected to pack this necessary thing? Will it be at work, in the car going to the gym, doing exercises in the gym, or when you are just about to take a shower? The answer is obvious; you will discover your need when the need is present. In any other situation, you are much less likely to become cognitively aware of your need.

In summary, users should be equipped with tools so that they can create the solutions that they want on their own. They should make their idea prototypes at a location where the need is located (Gladwell, 2005) since the need is much more easily discovered and expressed when the user is actually experiencing it.

7.4.   User Innovation at Telia — or 74 "Product Developers" Generating Innovative Ideas Rapidly and Free of Charge

In the research project at Telia, the overall aim was to find new ways of creating value for customers. More specifically, Telia was interested in innovating new non-voice mobile phone services but faced the usual problem of not knowing what the typical customer wanted. At Telia, getting into the minds of potential and existing customers was crucial. One excellent way of doing so is, of course, to let customers initiate what the company should develop in the future. In October 2003, CEO Anders Igel stated that "in the future our users will be developing the larger part of our innovations ... " (Computer Sweden, 2002). Indeed, having several actual and potential customers carving out ideas, in the immediate environment of use for the customer, is likely to provide the company with many opportunities for new services.

Because mobile phones and their associated services are technical in nature, market research techniques that are categorized as *say* and *see* methods did not function well. Customers simply stated that they were satisfied with the product as it was or they came up with solutions that the product developers were already aware of. Due to this situation, the new project was set up where customers were asked to be the inspiration for new cell phone services, much in the way that is mentioned in the previous "make" method description (see "About the research" regarding how the project was set up and conducted).

7.5.   About the Research

An experimental design was used where users were given the assignment to create new value-adding services (Kristensson *et al.*, 2002). The outcome, that is, the ideas about new mobile phone services, was to be compared with service ideas generated by a group of in-house developers at Telia.

The research project contained four phases. *PHASE 1* — In the first phase, all users listened to a brief lecture about telecom and its technology to provide a sense of understanding of the possibilities (and limitations) that today and tomorrow's mobile technology will enable. All users were also equipped with mobile phones and a free subscription so that they could use the cell phone whenever they needed. *PHASE 2* — In the second phase, all participants were to create ideas for new services. This phase lasted 12 days, and all ideas were recorded into a notebook. It should be noted that since the participants were instructed to create services that would provide benefits for themselves they were told to not sit at home and simply engage in an individual brainstorming process. Rather they were to function as usual, and whenever a problematic situation occurred, they were instructed to consider if, by any chance, they estimated that the mobile phone could play a value-adding role for them. If so, they recorded their idea about this in their notebook. Interviews carried out after the project was over showed that this process worked rather automatically for the users. Since they had learned about the possibilities regarding mobile phone opportunities in the future, whenever a small problem or situation of some kind occurred they came to think about how a mobile phone service could solve these situations in a smoother way. *PHASE 3* — In the third phase, all the participants were asked to transcribe their ideas from the diary into a more detailed service description. In the service description, the participants were asked to write a brief description of the service idea and state how the service would create value for them. *PHASE 4* — In the fourth phase, all ideas were taken to a screening phase. The ideas were ranked on a scale of 10. Three dimensions of originality, value, and ease of implementation were used. A score of 1 represented the least original, least valuable, and most difficult to produce. Similarly, a score of 10 corresponded to the most original, most valuable, and easiest to produce. There were four panels, consisting of three people in each panel, judging the ideas against the three criterions. All ideas were made unidentifiable so that judges did not know whether the idea was invented by a user or by a professional R&D member.

From a research point of view, it was of interest to investigate what a group of users would be able to identify in terms of ideas compared to a group of in-house developers. Our question was whether ideas generated by professional service developers were more original, valuable, and realizable than ideas generated by users. From Telia's point of view, it was of interest to discover new ideas for new mobile phone services. Both of these questions (in this project answered by the same set of data) are important because customer behaviors, needs, and wants, in light of the invasion of technology based products, are becoming more difficult to grasp (Parasuraman and Colby, 2001).

As shown in Figs. 1 and 2, the results from the customer driven project at Telia clearly indicate that users can be a useful source for innovative ideas (i.e., original, valuable, and realizable ideas). Users are capable of being creative if they are asked to be in a different manner and at a different location than what is usually the case in market research.

According to another group of in-house developers at Telia and a group of externally recruited technology consultants, the ideas from users were assessed as being more original (new) and more valuable (solving a user problem) than those of developers. To further validate this pattern, we also let a panel of analysts at the market department and a panel of customers, carry out the same screening procedure (described in the box "about the research"), and the results obtained were similar. If the three criteria of originality, value, and realization are taken apart, it can be seen that users derived ideas that were significantly more original and valuable, but the in-house developers derived ideas that were easier to implement (Kristensson *et al.*, 2004).

These results are impressive, but it is important to remember that users outnumber members of R&D departments and thus represent a much more diverse group of people (e.g., regarding education, age, home setting, interests, and so forth). Therefore, user ideas will not only be of more value, but they will also be more heterogeneous, diverse, and varying than the ideas from the R&D department (for a thorough presentation of all data, see Kristensson *et al.*, 2004; Franke and von Hippel, 2003).

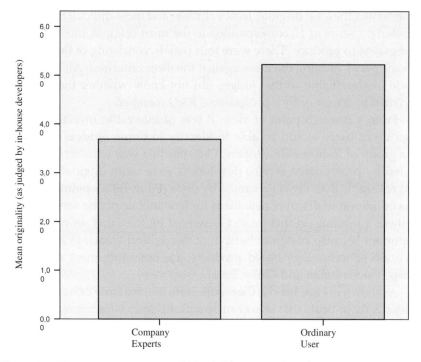

Figure 1:   How company experts (Telia in-house developers) and ordinary users perform on the task of identifying original ideas, assessed by in-house developers (other than the ones participating in the study).

The Telia case illuminates how a make method, here in terms of a customer involvement project, may lead to ideas that are unlikely to be thought of beforehand. These ideas would never have developed if the department had called customers into a focus group, or observed them using mobile phone services live.

7.6. Managerial Implications

Since what a customer really values is often hidden, both to the customer herself/himself and to the companies, new improved methods of under-standing customer value are needed. This article has provided a conceptual case that shows different situations where market research might create such knowledge. The managerial implications of this article are for com-panies who are trying to proactively come up with ideas for new products

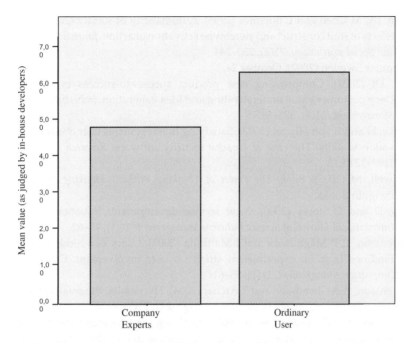

Figure 2:   How company experts (Telia in-house developers) and ordinary users perform on the task of identifying valuable service ideas for mobile phones, assessed by in-house developers.

and services that will generate value for their customers in the future; these companies should avoid using traditional market research methods but should instead look to actively involving users early in the product development process.

In light of the Telia project, the message of involving customers to create on their own will inform a company about what a user may do in a new set of circumstances with a relatively unknown product (Trott, 2001). Therefore, by involving users/customers with tools in a new product development project, ideas that seem unthinkable in advance may pave the way for more non-traditional market research techniques.

References

Amabile, TM (1996). *Creativity in Context*. Colo: Westview Press.
Anderson, HC (2000, originally 1837). *The Emperor's New Clothes*. London: Walker Books.

Bargh, JA, M Chen and L Burrows (1996). Automaticity of social behavior: Direct effects of trait construct and stereotype activation of action. *Journal of Personality and Social psychology*, 71(2), 230–244.

Computer Sweden (2002). October 24.

Flint, DJ (2002). Compressing new product success-to-success cycle time — Deep customer value understanding and idea generation. *Industrial Marketing Management*, 31(4), 305–315.

Franke, N and E von Hippel (2003). Satisfying heterogeneous user needs via innovation toolkits: The case of Apache security software. *Research Policy*, 32(7), 1199–1215.

Gladwell, M (2005). *Blink. The Power of Thinking Without Thinking.* New York: Penguin Books.

Kelly, D and C Storey (2000). New service development: Initiation strategies. *International Journal of Service Industry Management*, 11(1), 45–62.

Kristensson, P, P Magnusson and J Matthing (2002). Users as a hidden resource: Findings from an experimental study on user involvement. *Creativity and Innovation Management*, 11(1), 55–61.

Kristensson, P, A Gustafsson and T Archer (2004). Harnessing the creativity among users. *Journal of Product Innovation Management*, 21(1), 4–14.

Kristensson, P and PR Magnusson (2005). Involving users for incremental or radical innovation — A matter of tuning. Paper presented at the *12th International Product Development Management Conference*. In Copenhagen, Denmark, 12–14, June.

Khurana, A and SR Rosenthal (1998). Toward holistic 'front end' in new product development. *Journal of Product Innovation Management*, 15, 57–74.

Leonard-Barton, D (1992). Core capabilities and core rigidities: A paradox in managing new product development. *Strategic Management Journal*, 13(5), 111–125.

Magnusson, P, J Matthing and P Kristensson (2003). Managing user involvement in service innovation: Experiments with innovating end users. *Journal of Service Research*, 6(2), 111–124.

Marsh, RL, JD Landau and JL Hicks (1996). How examples may (and may not) constrain creativity. *Memory and cognition*, 24(3), 669–680.

Marsh, R, T Ward and J Landau, (1999). The inadvertent use of prior knowledge in a generative cognitive task. *Memory and cognition*, 27(1), 94–105.

Parasuraman, A and CL Colby (2001). *Techno-Ready Marketing, How and Why Your Customers Adopt Technology.* New York, NY: The Free Press.

Sanders, EGN and CT Williams (2001). Harnessing people's creativity: Ideation and expression through visual communication. In *Focus Groups: Supporting Effective Product Development*, J Langford and McDonagh-Philip, D (eds.), UK: Taylor and Francis.

Trott, P (2001). The role of market research in the development of discontinuous new products. *European Journal of Innovation Management*, 4(3), 117–125.

Tyre, MJ and E von Hippel (1997). The situated nature of adaptive learning in organizations. *Organization Science*, 8(1), 71–83.

von Hippel, E (2001). User toolkits for innovation. *Journal of Product Innovation Management*, 18(4), 247–257.

Wiley, J (1998). Expertise as mental set: The effects of domain knowledge in creative problem solving. *Memory and Cognition*, 26(4), 716–730.

Zaltman, G (1997). Rethinking market research: Putting people back in. *Journal of Marketing Research*, 24, 424–437.

Zaltman, G (2002). Hidden minds. *Harvard Business Review*, June, 26–27.

Zaltman, G (2003). *How Customers Think. Essential Insights into the Mind of the Market.* Boston: Harvard Business School Press.

8

Learning from Experiments Involving Users in Service Innovation

Peter R. Magnusson

Service Research Center, Karlstad University, Sweden
peter.magnusson@kau.se

8.1. Introduction

The literature is filled with examples of organizations testifying how they utilize customers and users in the development of new products or services. Being "customer driven" has almost become a mantra. Nevertheless, a critical review of the literature reveals that there is rather limited knowledge concerning the actual contribution made by users. Much of the reading material is on "success stories" describing the successful involvement of users. But is user involvement in service innovation always beneficial? Are there situations when involving users does not contribute anything, or even worse, becomes a burden? These issues form the basis for this chapter.

The purpose of this chapter is to account for some of the findings in the CuDIT study. CuDIT (Customer Driven IT-development) was a joint research effort conducted by Per Kristensson, Jonas Matthing, and the author. The study formed the empirical input for our individual doctoral theses (Magnusson, 2003a; Kristensson, 2003; Matthing, 2004). The experimental part of the study was common. The data, however, were analyzed individually with different research questions and focuses that formed the individual dissertations. This chapter accounts only for the research questions and focus of the author.

8.2. Scope

The chapter discusses the effects of involving users in creating new service ideas for mobile telephony, based on the CuDIT research study. It deals with three themes:

- The first theme concerns *whether* or not services developed with user involvement are *better* than those developed by professionals alone and if so in what way.
- The second theme investigates whether or not user involvement can be *optimized*; that is, what is the best way of involving users?
- Finally, the chapter discusses how the *product development* process needs to be adapted when users are involved. In other words, how should companies implement user involvement? The questions elaborated upon in the thesis are the following:

- Does user involvement produce better service ideas?
- If so, in what way are the service ideas better?
- Are certain users better suited to be involved?
- How are users best involved?
- Does the product development process need to be adapted when users are involved?

8.3. Method — Knowledge through Experiments

To investigate the research questions, we arranged five different trials (experiments). The first trial consisted of 12 professional service developers from Telia Mobile (Sweden's largest mobile telephony operator); the four remaining trials consisted of different setups of 72 users represented by students of the Karlstad University.

The participants were given 12 days to come up with at least one idea for an SMS-based service idea that would be beneficial to themselves.

The professionals were given 12 days to come up with service ideas they believed to be suitable for students of the Karlstad University. Consequently, all trials had the same target group. It was thus possible to compare the service suggestions and draw conclusions regarding the contributions made by user involvement.

Each trial started with a two-hour introduction. The participants were first asked to do three personal tests in the form of written inquiries. The participants listened to a lecture on the application platform for which their service suggestions would hopefully be realized. The application platform was essentially a server that could handle user originated commands transmitted via SMSs (mobile phone text messages). The commands were translated into http calls on the Internet to retrieve information. The retrieved information was then packaged in the form of an SMS and sent back to the user.

About 10 implemented test services were available to create an even deeper understanding of the opportunities provided by the underlying application platform. One of the sample services, for example, was a bus timetable service. The command for finding out when the next bus to town was due to depart was executed by sending an SMS with the text "BTT." Within a few seconds, this resulted in an SMS response with the time for the next bus, for example, "The next bus to the city center will leave at 17:06 from the University Campus" (text translated from Swedish).

Each participant borrowed a mobile phone topped up with about 25 euros so they could try out the test services during the trial. This enabled the participants to send at least 170 SMSs during the trial.

To encourage the submission of ideas, all ideas remained the intellectual property of the *creator of the idea*. To motivate the participants, an award of 80 euros was given for the best service idea in each trial.

It was also stated that one could choose to work alone or collaborate with others. If one collaborated with other participants, this was to be noted in a diary. Each individual was expected to produce at least one service idea of his or her own.

8.3.1. *The different trials (groups)*

Group A (Professionals) consisted of 12 professional service developers and was used as a reference; the group represents the outcome when users are *not* involved in the development process.

Group B (Technically Skilled Users) consisted of 16 computer technology students. The aim of this group was to investigate how the participants' technical skill affected the resulting ideas. The group also had access to a developer's toolkit (von Hippel, 2001) used to implement the US services. They were thus able to implement their ideas.

Group C (Ordinary Users) consisted of 19 "ordinary" users who were students in non-technical courses such as economics, teaching, and political science, meaning that they had no formal technical education.

Group D (Consulting Ordinary Users) consisted of 20 students of the same type as group C except that during the trial these participants had two one-hour consultations with a professional service developer. They were thus able to obtain qualified feedback about their ideas.

Group E (Creativity Trained Ordinary Users) consisted of 17 students with no technical background. Before participating in the trial, they had passed a course in creative methods.

8.3.2. *Assessment by experts and laymen*

The participants were assembled after 12 days of idea creation. A total of 429 ideas were submitted, of which 374 came from the "users." All ideas were assessed by independent judges: three experts from Telia, three non-Telia telecom experts, three technically skilled university students, and four non-technical university students (in this paper, only the results from the two expert panels are used).

8.3.3. *Three assessment dimensions*

Based on previous research (Hart *et al.*, 2003; Hauser and Zettelmeyer, 1997; Kelly and Storey, 2000) and input from experienced service developers, three dimensions were stipulated (Magnusson, 2003a, p. 62):

(A) originality,
(B) user-value,
(C) producibility.

Originality or innovativeness is, by definition, important in all new product development; a new product or service must "stand out" to be noticed. User value represents the value that a user is willing to pay for. Although an idea can be both original and possess a high user value, it will have no commercial value if it cannot be realized. The judges used a scale from 1 to 10 where one 1 was the least original, had the lowest user value, and was the most difficult to realize.

8.4. Results — The Contribution Made by User Involvement

Were the users' ideas better than the professionals'? The simple answer is that at least they were different. They were better if the users were involved *"the right way."* If involved incorrectly, there was no contribution by the users; this will be elaborated on in Section 8.5. First, however, we will see what users *can* contribute when invited to discover new ideas for services.

8.4.1. *Originality, user value, and producibility*

The users' ideas were on average found to have a higher perceived user value. Perhaps not so surprisingly, the users ought to be the "experts" when it comes to suggesting services that are useful for them. It is more surprising that under certain circumstances, users seem to be more innovative, creating more original ideas than the professional developers. However, there is a problem; the more original the idea — the more difficult the service would be to realize. Essentially, none of the ideas were assessed as both original and readily producible.

8.4.2. *Other types of services*

To ease the assessment, all service ideas were structured into 12 categories (Magnusson, 2003a, p. 68). Table 1 shows how the ideas from the different experimental groups were distributed across the 12 categories. The seven items that had significantly more or significantly fewer ideas than expected in a chi-square test are marked by indexes 1–7 in the table. A plus sign in the residual indicates significantly more ideas than expected, whereas a minus sign indicates significantly fewer ideas than expected.

Most remarkably, about 60% of the professionals' ideas fell into two of these categories *"communications & telephony"* and *"public information gathering"* (see Table 1). These two categories correspond to the traditional type of services provided by a telecommunications operator. The professionals thus seemed to fail in breaking the ingrained technological trajectory (Dosi, 1982). The users induced a new mindset; users want to use their mobile phones for new applications such as alerts/alarms, gambling, and remote control. Notable is that the two groups that learned more about the underlying system's possibilities and limitations, namely, groups B and D, submitted many ideas in the category *"public information gathering"*, that is, the same proportion as for the professionals.

Table 1:   Category distribution of ideas for the groups.

Category	Group A		Group B		Group C		Group D		Group E		Total	
	n	%	n	%	n	%	n	%	n	%	n	%
Public information gathering	27	49.1[2]	30	41.1	34	27.6[4]	55	49.5[5]	12	17.9[6]	158	36,8
Others	1	1.8	1	1.4[3]	13	10.6	5	4.5	14	20.9[7]	34	7.9
Self-service and reservation	4	7.3	5	6.8	11	8.9	6	5.4	5	7.5	31	7,2
Remote control	2	3.6	7	9.6	9	7.3	5	4.5	7	10.4	30	7,0
Communications & telephony	7	12.7[1]	6	8.2	9	7.3	3	2.7	3	4.5	28	6,5
Games and entertainment	3	5.5	3	4.1	7	5.7	9	8.1	5	7.5	27	6,3
Private information handling	2	3.6	8	11.0	4	3.3	9	8.1	3	4.5	26	6,1
E-business	4	7.3	1	1.4	11	8.9	5	4.5	4	6.0	25	5,8
Alert/alarm	0	0	3	4.1	10	8.1	4	3.6	6	9.0	23	5,4
Info + position	3	5.5	3	4.1	6	4.9	5	4.5	5	7.5	22	5,1
Personal assistant	2	3.6	4	5.5	8	6.5	4	3.6	2	3.0	20	4,7
Gambling	0	0	2	2.7	1	0.8	1	0.9	1	1.5	5	1,2
Total	55	100	73	100	123	100	111	100	67	100	429	100

A = professionals; B = technically skilled users; C = ordinary users; D = consulting ordinary users; E = creativity trained ordinary users.
Significant adjusted residuals and p-values (Haberman, 1973): $^{1}R_{adj} = 1.994$; $p = 0.046$; $^{2}R_{adj} = 1.994$; $p = 0.043$; $^{3}R_{adj} = -2.276$; $p = 0.023$; $^{4}R_{adj} = -2.501$; $p = 0.012$; $^{5}R_{adj} = 3.227$; $p = 0.001$; $^{6}R_{adj} = -3.495$; $p < 0.001$; $^{7}R_{adj} = 4.278$; $p < 0.001$.

Many of the users' ideas (17%) were, interestingly, not suggestions for new services but rather proposals for modifications to their mobile phones which would give them new functionality. Notable is that all of the professionals' submitted ideas were regarded as actual services.

The data indicate that many users cannot, or do not want to, separate the services from the equipment. For them, it seems to be the total offering consisting of both equipment and service that is of interest. This implies a strong dependency between the service supplier and the equipment manufacturer. Consequently, operators and mobile terminal manufacturers should consider co-operating with each other in order to accomplish better end-user offerings.

8.4.3. *Mixing service ideas and equipment*

Although the task of the users was to think of new ideas, several of the users' submissions were not new service ideas. The submissions could be divided into either (1) error reports, (2) suggestions of improvement in the sample service, (3) context translation, or (4) totally new service.

Table 2 illustrates the different types of proposals by using the previously described sample service the *bus timetable*. The service consisted of two commands: The first was to get the time for the next bus leaving from the city center to the university campus. The second command was to get the time for the next bus in the opposite direction. A dozen of the submitted services concerned modifications of the bus timetable. The type of proposal decides how the information can be further elaborated. Type 1 proposals, error reports which are not service suggestions, are still valuable for fixing bugs in the original prototype. Type 2 proposals (functional improvements) can also be used to improve the original prototype by adding new functionality. Type 3 (context translations) can be the seed for new prototypes, for example, a train timetable. In this case, most of the primary service's logic can be re-used. The last type, type 4, however, is a proposal that has no obvious relationship with the tested prototypes. By using the sample services, the users understood the possibilities and started a creative process.

Table 2:   Types of proposals exemplified.

Type of proposal	Example using the bus timetable
1. Error report	"The service told me a time for the next bus that had expired two minutes ago, useless."
2. Suggestion for improvement in functionality	"When I was at the library, I wanted to know when the bus would leave two hours from now. This was not possible since the service only tells you when the *next* bus is leaving. I would like to have a time parameter included in the service."
3. Context translation	"I liked the concept of the bus timetable. It would be very useful for me to be able to get access to the train timetable as well."
4. Totally new service	*Not applicable*

8.5. Optimizing User Involvement

Can the effects on user involvement be optimized? We have already seen that it seems to matter *how* users are involved. More surprisingly was that in this study *none of the participants' personal characteristics affected how the users performed.*

8.5.1. *No influence from personal characteristics*

In the CuDIT, we analyzed several personal characteristics in order to examine whether or not any of these could be used as a suitability indicator for user involvement. All participants underwent three tests aimed at measuring their creativity: FS test (Holmquist and Ekvall, 1986), technology readiness: TRI (Parasuraman, 2000), and whether they had an optimistic or pessimistic attitude toward problem solving: LOT (Scheier and Carver, 1985). Additionally, age, gender, and previous experience of mobile telephony were recorded. For a more detailed description of the different tests and data collected, see Magnusson (2003a, pp. 57–58).

None of the personal characteristics was found to affect the quality of the created ideas. This does not necessarily imply that personal characteristics are of no interest. There can be tests measuring other significant aspects that our tests failed to capture.

8.5.2. *It matters how users are involved*

The decisive factor for successful user involvement was *how* the user was involved, in other words, the process. This can be illustrated by trials C (Ordinary Users) and D (Consulting Ordinary Users) (see Magnusson *et al.*, 2003). Both groups consisted of the same type of users randomly selected and assigned to either of the two groups. The participants in group C received a minimum amount of support during the trial, whereas those in group D were able to consult an expert on two occasions during the trial. Those in Group D thus received significantly more support and aid than did group C participants. A reasonable assumption should thus be that those in group D would also produce better ideas. This was, however, not the case.

When analyzing the higher quartile, those in Group C produced ideas deemed more original and having a higher user value than did the professionals. For group D participants, the consultation seems to have ruined their ability to produce good ideas. Their ideas were less original than the professionals'; it could even be concluded that the perceived user value of the suggestions was negatively affected.

An important reason for this lack of originality was probably the fact that the more the users learned about the technology, the less they dared to think "outside the box." The decline in user value seems to have been caused by the users thinking more about the good of the company than about being a representative of the users.

One of the participants when subsequently interviewed told us that he had ignored to submit a "super idea" for the reason that he could not imagine how a company would make any money from it. His task had been to function as a representative of the user community. Instead, he had started to identify more with the company's service developers and began to represent their perspective.

The desire to help the users involved can thus have the effect that they become quite useless. As described, the two consultations resulted in different ideas from those not receiving any consultation.

8.6. Pioneering vs. Guided Users

The experimental user trials can be synthesized into two categories: "guided users" and "pioneering users." The main difference between these is the way that the users were involved. The guided users received a higher degree of training and guidance concerning the *possibilities* and *limitations* of the underlying technology. The guided users made up groups B and D, whereas the pioneering users made up groups C and E (see Section 8.3.1).

The guided users mainly produced ideas of the type *stepwise refinements*. This means proposals for minor changes which were easy to implement. Compared to the professional developers, they contributed ideas containing a greater user value.

The other involvement approach, that is, pioneering users, resulted in more *radically* new service ideas. These ideas were more original than those of both the guided users and the professionals. These ideas, however, suffered from a severe drawback; they were difficult to realize. The contributions made via the respective approaches are graphically illustrated in Fig. 1.

An idea must meet at least two basic criteria in order to be of commercial interest. It must be possible to realize (producible), and the service being implemented must create value for its user. This corresponds to the area

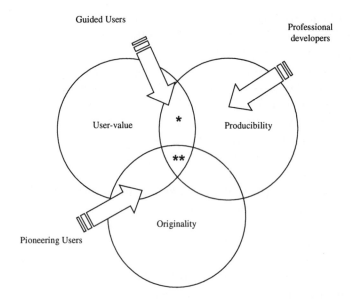

Figure 1:   The contributions made by the different types of involvement.

marked by a single asterisk (*) in Fig. 1 (stepwise refinement). Ideas also perceived as original will end up in the area marked by a double asterisk (**) in Fig. 1 (radical innovation). The guided users contributed stepwise refinements more than the others did. The pioneering users, on the other hand, were stronger on originality and user value but suffered from a low level of producibility.

It is, however, a partly gloomy view that Fig. 1 conveys. Only the guided users came up with producible ideas. The pioneering users' ideas tended to be more amusing but were out of the blue and almost impossible to implement. Is the creative input of the users thus of no practical use . . . or is it?

There is hope that the pioneers' ideas also could be useful. The key lies in how to manage (assess) the incoming ideas, which will be discussed in the following section.

8.6.1.   *User ideas must be evaluated in a new way*

Traditionally, the idea evaluation process is described as a funnel (e.g., Wheelwright and Clark, 1992) (see Fig. 2). "Bad" ideas are filtered out

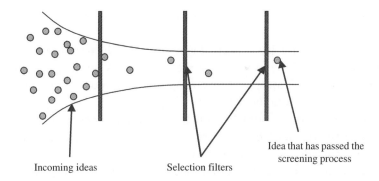

Incoming ideas   Selection filters   Idea that has passed the screening process

Figure 2:   Traditional idea screening.

because they fail to meet certain criteria. At the end of the funnel are the remaining "good" ideas.

A problem with users is that they are normally not capable of bringing up technically feasible ideas. They do not normally have a sufficient knowledge of telecommunication systems to specify ideas that are viable. Therefore, few users' ideas will run the course and be accepted when the funnel model is used to evaluate them. This shortcoming, however, can actually be turned into an opportunity. The users' ignorance regarding technological limitations makes them propose ideas that reach beyond what is currently possible. Instead of thinking of the incoming ideas as seeds to a development process and instead see them as potential *rough diamonds,* new possibilities arise.

The value of a rough diamond cannot be decided until it has been cut and polished. Applied to original ideas, this implies that they will instead be input into a design process where they can be polished and modified into something realizable. This was actually something that occurred in the study.

One participant in the trials had received the wrong morning paper several times in succession. His solution to the problem was a mobile service that would enable him to induce an electric shock of 440 V in the newspaper boy; a service that would be fraught with severe technical, moral, and legal problems. Despite this, the idea worked as input into a design process.

The idea was presented to a group of eight professional developers. The intention was to illustrate how original, yet unusable, some of the users' ideas obtained in the experiments could be. However, within a few minutes, the group had redesigned the proposed idea into something original, as well as producible, and with intact user value (see Magnusson, 2003a, pp. 84–85).

The idea would have been deemed as totally uninteresting when assessed with traditional methods, that is, using a number of criteria to evaluate the idea. However, introducing the "rough diamond" metaphor will yield a totally different result.

It could thus be ignorant to think that the users' ideas could actually be correctly valued in their initial form. Among the users' ideas could actually be *rough diamonds* just waiting to be cut.

When applying the rough diamonds metaphor, idea processing is no longer a pure *selection process* and is turned into a *design process* (Le Masson and Magnusson, 2002). This transformation makes it possible to utilize the innovative potential of more ideas.

8.7. Managing User Involvement — Some Advice

How will the results affect a company's development process? First, the results of the study lend support to those advocating the involvement of users in service development. At the same time, a warning must be given; user involvement must be handled carefully to avoid unwanted effects. Some aspects to bear in mind will be mentioned next.

8.7.1. *Regard user involvement as a learning process*

The purpose of inviting customers or users to take part in the development process is essentially to *learn* more about them, for instance, their needs and wishes. To utilize this knowledge, it must first be transformed into products or services that are offered to the market. The way in which users were involved in our study entailed different competencies (functions) being linked together.

Research, development, and marketing are, in practice, integrated when working in close collaboration with users. For instance, we will need *research competence* to understand the available technological possibilities, *development competence* to develop prototypes or demonstrators to be tested by the customers, and *marketing competence* to evaluate ideas and concepts and to package new offerings.

This way of working is different from the "traditional" way of conducting development and marketing where these functions are separated.

I also advocate for a more flexible form than the development models that dominate today, that is, stage-gate based. Involving customers' demands an iterative procedure which includes *testing, learning, changing, testing, learning,* and so on. In the literature, this activity is commonly referred to as the "fuzzy front end" (Kim and Wilemon, 2002; Koen *et al.*, 2001; Montoya-Weiss and O'Driscoll, 2000; Reinertsen, 1999; Zhang and Doll, 2001). The output will be a customer or user-proven concept that can be further developed via a sequential implementation process (see Fig. 3).

The implementation process will result in an almost finished product or service which is the so-called beta release. It is now time to open the customer involvement window once again, this time not to catch new ideas but to get help in adapting the beta release to the wishes of the customers. CuDIT did, as previously mentioned, focus on the first "customer involvement window."

8.7.2. *Adapt customer or user involvement to its intended purpose*

Previously, we saw how the two different approaches of guided users and pioneering users provided different results. Both approaches are useful. On a mature market where the focus is on keeping development costs low while maximizing customer value, the guided user approach would be preferable. When it is important to create innovative offerings, which is more common on emergent markets, the pioneering user approach would be the best choice (see also p. 91 of Magnusson, 2003a for a discussion).

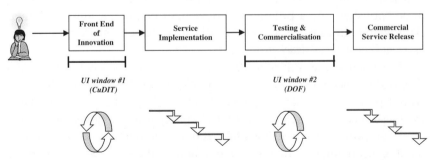

Figure 3: The windows for customer/user involvement in the product development process.

8.7.3. *Clarify the intellectual property rights*

As further elaborated on in Chapter 14 by Hipp and Herstatt, an important issue is the intellectual property rights concerning the users' ideas. This is an important practical issue to deal with before involving users for innovation.

8.7.4. *Users are not a substitute for professional developers*

The results should not be interpreted as dismissing the professional service or product developers and putting all of our trust in users and customers to supply the company with all its future products and services. The professional developers will remain a crucial asset, but they might need to work in a slightly untraditional way. The experimental trials in the study were dependent on an underlying technological platform. This platform was not invented by a user, but by a creative developer at Telia Mobile, Håkan Blomkvist. He saw the opportunity to convert SMSs into calls on the Internet, thus enabling access to a lot of information on the Internet directly from an ordinary GSM mobile phone (Magnusson, 2003a, p. 91). Håkan thus created a platform enabling the development of a virtually unlimited number of services.

So far, the development could be regarded as *technology-driven*. In the next step, Håkan, together with some colleagues, developed a portfolio of services to illustrate the potential of the platform. These sample services were made available to a number of students at the Karlstad University to test and gain inspiration from in order to create new services that would be of value to them. This resulted in 374 proposals being made by the users which was *market-driven* development. Most of the ideas, however, needed to be "polished" by a professional developer before becoming commercially viable. In practice, successful user involvement is *interplay between users and professional developers*.

Most of the ideas submitted by the users would never have occurred if they had not been inspired by the sample services. Inquiries or interviews would probably not have been sufficient to trigger the users into creating these service ideas. Sometimes, technology must be developed before users can provide any sensible ideas. It does not matter whether development is technology- or market-driven; there will always be a necessity to *match customer needs with technology*. This will require interaction between developers, marketers, and users.

Developers of technology based services should be encouraged to meet the users in their own environment. They must, for example, demonstrate the possibilities provided by new technology, using prototypes. When users understand the potential, they can start to discover suggestions that are of value to them.

References

Dosi, G (1982). Technological paradigms and technological trajectories. *Research Policy*, 11(3), 147–162.

Haberman, SJ (1973). The analysis of residuals in cross-classified tables. *Biometrics*, 29, 205–220.

Hart, S, EJ Hultink, N Tzokas and FR Commandeur (2003). Industrial companies' evaluation criteria in new product development gates. *Journal of Product Innovation Management*, 20(1), 22–36.

Hauser, JR and F Zettelmeyer (1997). Metrics to evaluate RD&E. *Research-Technology Management*, 40, 32–38.

Holmquist, R and G Ekvall (1986). BPE: bedömning av personliga egenskaper. Stockholm: Psykologiförlaget.

Kelly, D and C Storey (2000). New service development: initiation strategies. *International Journal of Services Industry Management*, 11(1), 45–62.

Kim, J and D Wilemon (2002). Focusing the fuzzy front-end in new product development. *R&D Management*, 32(4), 269–279.

Koen, P, G Ajamian, R Burkart, A Clamen, J Davidson, R D'Amore, C Elkins, H Kathy, M Incorvia, A Johnson, R Karol, R Seibert, A Slavejkov and K Wagner (2001). Providing clarity and a common language to the "fuzzy front end". *Research Technology Management*, 44 (April–May), 46–55.

Kristensson, P (2003). Creativity in applied enterprise — bringing impetus to innovation. PhD dissertation, Department of Psychology Göteborg University, Gothenburg.

Le Masson, P and P Magnusson (2002). Towards an understanding of user involvement contribution to the design of mobile telecommunications services. Paper presented at the 9th International Product Development Management Conference, May 27–28, 2002, Sofia Antipolis, France.

Magnusson, PR (2003a). Customer-oriented product development — experiments involving users in service innovation. PhD dissertation, EFI — Stockholm School of Economics, Stockholm.

Magnusson, PR (2003b). User involvement and experimentation in collaborative research. In *Collaborative Research in Organizations*, N Adler, ABR Shani and A Styhre (eds.), pp. 215–236. Sage.

Magnusson, PR, J Matthing and P Kristensson (2003). Managing user involvement in service innovation: experiments with innovating end-users. *Journal of Service Research*, 6(2), 111–124.

Matthing, J (2004). Customer involvement in new service development. PhD dissertation, Service Research Center — Karlstad University.

Montoya-Weiss, MM, and TM O'Driscoll (2000). From experience: applying performance support technology in the fuzzy front end. *Journal of Product Innovation Management*, 17(2), 143–161.

Parasuraman, A (2000). Technology Readiness Index (TRI) — a multiple-item scale to measure readiness to embrace new technologies. *Journal of Service Research*, 2(4), 307–320.

Reinertsen, DG (1999). Taking the fuzziness out of the fuzzy front end. *Research Technology Management*, 42 (November–December), 25–31.

Scheier, MF and CS Carver (1985). Optimism, coping, and health: assessment and implications of generalized outcome expectancies. *Health Psychology*, 4(3), 219–247.

Wheelwright, SC and KB Clark (1992). *Revolutionizing Product Development: Quantum Leaps in Speed, Efficiency and Quality*. New York: Free Press.

von Hippel, E (2001). User toolkits for innovation. *Journal of Product Innovation Management*, 18(4), 247–257.

Zhang, Q and WJ Doll (2001). The fuzzy front end and success of new product development: a casual model. *European Journal of Innovation Management*, 4(2), 95–112.

9

Customer Involvement — Lessons Learned: A Study of Three Customer Involvement Projects at Volvo Cars

Fredrik Dahlsten

Volvo Cars, Gothenburg, Sweden
Chalmers University of Technology,
Gothenburg, Sweden
fdahlste@volvocars.com

9.1. Introduction

Customers are seen as a new source of competence for companies (Prahalad and Ramaswamy, 2000). Among technology researchers and innovation management practitioners, involving customers in innovation projects has become somewhat of a leap of faith (Gales and Mansour-Cole, 1995). Several approaches for the collaboration between the company and customers, and the potential benefits of these relationships, have been launched and described in the literature (e.g., Kaulio 1998; Neale and Corkindale, 1998; von Hippel, 1986). Wikström (1995) concludes that intensive interaction with potential customers is a source for generating new ideas and ways of doing business. Through spending time with customers and taking part in activities with them, deep insights guiding new product and service development may emerge (Flint, 2002). The poor connectivity between firms and customers, recognized as the main obstacle for customer involvement (Nambisan, 2002), is increasingly being resolved. There is a shift taking place from a perspective of exploiting customer knowledge to a perspective of knowledge co-creation with the customers (Sawhney and Prandelli, 2000). Customer involvement could, in other words, constitute a participatory learning approach for increased customer orientation in organizations, proactively integrating the customer into the new product development (NPD) process, and in turn improving customer value.

Despite the perceived importance of customer involvement, research intended to increase the understanding of the customer involvement process remains relatively underdeveloped (Alam, 2002; Neale and Corkindale, 1998; Tomes *et al.*, 1996). Accounts from within customer involvement processes are rare. In general terms, it could be argued that customer focus has not been developed as a research question, but has instead been dominated by fairly ungrounded prescriptions (Hennestad, 1999). Practical advice on how to achieve and utilize customer understanding is scarce (Flint, 2002).

This chapter is intended to shed some additional light on customer involvement processes from a more empirically grounded perspective. There are not only potential pitfalls but also opportunities for companies wanting to increase their new product and service development effectiveness through increased customer involvement. This chapter will analyze three different cases of customer involvement at Volvo Cars, illustrating both lessons learned and the gradual development of customer involvement methodology.

9.2. Research Methodology

The three cases in this chapter are all from the Volvo Cars NPD process. First, during the development of XC90, a sports utility vehicle (SUV), the project management team interacted with a group of female Californian customers throughout the project. Second, for P14, a smaller car, codenamed and not yet on the market, the project management team tried to replicate the approach of the XC90 team using a low-key approach to customer involvement. Finally, in the development of a concept car,

Your Concept Car (YCC), the project management team acted as virtual customers themselves.

Those projects took place between 1999 and 2004, at a time where the author of this chapter was working part- time as an inside action researcher (Coghlan, 2001), completing his PhD in the Fenix Research Program (see Hart *et al.*, 2004 for a description of the program), and working part-time within the marketing organization of Volvo Cars. Traditional academic data gathering has complemented direct or in-direct involvement in the respective NPD projects.

Albeit not participating in the meetings between the XC90 project management team and the female customers, the author was involved in other market research initiatives within the XC90 project. Full access to reports from the meetings, written by the moderator, as well as video recordings, has facilitated an understanding of the atmosphere in the meetings. In total, four formal interviews were conducted with members of the project management team. Data analysis was examined and validated by the manager of the female customer group initiative. An underlying intention with the XC 90 research was to produce actionable knowledge (Argyris *et al.*, 1985), and the results of this study (Dahlsten, 2004) served as input to the P14 project management team in a kick-off workshop.

Apart from working closely together with the market researchers moderating the P14 customer involvement, three formal interviews have been carried out with project members. For the YCC project, data have been gathered through two customer focus workshops held with the project management team and two formal interviews with Project Managers. In addition, researchers from Fenix have carried out a large scale research project within the YCC project team (Backman, 2005). The associated research team seminars and discussions are likely to have affected the account of YCC in this chapter.

9.3.   Three Approaches to Customer Involvement

9.3.1.   *Customer information in new product development at Volvo Cars*

Car companies and car customers have a special relationship. To many customers, the car is their second biggest investment after housing. Cars express not only what you drive but also who you are. Therefore, car companies do not only sell cars but they also sell something that customers relate to. Buying and using a car is as emotional as it is rational. Some 40 million new cars are sold around the world each year (Volvo Cars sells 450 000 cars), resulting in many moments of truths in the relationship between the industry and the customer.

Improving the relationship with their customers and understanding them better, quite naturally offers a great potential for car companies. It is not only the sales experience itself that offers opportunities for tightening the bonds with customers, but also the after-market experience of service, repairs, and spare parts. Bringing customer understanding into new product and service development has the potential of significantly improving customer value. Some suggest that a new business model for the Automotive Industry should be built on the concept of a high-performing collaborative community, including customers, instead of relying on the traditional and transactional economy of scale models (Blake *et al.*, 2003).

In terms of learning from and about customers for new product and service development, there are a number of mechanisms in place. The Automotive Industry is one of the biggest spenders in terms of market and customer research. For example, they pioneered the use of customer satisfaction surveys and probably spend more money on customer satisfaction research than any other industry. The market research activity level is therefore high. At Volvo Cars, which is a relatively small car company, approximately 400 major market research activities are conducted each year.

The New Product Development (NPD) process is heavily regulated through the use of stage gates, as is the detailed framework regulating which customer information should be used in the NPD process. Cars are tested in clinics with customers in a number of stages of the NPD projects, although it might vary between different products and projects. If the car is innovative and novel, testing might start in the earliest phases, using renderings or animations to capture customer input. When the design work has progressed further, customers assess the design proposals often using full-scale models of the car. During the development phase, the appearance and some of the functionality of the car can be tested, often with a market positioning perspective, for example, discussions of price positioning, product specifications, and advertising messages.

NPD is guided by specific target customer imaging for each project. Customer targeting often begins with research on the wider target group of the brand. Following this analysis in the earliest phases, customer potentials are identified. During the pre-study phase, the image of the target customer becomes clearer, resulting in a firm target group description before the project enters the development stage. A number of methods and formats are used to portray the target customer. Numerous surveys are conducted to profile customers of present cars in the market, both in terms of buying behavior, usage situations, and personal data. Often these studies are used for the development work with new cars, forecasting customer development, and benchmarking competitors. Customers' product needs and wants receive much research attention, supporting the development of an elaborate product attribute list in the pre-study phase.

There is also on-going method development in terms of customer and market information acquisition and utilization at Volvo Cars. In the earliest NPD stages, business environment scanning can be used to give a broader view of what is affecting the customer and, as such, can stimulate ideas on expansion proposals in the car line-up (Börjesson *et al.*, 2005). Concept Engineering (Burchill and Fine, 1997) has been used in some projects in the earliest phases of product development, integrating customer input and concept development in a systematic way. Volvo Monitoring and Concept Center, a small think-tank organization with a design studio, integrates customer information directly into the design process.

Overall, Volvo Cars has a wide portfolio of customer and market research activities in place, as do many other organizations in the Automotive Industry. These activities are, however, not the only way of acquiring customer information, as the three following cases will show. By bringing customers closer to the product development process, deeper customer knowledge can emerge.

9.3.2. *Case one: XC90 and the female customer group*

Management of Volvo Cars had considered the development and launch of an SUV several times. The growth of the light truck segment, especially on the American market, had received attention for many years. When the NPD project finally began to develop an SUV in 1998, to be called XC90, the market potential was clearly there. The project team, however, quite immediately realized that knowledge was lacking about the potential XC90 customer. Women were driving SUVs in increasing numbers in the US, and the project team did not have an understanding of this market. One of the project team members began discussing the idea of genuine customer interaction.

Initially, this idea was not popular within the XC90 project. The project leader commented, "It is so easy to get a customer group to discuss with—but what to use it for?" Reluctantly, it was decided to carry out a trial and initiate a first meeting with a group of female customers in California. Meeting a customer group would complement the normal market research activities in the project. The criticism toward the idea of a customer group also included a notion that, as one marketing manager said, "This is not scientific."

A moderator was contacted in order to set up the first trial and error meeting between female customers and the project management team. The long-term ambition was to establish a small group of customers for continuous contact during the three-year duration of the project. The moderator seemed ideal for the task. Before becoming a consultant, she had led the Volvo Monitoring and Concept Center in California. She lives in Hollywood and has a wide network of contacts in the area. Knowing both NDP processes at Volvo Cars and female consumer reality in California, she immediately had an idea what the project team was searching for and what the contribution of the female customer group might be.

Recruitment of group members started in the moderator's circle of acquaintances. She recruited affluent women in highly professional fields that were likely to make independent decisions regarding the purchase of a vehicle. They were screened for willingness to participate in future meetings as well as for confidentiality matters. A range in age and professions was desired. This was not a random sample of female car customers in California, but instead of female professionals owning cars and having distinct views on cars, making the group a representation of the target customer in a qualitative sense rather than in an absolute sense.

9.3.2.1. *Meetings*

The first meetings were held in March 1999 in the moderator's home. Two groups of female customers met with the XC90 project management team the same day. The general purpose of these meetings was to elicit opinions and expectations of SUVs for the concept development phase of the project. Sessions were organized in an informal dinner setting in order to use a less clinical approach. The meetings started off in a positive manner, with participants engaged in discussion from the start and very willing to voice their opinions. The presence of Volvo Cars' managers gave a strong sense of seriousness to the subject. For the project team, the first meetings resulted in that they received a good framework for the start of vehicle design. Primarily these meetings resulted in the confirmation of some of the project management team's beliefs. The customers acknowledged that an SUV should not be intimidating and emphasized interior flexibility, comfort, and safety.

The first meetings were deemed successful, so a second meeting was scheduled for October 1999. The management of the female customer group continued to be pragmatic. When the project management team had something to discuss, a new meeting was arranged. The second session was held in a consumer research facility, because interior and exterior concepts needed to be presented in a professional way. Initially, a normal focus group setup was used, with the female customers studying videos and renderings of the XC90, while the project team observed in an adjacent room behind mirrors. An open discussion then followed between the groups. In addition to getting opinions on the displayed material, more implicit views on SUVs in general and the XC90 in particular were captured. There seemed to be a fine line between an attractive dynamic vehicle and a constrained family vehicle. The group said that the seven-seat setup of the XC90 risked turning the car into only a family vehicle. Paying extra for features annoyed the customer group — "just include it in the price." The notion of having e-mail and fax in the car was unanimously judged as a bad idea — "my car is the only place left for some privacy."

The third meeting, in November 2000, was held in a hotel ballroom, since a full-scale plastic model of the XC90 was to be displayed. The emphasis at this meeting was on exterior and interior design, pricing, and options. The two sessions were held over lunch and dinner. At this time, there had been some negative press coverage about SUVs in the US, but the female group still praised the overall concept and SUVs as being fun to drive, having a high seat position, comfortable, and great to throw things in — "an extra closet." The question of power appealed — "I like power when I am driving on Mulholland Drive." The exterior styling was well received and the balance between ruggedness and elegance was also noted — "it can do the job," "not intimidating, yet still looks safe." The interior received more mixed impressions, as it looked cramped in a 7-seat setup. Pricing concerns were not as important to the customer group, although petrol-pricing concerns were discussed. The project management team also received specific feedback on the tailgate design, night vision system, and rollover protection system.

9.3.2.2. *Outcome*

In the meetings, the female customer group judged the atmosphere to be easy-going and Fun, while making them feel specially selected. At the same time, the forum was a familiar one which they felt gave them an opportunity to contribute. In total, 24 female customers participated, of which 16 followed the project from start to finish. The moderator claimed that this was remarkable since all of these women are in demanding professions. At each session, the participants were paid $50 each to cover expenses. This sum barely covered the actual expenses for the group members, who instead enjoyed the social value of the sessions. The presence of the project management team was not perceived as being intimidating; on the contrary, the female group members were glad to be heard. Another important explanatory factor for the positive atmosphere at the meetings was the subject matter. Cars hold a high interest in Southern California. Also, the project management team was relatively intact during these two years. As a result, nearly all the same managers were present in all meetings, giving them the opportunity of creating and sharing a common picture of the customer.

In February 2002, a final meeting was held, and at this time, the female customer group got the opportunity to drive the final version of the XC90. This session was more emotional than the previous ones, with the project team proudly presenting the new car and the customer group eager to see the result of their joint efforts. One woman said, "I'm impressed by the fact that they really did listen to us." Other participants in the customer group also recognized results of their personal ideas in the ready-to-drive car.

In terms of concrete action taken based on input from the women, the interviewed project team members have some difficulties in recalling them. When prompted however, some concrete results appear, but more often in terms of confirmation rather than idea generation. The split tailgate design, choices of textiles, fuel consumption considerations, overall exterior design choice as not being too aggressive, and the flexible child seat could all be attributed to the interaction with the women. There are also examples of counteractions to the customer input, such as the continued development of the seven-seat layout and night vision system. The female customer group has been a frequent discussion topic in project meetings. The project management team has often used the customer group input as support in argumentation within the Volvo Cars organization. The project leader stated, "We got to know these women." Project managers also recognize the value of having a common view of the customer as a result of having participated in the customer group meeting together. The female customer group is viewed as an important tool for creating customer presence throughout the project.

9.3.3.   *Case two: P14 and the international customer group*

In the wake of the successful XC90 project, other efforts to widen the Volvo Cars product portfolio followed. The success of other premium car manufacturers in the segments for smaller cars was noticed at Volvo Cars. Audi had success with its A3 and A2, MB with its A Class, and BMW planned for the 1 Series. In a new product development project for a smaller car, the commercial project leader was aware of the success of customer involvement in the XC90 project. He began to consider involving customers in his project, codenamed P14.

The conditions of this project differed somewhat from XC90. P14 was in a later stage in the NPD process, although still in a pre-study mode. Commonality with other car models was said to be as high as 80%. Freedom of styling was limited due to the fact that the project car was to resemble a previously displayed concept car. In addition, budget was clearly limited for arranging the customer involvement.

The rationale for customer involvement in P14 was to be able to paint a clearer picture of the potential customers for the engineers engaged in the project. They wanted to make it evident that "this is not your next company car that we are developing." The customer characteristics of competitive cars indicated a share of more than 50% female buyers who were on average below the age of 35 — not the demographics of the average Volvo Cars engineer. In addition, the target markets for P14 primarily included Central and Southern Europe. "The importance of visualizing the customer cannot be underestimated — and the earlier in the project the better", that is, making sure that the target customer for the development work is clear to everyone involved. Customer involvement could also be an effective method to stop personal agendas among project leaders. "In a way, for a car like P14, if the project leader personally thinks the concept and contents are ok, they are probably not ok to the target customer."

Starting off as a low-cost endeavor, relationships with customers had to be developed locally in the Gothenburg region of Sweden. Market research agencies, extensive travel, and compensation for the customers were out of the question. Through colleagues, the project team was advised to contact a network of international professionals living and working in Gothenburg for a sample of customers. The in-house market research function was tasked to run the recruitment. The network members were screened for age (25–35), education (university), primarily Southern or Central European origin, and for no previous connection to the Automotive Industry. It was also decided to use the corporate market researchers for moderating the sessions that would be held on the Volvo Cars premises.

9.3.3.1. *Meetings*

When customer contacts had been established and recruitment was completed, the ambition of the planned meetings increased. A full-scale model of the car was developed for the first meeting, as well as models of interior components. Desk research was conducted to dig deeper into the attributes of the target customer profile. In total, a series of three meetings were planned.

The first meeting, in July 2002, dealt with the exterior and the interior of the car, as well as accessories, and was seen as a test that the project was on the right track. Two parallel group discussions were held, with approximately 10 customers in each and 15 project team members attending. One major finding was that the interior that the project management team considered to be radical was not perceived in this way by the customers. The full group then summarized the discussions. A problem occurred when a customer bluntly asked the project management team "who is responsible for this design?" The designer became defensive and tried to motivate his decisions, which had a negative affect on the overall atmosphere of the meeting.

During this meeting, some additional practical problems occurred. Lighting was not ideal for capturing both the customer dialog on video and presenting the exterior and interior models professionally. As well, the sound recording was of low quality, leading to a market researcher spending quite a few days trying to capture what was said.

The second meeting, in January 2003, dealt with the interior in more detail, co-branding issues, and detailed design proposals. The second session was aimed at trying to portray and understand customers through discussions on how they lead their lives, usage of the intranet, and appropriate marketing approaches to reach them. There was fewer of the project management team in attendance. The designer community was less represented as well. Since all major design decisions were already made, they did not understand the purpose of the meeting. "Everything is fixed anyway."

9.3.3.2. *Outcome*

Just after the second meeting, the overall Volvo Cars product cycle plan changed, delaying the launch of P14, and ending customer meetings. An evaluation was done of the initiative and the project management team generally judged it positively. The project leader added that it would have been better to start with customer involvement earlier in the project, that additional meetings would have been beneficial and that practical considerations would need more attention if he would carry out the same project again.

The P14 is not yet on the market, and the tangible results of this customer involvement initiative are still to be seen. Given the most reasonable efforts that were put into the customer involvement initiative, and the customer exposure and interaction achieved, it is not surprising that other car projects at Volvo Cars are planning to follow suit in developing customer involvement initiatives. There are also different ways of arranging customer involvement, as in the next case of YCC — bridging the gap between customers and project managers more radically.

9.3.4. *Case three: YCC and the reference customer*

In October 2001, a top management seminar at Volvo Cars pointed at the need to develop cars while taking female customer needs and wants into account. Strong evidence supported the growing market segment of independent women demanding premium cars. An association for business women at Volvo Cars picked up the idea and an informal investigation began as to how Volvo Cars could capitalize on this growing demographic segment. In August 2002, a suggestion of a concept car, that is, a one-off car showcasing innovative solutions and design at a Motor Show, was presented to Volvo Cars' management team. Having the theme from the management seminar in mind — "if you meet the expectations of women, you exceed the expectations of men" — it was also suggested that the project developing the concept car consist only of women. The corporate management team approved a pre-study conducted by an all female team. In January 2003, the concept car development was fully approved and targeted to deliver a concept car to be called Your Concept Car (YCC) at the Geneva Motor Show in April 2004.

Stakes were high for the five women on the project management team. The project was not only dealing with concept car development, but it was also dealing with many inherent gender issues. Promoting female competence and Volvo Cars' position on this, a high profile press conference and press release went out in March 2003, telling about the project and its ambitions, even though it had barely started. Leaving the gender issues of the project aside, analyzed and reported elsewhere (e.g., Styhre *et al.*, 2005), the project team had a year to design an innovative concept aimed at a specific customer group. By closely resembling the target customers, and using specific tools and techniques to target customer insight, it could be argued that the personal involvement of the project management team had clear parallels to conventional customer involvement. This experimental approach of mirroring the notions of customers, product, and project management will be presented.

9.3.4.1. *Creating the customer and the car*

As with regular product development, the project management team did their homework in terms of target customer knowledge. Desk research on female vs. male car buying and using behavior in the premium segment was analyzed thoroughly. In general terms, women focus more on safety and driving, whereas men seem to be more oriented toward status and comfort. Another interesting finding was that female premium car customers not only want everything men want, but they also have additional demands. This research gave insight in terms of focus areas for potential innovation, for example, women seem to have more needs in terms of interior flexibility and storage. Research also showed that men do not seem to report parking as an issue, whereas women sometimes are concerned about parking, leading to visibility from within the car as an area for innovation.

Using idea generating seminars qualified the notion of what the project team wanted to offer the target customer (and maybe themselves). They predicted that she is not so interested in cars, but in the convenience the car can offer. One of the designers described the role of the potential customer:

> *The customer stands in the centre of this project. Everything we do, we do for her! We don't just give her an attractive product; we also offer her an attractive ownership scenario and a customer profile that she can identify with (Backman, 2005).*

The project management group knew basically what they wanted from the start. Early in the process, they created a common vision of the car they wanted to make, and they often talked about the concept as if it was a clearly defined framework. They did not have, however, a documented objective; instead, they have nurtured the common idea as a base for developing the car. One of the designers felt this was not quite enough, so she developed a more detailed image of the person who could own the concept car. She used a target customer notion of the independent premium woman, called her Eve, and froze a second in her life saying that she has

> *a great hair day today, to find a parking spot, demands for quality, style, money to spend, a laptop in her hand, a jean skirt, a lunch meeting with her sister, yoga class this evening, been shopping, very little time, phone calls to make, a desire to have things her way, hopes and dreams.*

This image, on a single page, became central to the project.

Eve became the reference customer of the project as an example of a credible buyer from the premium segment with high demands. The reference customer was developed on a detailed level. If they succeeded in meeting her needs, the other customers in the premium segments would also be more than satisfied. An understanding of her preferences on an emotional level was developed and this understanding guided the project management team in decision-making situations. For instance, the concept car does not contain a child seat because the project management team felt that this was not a car for transporting children or even more people than one or two. The rear seat was thus primarily designed to carry luggage. One of the project managers described the relationship they wanted to achieve between the reference customer and the car:

> *It is like when you see a fantastic shoe when out shopping. It is very beautiful but extremely expensive. But you decide to try it on anyway. You only live once you think. You discover that it is not only fabulous, but it also fits perfectly and you'll be able to walk in it without problems. That's how our car should be. First you will find it attractive, then you'll discover all the convenient features and then you'll realize you not only need it, you want it (Backman, 2005).*

The reference customer that the project managers described is a professional woman with enough money to buy her own car, a woman who knows what she needs and what she wants. This description also fits very well with the women designing and developing the concept car. One of the project managers expressed their relation to the reference customer like this: "We could all be our reference customer, or at least we would like to be like her" (Backman, 2005).

9.3.4.2. Outcome

When YCC was presented at the Geneva Motor Show 2004, media attention was intense. It was judged almost unanimously as a success. YCC displays a number of innovative product solutions, such as interchangeable seat pads for an individual interior flexibility and back seats which fold down like cinema seats when needed for passengers which leaves room for sport bags. Features for storing are in focus, and the car is full of clever solutions such as storage space in the pillars and a tunnel console with multiple compartments instead of the traditional gearshift between the seats. Features for low maintenance are also in focus, for instance, the car has a fixed hood that can only be opened by the mechanic, the washer fluid is filled up next to where you fill up the gas and the paint is self-cleaning. The "ergo vision system" allows smaller women (and men) to have a good driving position and yet obtain a good visibility. Practical details include the ponytail split headrest and the possibility of driving with high heels. Many of these product features could be considered truly innovative by industry standards, especially in combination. The innovative concept of YCC rests upon features offering unique customer value, in turn relying on how the reference customer was managed.

9.4. Analysis

9.4.1. Different approaches to customer involvement

The three cases of customer involvement at Volvo Cars quite evidently illustrates that there are different approaches for customer involvement with different results. Alam (2002) offers useful distinctions between different customer involvement initiatives along four dimensions that will illustrate this point even clearer.

The objective of the customer involvement initiative is the first dimension. There is a common factor between the three projects at Volvo Cars, as they are trying to qualify and deepen the picture of the customer compared to regular market research and guide the product development efforts more sharply. For X90, the initial objective was to learn about the women buying SUVs in increasing numbers in California. As the learning process between the customers and the project management team worked positively and the managers felt that the meetings were useful, the objective changed into more active and joint support for the development process of XC90. P14 had a more internal objective to start with, that is, to create a more vivid picture of the customers for the project management team and engineers. This objective did not develop during the two sessions. The overall YCC involvement process, with its close interrelations between the roles of product, customer, and project management team, had the overall objective to create innovation in a very public way.

Alam's second dimension, in which project stage the involvement takes place, also differs between the projects. The XC90 Californian customer group was involved throughout the project, from the early concept phase to the actual launch of the car. Kaulio (1998) reports that it is rare for customers to be involved in all NPD stages. The P14 involvement had a point in time character, infusing contacts with potential customers when the project was about to go from concept development into product development (which was then delayed). For YCC, the customer was an integral part of the project from the start. Although developing a concept car, the project management team used the normal Volvo Cars' product development process to a great extent in their work. What differed from the regular Volvo Cars' practices was that in this case the customer was the guiding principle from early ideas to Motor Show Launch.

Intensity of the involvement, Alam's third dimension, displays additional differences between the projects. Although both XC90 and P14 were not particularly intense, the XC90 involvement was judged to be sufficient for the needs of the project management team. Seven meetings took place on four occasions, which is relatively sparse for a customer involvement initiative. The continuous impact of these meetings on the work of the project management team was, however, higher. For P14, the customer interaction stopped prematurely. The YCC project was as intense as a product development project can be. The project management team, virtually taking the customer's role, lived their project for more than a year.

9.4.2. *Interaction*

Mode of interaction is the last dimension from Alam. The intensity ranges from passive acquisition of customer input via feedback on specific issues and extensive consultation with customers, to full customer representation in the project. This range of interaction is represented among the studied projects. For the P14, the interaction was almost clinical, inviting customers to the Volvo premises for a short discussion on specific design concepts and product solutions on display. For XC90, the social interaction was considered from the start, that is, getting to know each other before discussions started. The role of the moderator was critical to establishing this rapport. This, in turn, can lead to innovation potential by being able to harness tacit knowledge, that is, knowledge that cannot easily be expressed and which is seen as difficult and costly to transfer (Mascitelli, 2000) and often transferred between individuals by socialization (Nonaka and Takeuchi, 1995). Task orientation was at least partly exchanged into social orientation. The importance of peace and quiet in the car, the fear of being perceived as intimidating when driving an SUV, or the independence of female decision making about cars is not likely to have been co-opted by a series of focus-group meetings without social interaction. Nambisan (2002) reports that longitudinal and informal customer involvement data have been found to be more beneficial than cross-sectional and formal data provided by structured enquiry tools, which illustrates the merits of the chosen approach of the XC90 team. The customer consultation was extensive.

The YCC mode of interaction was clearly influenced by the role of the total project as an organizational and process experiment as well as by the role of the project managers embodying customers. Intense customer oriented interaction among the project managers was omnipresent because of the experimental setting on the Volvo premises, working around the clock, living the project, and Eve. Although they were not customers, the project management team made sure that the "customer" was fully represented.

Kaulio (1998) elaborates further upon interaction types. "Design for" denotes a product development approach where products are designed on behalf of the customer and traditional market research methods are used. "Design with" includes a display of different solutions/concepts for the customers so the customers can react to various design solutions which is a way of maintaining a formal dialog with the customers. "Design" by denotes a product development approach where customers are actively involved and partake in the design of their own product. The sharp distinction between customers and designers ceases to exist.

All three projects from Volvo Cars were initiated as complements to the "design for" development approach, aimed at developing deeper customer knowledge than was possible from traditional market research. The formal dialog and displaying of concepts from the "design with approach" were sustained in the XC90 project, but stopped early for P14. It could be argued that the quality and impact of the female group interaction affected the XC90 project further, although in an implicit way and by creating continuous customer presence in the project, that is, "implicit design by customer presence." The distinction between the role of customer and designer was not particularly sharp in the YCC project suggesting a meta "design by" approach.

The final factor used for positioning the three Volvo Cars cases is the degree of uncertainty associated with the projects. Gales and Mansour-Cole (1995) suggest that uncertainty can be reduced by having higher frequency, intensity, and contacts with a greater number of customers in the customer involvement initiatives. Both XC90 and P14 were intended to reach new market segments but from a technological point of view, the uncertainty was relatively low. For P14, both styling and components were almost frozen, leading to no apparent need of reducing uncertainty by intense customer involvement. The YCC is different, with as high uncertainty as possible for a development project. Intense customer considerations might have been one way of dealing with this uncertainty.

In summary, P14 can be seen as an expansion of a regular point in time market research activity in a car project, where the benefits of customer involvement were not fully utilized. XC90, through its continuity and quality of interaction, affected customer value of the final product to a higher extent. The experimental approach of YCC in a concept car setting, displays even clearer the potential impact of developing and integrating customer knowledge in new product development. The accounts from within the black box of customer involvement processes offer not only different characteristics indicating that there are many potential routes for development of customer involvement, but there is also some guidance from a more practical point of view.

9.4.3. *Practical lessons learned*

Successful customer involvement is demanding to the organization that is managing the process. This perspective is often neglected in the literature. Some critical success factors for customer involvement management are the following: competence in customer group management (Tomes *et al.*, 1996), relationship capabilities (Athaide and Stump, 1999), collaborative skills (Leonard and Rayport, 1997), and transferring knowledge across borders (Prahalad and Ramaswamy, 2000). The studies of this chapter have all been carried out to try to understand project leaders' perspectives on customer involvement. It might be easier to learn from mistakes. The commercial project leader of P14 alluded to what could have been done differently: "It would have been good to start earlier in the project." This view is also found in the literature, for example, Veryzer (1998), who claims that customer involvement is more effective the earlier it is conducted in the NPD process. For the XC90 project, it was a major benefit to start in the earliest concept phase, getting confirmation that a car-like SUV was an accepted concept. For YCC, the customer was fully integrated in the setup, as a raison d'être, from the start. "The sooner the better" are appropriate words for customer involvement.

"Project management teams need to be better prepared" is a key issue from the P14 project leaders' perspective. Running customer involvement initiatives and utilizing the full learning potential requires more efforts than ordering a regular focus group. The experienced project leader in the XC90 project immediately realized that setting up a group of customers was only a minor part of the job of running and utilizing customer involvement. The P14 project leader continues: "the team needs to think through what the resulting knowledge will be used for" and "is there a mandate to use the knowledge?" With most of the car pre-determined, customer involvement might not be an ideal approach. YCC is contrasting this situation, starting with a blank sheet of paper in the creation of innovation. Customer involvement is therefore likely to better suit explorative purposes. This requires open-mindedness to the results of the real or virtual customer meetings. The P14 manager noted "Sometimes especially engineers are afraid of the customers' perspective, which just adds uncertainty."

The in-direct use of customer involvement results is a common factor for both P14 and XC90, that is, not necessarily to guide the development of specific product features, but rather to create a more vivid picture of the customer or to create customer presence in the project. Internal corporate considerations and decision making procedures could therefore be important reasons for customer involvement. The internal image of the product and its underlying ideas could be strengthened by using customer involvement. There is also a political agenda in NPD. In the worst case, customers could be taken hostage and used in the internal debate. One role of the Californian customer group in the XC90 project was to secure credibility of the project that had been previously cancelled.

"Truly practical considerations should not be underestimated — moderators, venues, and technical equipment must be professional." In the

XC90 project, the role of the moderator was critical to the customer involvement success, especially her unique ability to know both what the customers could offer and what the project needed. The distance between project managers and customers must be bridged, which the YCC project illustrates in its unique way.

In terms of venues, XC90 was successful in having the meetings within the customer paradigm, that is, the market. The clinical approach at the corporate venue of P14 did not work well. Meetings could be set up at the customer's home ground. A neutral playing field is likely to be preferred. Technical equipment is often taken for granted, but it might require both specific attention and discussions. How should meetings be documented and what should the documentation be used for? Should there be written reports and how much conventional market research rigor should go into the customer interaction? It is likely that the methodological efforts should be relaxed and the focus put on achieving successful meetings and dialog. The P14 manager stated, "The relation to other methods also needs to be checked, e.g., what is the role of a regular customer clinic and what is the role of a customer reference group?" To learn not only from but also about customers (Slater, 1997) is one distinguishing factor between conventional market research and customer involvement. This, in turn, puts demands on the venue, and the general setup of the meetings in terms of offering room for socialization and not just task orientation.

Another related issue is "how to create motivation among the customers and a true sense of involvement?" In the XC90 project, the long process of meetings finally seemed to create a feeling among the customers of actually affecting the launched car. For P14, two brief meetings did not create a relationship. One way of creating a more active dialog is to communicate between meetings, for example, through e-mails or via dedicated web sites. To create a sense of real involvement, ownership of the overall customer involvement process could be discussed. Joint process ownership between customers and project management team is an interesting thought.

The final practical observation from the cases at Volvo Cars is that someone in the project management team needs to fully believe in the concept of customer involvement. They must believe that it is possible and worthwhile to improve end customer value by consulting the customers in a dialog. Belief is, however, not enough. Both the P14 and XC90 cases show that some internal fighting is needed for securing the implementation of customer involvement.

9.5. Discussion and Conclusions

9.5.1. *Allowing experimentation*

The cases in this chapter were presented in chronological order, and they also illustrate a development of customer involvement at Volvo Cars. In-depth customer research is not new in the Automotive Industry. When Toyota's luxury brand Lexus entered the American market in the 1980s, the introduction was preceded by having many project members living as potential customers in the US. This was accomplished before the actual design work started. It was the Lexus case that inspired one of the project managers in the XC90 team to consider customer involvement. Luckily, the project management was willing to start experimenting.

A more experimental approach to gathering and utilizing customer knowledge for innovation is suggested in the literature (Christensen, 1997; Trott, 2001; Thomke, 2001), but to implement it might be a more compli-cated issue. customer involvement as a vehicle for experimentation also requires organizational innovation. Neither of the Volvo Cars cases illus-trates how customer knowledge is normally created at Volvo Cars. The project managers had to act entrepreneurially and not following the stan-dard NPD routines. The XC90 team proved that a closer cooperation with customers affected the final product positively, which created attention within the company. The P14 team carried out their "home-made" cus-tomer involvement initiative in an informal way. The YCC project was one of the most high-profile concept development experiments in the Automotive Industry in recent years. A common denominator among all three projects is that, through the different sorts of customer involvement experiments, customer knowledge have been significantly improved, which affects the final products.

To maintain development of customer involvement practices, it is important to create mechanisms for learning and discussing customer involvement methodology between projects. One way of creating this orga-nizational learning is to introduce customer involvement as a requirement in the regular NPD process. This has been discussed at Volvo Cars. There are both risks and opportunities. The truly experimental approach to cus-tomer knowledge creation might be lost if it is mandatory. Task orienta-tion might follow, reducing the social orientation which is critical to the learning that occurs between project members and customers. There are different contexts for different NPD projects and customer involvement might be most beneficial when used as an explorative approach for creating in-depth customer knowledge, that is, to be used when qualified customer knowledge can stimulate innovation.

Customer involvement initiatives must also be seen in relation to conventional market research activities. In the Automotive Industry, there is a wealth of customer information, often from large-scale surveys, almost running continuously. Concepts are regularly tested on customers before reaching the market. Focus groups deal with many issues. The literature suggests that those traditional market research tools are not likely to be sufficient for developing innovation (Slater and Narver, 1998).

It could be argued, however, that incremental NPD projects could benefit from customer involvement. The P14 project clearly illustrates that there are customer involvement benefits for the project management even when the project direction is pre-determined. The information acquired at a closer distance to the customer is not available from the traditional market research.

9.5.2. *Deepening customer knowledge*

Khalifa (2004) elaborates upon different depths of customer knowledge, which helps to further discuss the characteristics of customer involvement at Volvo Cars. Dimensions include whether the relation between customer and company is based upon a transaction or on interaction, whether customer benefits are tangible or intangible, whether customer needs are utilitarian or psychic, and if the customer is viewed merely as a consumer or a person. To create traditional and functionally oriented customer value is based upon knowledge with a transactional mass consumer perspective. Creating more complete customer solutions requires more customer understanding and acknowledgment, and affecting the customer experience requires even deeper customer knowledge. To create new meaning, the essence of innovation requires interaction, attention to psychic needs, intangible customer benefits, and recognition of the customer as a person.

The deepest customer knowledge among the projects studied was in the YCC project. The YCC approach to customer knowledge creation, clearly resulted in the creation of a new meaning. Customer presence permeated the project, and value was co-created by the "customer." The first rationale of how this was possible lies in the way the project management team viewed the customer. The YCC team viewed the customer as neither a consumer nor a person but more as a concept or an image. The second rationale lies in how this customer image was continuously mirrored in the team. The traditional form of customer involvement was short circuited by having the project management team playing the role of customers. The customer concept was a ubiquitous theme throughout the project development work which continuously reflected in the team's own values and ideas, and was an important driver for the work. Compared to traditional new product development projects, this notion — customer-oriented concept development — is unique; customer knowledge is not normally fully used as a design and development criteria.

In the XC90 project, customer involvement resulted in actively learning about persons, rather than passively learning from consumers. The discussions based upon informal interaction, included intangible customer benefits as well as the psychological needs of the customer group. Perhaps not discussing deeper meanings of cars to customers, the customers' experience was fully covered. For P14, the large distance between the groups remained, resulting in a more shallow form of customer knowledge, although still resulting in complementary information from the traditional market research. Figure 1 illustrates the differences in customer knowledge depth for the three projects. It also illustrates the NPD process coverage of the customer involvement projects.

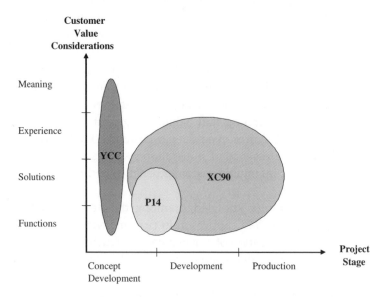

Figure 1:   Customer involvement project footprints.

Differences between the projects are illustrated by the customer involvement footprints in the chart, deep customer knowledge but never leaving the concept phase for YCC, shallow customer knowledge based upon limited customer interaction offering point in time data for P14, and the continuous high-quality interaction for XC90. The footprints also point at the impact of the customer involvement initiatives. For YCC, the innovativeness of the project could be derived from the deep customer value considerations, although the concept car is not likely to be launched. The well planned alignment between project needs and the customer involvement approach for XC90 shows that it is possible to impact a large scale project by a relatively limited customer involvement effort with deep customer knowledge. The exhibit also illustrates the issue of trade-off between scale and scope of customer involvement. Organizations need to plan in advance for the depth of customer knowledge that should be brought into the stage of NPD they choose. In all the cases from Volvo Cars, however, the image of the customer was made clearer to the project teams thanks to the real or meta customer involvement activities. This might be the most immediate benefit of customer involvement.

9.5.3. *Allowing role ambiguity*

To have the customer as the focal point for product development is as evident in theory as it is in practice. Drucker's (1954) notion that it is more important to create a customer than a product, that is, a car, is, however, difficult to find. A rare exception is the YCC project, where the main result of the project is not the concept car but rather the developed notion of female premium customers. The roles of the product and the customers became more closely interrelated, if not integrated in the project. The same applies to the roles of project leaders and potential customers of the concept car.

This in turn put management of customer involvement in another perspective. To successfully operationalize customer orientation and innovation might require a broader and more active management attention. Closing gaps between the concept, constituents, and customers and blurring the boundaries of those components, might be a way to simultaneously develop customer orientation and innovation. The customer as a project leader, the product as a customer communication tool, and the customer as a concept are all examples of this re-framing which in turn widens the notion of customer involvement. There is more to the customer than a buyer, there is more to the concept than a product, and there is more to a project leader than a manager's role.

9.5.4. *Affecting customer value*

The ultimate receipt from customer involvement success is whether or not value creation in the development project changes. Ramirez (1999) claims that co-production is different from the traditional value-chain view in that co-production considers value creation as synchronic and inter-active, not linear and transitive. With the customer as co-producer, the interaction between the parties should generate more value than a tra-ditional transaction process. In the three cases studied, both XC90 and YCC present an improved customer value proposition as a result of the customer involvement. For YCC, with its meta customer involvement, the radical customer value proposition is a result of the customer knowl-edge created in the project. The customer value effects on XC90 are more subtle, for example, confirming the merits of the concept, indicating that the project was on the right path. This method was more interactive than in any previous NPD project at Volvo Cars. This customer involvement approach could be characterized as pragmatic, informal, and cost effective yet continuous and intense. The P14 results remain to be seen on the mar-ket, but it is quite clear that the results of the customer involvement did not affect the product to a great extent. In terms of project managers making sense of customers, the effect was there.

9.6. Concluding Remarks

In summary, the three cases from Volvo Cars firmly indicate that there is more than one methodology for customer involvement. In the litera-ture, customer involvement is sometimes presented a homogeneous con-struct. Customer involvement is highly contextual and requires serious and adapted attention from project management if it should be success-ful. There is also a great variety of practical considerations that need to be made in order for a customer involvement initiative to create improved customer value. Some of those considerations are primarily internal and do not deal with the customer interaction, for example, mandate for action and sometimes organizational politics.

Furthermore, this chapter has illustrated that customers could indeed be a new source of competence for a company. The company and its projects must, however, be willing to experiment to be able to utilize the potential of customer involvement. There must be room for innovation, generated by the customers themselves or by the resulting in-depth customer knowledge. Companies could expand and capitalize on the interrelations of the customer involvement roles, for the product, within the project, and in the relations with customers. The overall objective of customer involvement, to create a better customer value in an alternative way, must guide the initiatives continuously. Organizations, in addition, have to learn from the customer involvement activities and transfer knowledge between projects in order to secure development and utilization of customer involvement methodology. At Volvo Cars, project P15 has now recruited a new group of American customers . . . .

References

Alam, I (2002). An exploratory investigation of user involvement in new service development. *Journal of the Academy of Marketing Science*, 30(3), 250–261.

Argyris, C, R Putnam and D McLain Smith (1985). *Action Science — Concepts, Methods and Skills for Research and Intervention*. San Francisco: Jossey-Bass.

Athaide, GA and RL Stump (1999). A taxonomy of relationship approaches during product development in technology-based, industrial markets. *Journal of Product Innovation Management*, 16(5), 469–482.

Backman, M (2005). Projektledning i *Strålkastarljuset — en Studie av Volvo YCC*. Malmö: Liber.

Blake, D, T Cucuzza and S Rishi (2003). Now or never: The automotive collaboration imperative. *Strategy & Leadership*, 31(4), 9–16.

Burchill, G and CH Fine (1997). Time versus market orientation in product concept development: Empirically-based theory generation. *Management Science*, 43(4), 465–478.

Börjesson, S, F Dahlsten and M Williander (2005). Innovative scanning — Experiences from an idea generation project at Volvo Cars". To appear in *Technovation*.

Coghlan, D (2001). Insider action research projects, implications for practising managers. *Management Learning*, 32(1), 49–60.

Christensen, CM (1997). *The Innovator's Dilemma — When New Technologies Cause Great Firms to Fail*. Boston: Harvard Business School Press.

Dahlsten, F (2004). Hollywood wives revisited: A study of customer-involvement in the XC90 project at Volvo Cars. *European Journal of Innovation Management*, 7(2), 141–149.

Drucker, PF (1954). *The Practice of Management*. New York: Harper and Row.

Flint, DJ (2002). Compressing new product success-to-success cycle time — Deep customer value understanding and ideas generation. *Industrial Marketing Management*, 31, 305–315.

Gales, L and D Mansour-Cole, (1995). User involvement in innovation projects: Toward an information processing model. *Journal of Engineering and Technology Management*, 12, 77–109.

Hart, H, S Kylén, F Norrgren and B Stymne (2004). Collaborative research through an executive PhD Program. In *Collaborative Research in Organisations, Foundations for Learning, Change and Theoretical Development*, N Adler, AB Shani, A Styhre (eds.). Thousand Oaks, CA: Sage Publications.

Hennestad, BW (1999). Infusing the organisation with customer knowledge. *Scandinavian Journal of Management*, 15, 17–41.

Kaulio, MA (1998). Customer, consumer and user involvement in product development: A framework and a review of selected methods. *Total Quality Management*, 9(1), 141–149.

Khalifa, AS (2004). Customer value: A review of recent literature and an integrative configuration. *Management Decision*, 42(5), 645–666.

Leonard, D and JF Rayport (1997). Spark innovation though empathic design. *Harvard Business Review*, November–December, 102–114.

Mascitelli, R (2000). From experience: Harnessing tacit knowledge to achieve breakthrough innovation. *Journal of Product Innovation Management*, 17(3), 179–193.

Nambisan, S (2002). Designing virtual customer environments for new product development: Toward a theory. *Academy of Management review*, 27(3), 392–413.

Neale, M and DR Corkindale (1998). Co-developing products: Involving customers earlier and more deeply. *Long Range Planning*, 31(3), 418–425.

Nonaka, I and H Takeuchi (1995). *The Knowledge Creating Company*. New York: Oxford University Press.

Prahalad, CK and V Ramaswamy (2000). Co-opting customer competence. *Harvard Business Review*, January–February, 79–87.

Ramírez, R (1999). Value co-production: Intellectual origins and implications for practice and research. *Strategic Management Journal*, 20(1), 49–65.

Sawhney, M and E Prandelli (2000). Communities of creation: Managing distributed innovation in turbulent markets. *California Management Review*, 42(2), 24–54.

Slater, SF (1997). Developing a customer value based theory of the firm. *Journal of the Academy of Marketing Science*, 25(2), 162–167.

Slater, SF and JC Narver, (1998). Customer-led and market-oriented: Let's not confuse the two. *Strategic Management Journal*, 19(12), 1001–1106.

Styhre, A, M Backman and S Börjesson (2005). YCC: A gendered carnival? Project work at Volvo Cars. *Women in Management Review*, 20, 96–106.

Tomes, A, P Armstrong and M Clark (1996). User groups in action: The management of user inputs in the NPD process. *Technovation*, 16(10), 541–551.

Thomke, S (2001). Enlightened experimentation — The new imperative for innovation. *Harvard Business Review*, February, 67–76.

Trott, P (2001). The role of market research in the development of discontinuous new products. *European Journal of Innovation Management*, 4(3), 117–125.

Veryzer, RW (1998). Key factors affecting customer evaluation in discontinuous innovation. *Journal of Product Innovation Management*, 15(2), 136–150.

Von Hippel, E (1986). Lead users: A source of novel product concepts. *Management Science*, 32(7), 791–805.

Wikström, S (1995). The customer as co-producer. *European Journal of Marketing*, 30(4), 6–19.

10

Service Encounter Analysis Based on Customer Retrospection

Per Echeverri

Service Research Center, Karlstad University, Sweden
per.echeverri@kau.se

10.1. Introduction

Tuesday morning. Robert Jenkin's wife calls out from the bathroom: "Can I have the car today, love?" Realizes that this isn't the time for a discussion on the subject. He has to take the bus to work. Digs annoyed in the desk drawer after the bus schedule that came in the mailbox a couple of months ago. Reads on the front page that it must have come a year ago. Now, was it number 14 or 15? Isn't there an express bus? Leafs through the timetable. His eyes race over a myriad of departure times and street names...Main street...West street...minutes past the hour...except ordinary Saturdays proceeded by... 6 a.m.–7 p.m. see regular traffic...see night traffic, bus numbers 91–92...wrong table...evenings, Saturdays, Sundays and holidays . . . see bus numbers 31–35, 91–92 . . . low frequency . . . East street +14 min. . . . from North village +0 minutes. The bus is probably late too. Puts the bus schedule in his pocket and walks toward the bus stop. Looks longingly at the neighbor's two cars parked in their driveway. Positions himself at the bus stop. Looks absentmindedly at a blueprint . . . no, a route diagram . . . waits. Is the bus late or has it already left? A bus with another number than he is waiting for arrives. Headed for where? Fifteen college students move simultaneously in the same direction . . . only one of the two doors opens. The driver keeps his hands on the steering wheel . . . looks down to the right. Is quiet. Robert decides not to ask but changes his mind in the middle of the bus. Backs up to the driver with great difficulty. "Does this bus go to . . . should I change to . . . ?" The driver looks down at the ticket machine and answers "Yes." Behind Robert, two teenagers giggle. Will the next bus wait? Checks his watch. The driver mumbles something in the microphone . . . what did he say? No destination sign in the bus. Gets off. The other bus has just left. "Thank goodness, tomorrow I will have the car."

Travellers have many different contacts when using public transport services as in the previous example, such as confronting bus schedules, bus shelters, bus drivers, traffic information, vehicles, bus terminals, transit areas, and other elements of the service system. A bus ride consists of a number of activities/contacts, and that each separate activity/contact reflects the traffic company's internal organization made possible by underlying organizational activities. How are the customer's needs and processes reflected internally in the traffic company? How could the customer be used more intensively in analyzing specific service systems?

The point of departure in this chapter is that communication is the primary instrument for the coordination of human activities (Allwood, 1995). In service encounters, this is often referred to as "the moment of truth." The chapter illustrates how to use customers to not only respond to specific pre-defined questions but also to obtain an in-depth analysis of service encounter data as a starting point for service development. The basic ambition is to get close to the service experience and pose some questions as to what more specifically creates good demeanor from a customer's perspective. Specific information is often easier to assess and implement than more abstract or general concepts. The chapter contributes to the issue of using customers for developing communication in service encounters — specifically in the case of traveller perceptions of bus driver behavior. We will show how customers can be used both to identify relevant variables in the encounter and to interpret the meaning of actions from the perspective of service quality.

The discussion will be twofold: We first discuss some issues that make up the context in which the service encounter takes place. There are certain frameworks that set the standards for behavior and affect how a service encounter is experienced in a traffic environment. One can understand how a service encounter is experienced if we look closer at the context. Second, we discuss concrete behavior in the service encounter itself. We will consider what front personnel say and how they express themselves, and we will account for some research results regarding bus drivers' communication in the encounter with passengers. Following some excerpts from research on services in general, we will point to newer ways of understanding communication in the service encounter and some concrete details in this interaction that are easily overlooked but that can have a significant bearing on customer-experienced quality. Taking the customer's real-time experience as the point of departure can pave the way for new ideas and insights into service developments.

To pinpoint the word communication in this aspect, a short definition is needed to avoid any associations with vehicles, radio systems, telephones, computers, or other signal systems. Communication among people is different. We want to stress that communication is when individuals create a common understanding or meaning through cooperation, for instance in taking an initiative and responding. One important prerequisite is that the communicative actions are coordinated, and that this is done in a satisfactory way for both parties reaching some kind of common understanding.

There are unspoken "rules" for successful communicative coordination — although not always heeded. In most service encounter settings, the unspoken rule (which most service persons agree on) is that the interaction to some extent should be reciprocal. This means that service persons should be sensitive to customer perceptions and to what extent the customer wants to contribute to the conversation. This unconscious and socially accepted rule regulates how communicating individuals, in a specific face-to-face situation, give and take the spoken word (turn taking). In most cases, such rules are a result of successful social practices and are more or less agreed on. Following the rule is perceived as rational and effective for the interlocutors. Breaking the rule of reciprocity can have negative implications. One example is when a front-line employee repeatedly interrupts a customer. To break such a socially defined rule can be an expression of power or eagerness to persuade in a non-appropriate way. If existing or potential customers are "steamrollered" in service encounters, it will have implications for business. Sometimes, negative communicating patterns are established in such a way that it consequently hinder proper and rational interaction. Service encounters sometimes show such negative patterns. It could be a real blessing if the disregarded part (or parts) points out and questions the negative pattern. By openly questioning or breaking established (in-effective) patterns, rules can also be a way of reaching greater reciprocity.

10.2. Experiences from Different Service Organizations

Many studies have shown that appropriate treatment by the front personnel is important for customers to experience a feeling of satisfaction. This is true even of short and ritualistic service encounters (Patterson *et al.*, 1986; Sutton and Rafaeli, 1988). Expressions of empathy, willingness to serve, pleasantness, and professionalism have proven to be important in customer contacts (Berry and Parasuraman, 1991). Even in the early 1980s, one Scandinavian researcher claimed that there is a need to separate *what* a company and its front personnel deliver from *how* it is delivered and that both aspects are decisive for customer satisfaction (Grönroos, 1982). A company can offer quality service but can fall short in the delivery because of poorly designed work procedures, insufficient information systems, unclear rules for compensation to unsatisfied customers, or simply a lack of personal competence by the front personnel. To be careless with the quality in the service encounter is risky for a traffic company and can eventually lead to lost customer contacts, spreading of rumors, and undermined work morale. Even if the purpose of the service encounter is fulfilled, for instance to transport passengers from point A to point B, or to supply correct information regarding departure/arrival times, etc., a feeling of dissatisfaction can linger if the passenger is treated badly. How can quality be understood in such a situation? If a customer, however, encounters a happy and positive driver, but there were errors in the bus schedule, or if problems arose later on in the trip, quality is also lacking in the service encounter.

One practical way of correcting such shortcomings is to deliberately use the traveller's perspective and together with the company reflect on the type of information a customer receives and how it is communicated face to face and indirectly via other media. Thereafter, the employees can reflect on how the internal organization is adapted to customers' needs and expectations. This reversed logic puts new demands on the company's information spreading and information policy.

Research on communication in the service encounter is not new. Certain knowledge can be collected from other service industries than public transportation, and we will discuss three areas that have been of interest to researchers, all of them concerned with the service encounter (Brown *et al.*, 1994). The areas are actions of the employees, contributions from customers, and environmental issues. Areas such as these are challenging to measure and analyze using traditional methods of data collection.

10.2.1. *The employees' handling of customer contacts*

One aim of the research on employee behavior is to investigate how employees handle the contact with customers and how customers evaluate particular service encounters (Bitner, 1990; Bitner *et al.*, 1990; Czepiel, 1990; Lewis and Entwistle, 1990; Surprenant and Solomon, 1987). This is the classical and somewhat one-sided disposition. The employees act and the customers evaluate. This way of studying services originates in the observation of defective quality in a number of branches. Many companies work continuously on improving the performance in the service encounter. All organizations are, to a varying degree, dependent on this for survival.

For instance, within the framework of this research, we find studies of incidents that cause dissatisfaction. One example, where both dissatisfaction and delight are studied can be found in Bitner *et al.* (1990) who have studied positive and negative behaviors exhibited by front personnel. Some examples of positive behavior were attentiveness, quick response, and unusual actions of high moral and performance in stressful situations. The study shows that many times, compensation to unsatisfied customers causes a feeling of satisfaction as do extraordinary positive surprises. The opposite was seen in the unwillingness of personnel to respond to unsatisfied customers, which was because of poor attitude rather than a fault in the core service. Honest excuses, compensations, and explanations seemed to be the bearer of customer satisfaction. Forty percent of the incidents were related to unexpected personnel behavior, and the results were common for the branches studied (airlines, restaurants, and hotels). The importance of *how* something is done can be seen in the study. It is also important that the front personnel are empowered in a wide sense.

This means that, from the customer's point of view, the core in the service is the interactive communication itself. Still, many frontline employees are not educated for or aware of this. Nor are they paid in proportion to this responsibility; therefore, their motivation and work satisfaction could be lacking.

The importance of the interactive elements for service quality has been confirmed many times. A close study of the items that are included in the different dimensions of SERVQUAL, a popular measuring tool for quality (Parasuraman *et al.*, 1988), shows according to Bitner *et al.* (1990) that a majority of the items relate directly to human interactive elements in the service delivery. We must remember, however, that quality in communication does not necessarily influence an individual's choice of mode of travel. The motivation to use public transportation is the low price, or "The passenger loves you because you are an inexpensive catch, not for what you are." On the other hand, it is likely that public transportation companies and other buyers of traffic services will raise the standards for existing contracts when contracting new services. How does an entrepreneur show convincingly that the company actively and systematically works to secure and improve this type of quality?

10.2.2. *Customers also communicate*

Another research direction focuses on the customers' involvement in the service production (Goodwin, 1990; Kelley *et al.*, 1990; Larsson and Bowen, 1989) which is based on Bateson's research on self-service (Bateson, 1983). A considerable contribution from this research is the knowledge that the customer's own participation influences the quality experience. This becomes even more important when payment and information routines are automated with the help of intelligent card readers and real-time systems. Despite technical solutions, we remember that many customer contacts still remain and have an increased importance. The customers' own way of communicating with contact people and the company's ability to supply information at the right time in an appropriate way are important components in the service experience — "it takes two to tango." If the chauffeur greets the passenger and does not receive a greeting back, it affects not only the chauffeur's approach to that passenger but also his approach to the next passenger. On the other hand, if the passenger reciprocates, the chauffeur will feel elated for a moment and can become inspired to respond in an even more positive way. This mechanism is central to understanding how communication should work.

10.2.3. *The effect of the physical environments on customers and employees*

Since a service to a large extent is intangible, it has often been said that the physical elements in the service environment take on great importance. This third direction within the research of service encounters has shown how the physical environment affects behavior, that is, how interior decoration, atmosphere, design, clothing styles, etc. influence customers as well as employees (Berry and Parasuraman, 1991; Bitner, 1992). This research has shown that customers generally seek proof of the company's or the employees' competence and quality in the physical environment. Individuals often categorize and evaluate their observations mentally (categorization is the process through which we name objects and events). The physical environment can communicate something. Research in marketing has confirmed that the environment affects customer satisfaction, whereas organization theory research has observed that it also influences the employees' behavior, productivity, and motivation.

Thus, the service production is assumed to be directed to a large extent by the physical environment that surrounds it, and it is in the intersection between the internal and the external that many service companies operate. Employees and customers cooperate in the service production, and the environment can be seen as a communicative variable or a kind of communication that goes beyond the verbal. Even if buses and trains are physical objects, the service production is non-physical, widespread, and is constantly moving in the physical environment. Service can be poor even if the vehicles are of the latest design.

Based on research in environmental psychology, Bitner has formulated a number of theses about what kinds of behavior are affected by the environment and how they can be explained. Two kinds of behavior are included: approaching and avoiding. Approaching includes the desire to stay longer, discover more, and remain occupied, etc., whereas avoiding includes the opposite. Donovan and Rusell (1982) found that behavior that could be characterized as approaching was affected by the environment such as degree of consumer satisfaction, revisit to store, friendliness toward others, spending generosity, time spent on strolling in the store, etc.

Other studies have shown that the beat of background music can affect the pattern of customers' movement in grocery stores and restaurants.

Such behavior has also been studied in the realm of organizational environment. For quite some time, it has been known that patterns of social behavior are related to physical environment, and that people's behavior can be predicted based on the physical environment at hand (e.g., Baker, 1968). Group communications, forming of friendship, participation, aggression, withdrawal, etc., are all affected by the prerequisites of the physical environment. Lighting, temperature, noise, music, and color schemes are factors known to influence performance and work satisfaction (Holahan, 1982; Sundstrom and Sundstrom, 1986). The same is also true of spatial design, functionality, artefacts, signs, and symbols.

Who has not seen the line encircling the driver's work area on the bus and the sign saying that he must not be disturbed while driving? Have not these signs created an image of the driver as an appendage to the engine rather than a customer-focused empathetic service person? It is reasonable to believe that such signs and the interior itself has formed the traveller's conception of how the conversation on the bus is supposed to unfold, that is, fast, efficient, concise (or preferably not at all?). Few people expect to be greeted by the driver even if they think that it is nice when it happens. Focus group studies at Stockholm transit (SL) have shown that some think that the driver should take the initiative to greet the customers even though this is not necessarily their primary concern when they enter the bus. In interviews with drivers, however, they complain about the fact that passengers do not say hello or even seem to expect a greeting at the door.

We see from this brief review of three highly relevant research areas that there is a mass of concrete actions, service elements, and behavioral issues which are important when we analyze quality in service settings. New and innovative ideas could be unearthed by intensively using those who experience the service as the point of departure in service development.

10.3. Through Situational Retrospection Customers Identify Dramaturgical Aspects

We have examined some experiences from various service studies and indicated that they are generated in and through interaction between the parties and with the environment. We have seen that this interaction has certain functions in society and can be perceived both positively and negatively. We cannot be satisfied with knowing that the front personnel is professional, charming, perform well as drivers, show friendly personalities, and are capable of showing empathy for customer needs. There is reason to ask more specifically *how* a chauffeur shows friendliness and *how* he or she demonstrates empathy and competence. To answer such questions, the front personnel's behavior must be studied in detail. What do they say when they talk to customers and what kind of gestures do they use? Research has shown that body language often affects the other party, at least subconsciously. Thus, there are important issues beyond psychological perceptions in the service encounter. Some information comes from a research project about bus driver behavior in public transportation. What kind of behavior supported by what kind of gestures does the driver use when communicating with the customers? Is it more than words articulated by mouth that are of importance?

The dynamics and the flexibility in human communication are a potential source of innovation and enchantment as well as of misunderstanding and dissatisfaction. How is this noticeable on buses? In 1997/1998, a research study was carried out in Karlstad (a medium sized city in Sweden) on how bus drivers interact with their passengers. Almost all routes were represented, and service encounters were videotaped at different times of the day. Ten drivers participated, and passengers were interviewed about their perception of the service encounter, both what they spontaneously could remember after the trip and when they saw the videotaped encounter. The camera was discretely placed at the entry of the bus and the driver's behavior, body movements, and facial expressions were documented. The conversation with the driver could be about punctuality, information about time schedule, charging the bus card or problems regarding the card.

A few days after the video documentation, customers who were active in the interactions (the driver–passenger interaction in the video sequences) were interviewed in a two-step procedure. In the first step, they were asked to recapitulate from memory what happened, how they perceived the trip, and the service interaction. During the interview, the customer was asked to "think-aloud", which is to reconstruct relevant and important issues of the service procedure. In the second step, the customer was asked to comment on the video sequences which the customer (and bus driver) was part of. Looking at the videos repeatedly, commenting, pointing, and reflecting on the meaning and quality of actions (of both sides) elicited a long list of behavioral issues normally not found in the main stream service encounter literature. In such a way, customers did not only identify *relevant* issues, but they also contributed with *interpretations* present in the specific interaction. This is customer involvement *in situ*.

When reflecting closer on these occurrences, different patterns emerge. These patterns are abstract in their nature but are of great importance since they affect the quality of the service encounter in many respects. One recurring pattern is the dramaturgical: that the behavior is theatrical. We then use the interpretation pattern of the drama to make sense of the communication in the service encounter. Involving customers in reflecting on how proficient front personnel behave, we find that personnel have the ability to make the everyday service more exciting than it actually is. The service is charged with a certain degree of importance that structures both the behavior and how the behavior shall be perceived.

10.4. Dramatizing the Mundane

Many times this sort of dramatization creates a delight and even enthusiasm for the customers. We found one example of this in the Gothenburg transit system. When a traveller timidly complained that it was too hot in the bus the chauffeur replied in an astonished way — with a twinkle in his eye — with a series of rhetorical questions. "What do I hear? Is it too hot? I wonder why that is? I wonder if we can do something about it. I will adjust the radiator and you can tell me if it helps." Such a dramatic response to a timid complaint often makes the passenger get the point and smile. The driver did not take the heating problem so seriously and signalled this by the way he expressed himself.

The absence of non-verbal clues would have pointed to a problematic suspicion concerning the driver's mental health. The chauffeur reacted in such a way that in this context the event took on a humorous meaning. The pattern of behavior moved from one context to another taking on a new meaning. Whether it got cooler or not might be of secondary importance; the customer was met with good acting.

Some situations seem to be more suited than others for this kind of dramatization, for example, when a problem occurs and the outcome is uncertain. In this case, a somewhat dramatic situation is expected from the beginning which the chauffeur can utilize since the customer already is involved and more apt to perceive communicative signals. The creative employee should be able to find many situations that can be dramatized. As soon as an opportunity for improvisation presents itself and as soon as the front personnel have some extra time with the customers, there is room for performance and surprise. It does not take a lot of effort to make the daily service more stimulating for the customer as well as the driver.

Deighton (1994) is one of the people who developed these ideas for services, and he claims that the front personnel ought to seek opportunities to involve customers while increasing their ability of perception and to encourage the customers to become part of the drama for a moment. This can happen by introducing some uncertainty and can in some situations also decrease the distance between the self and the role being played. Engaging the customer sets the stage for effective communication in the service encounter.

10.4.1. *Have-a-good-day syndrome*

The kind of behavior described here should not be mistaken for a stereotypical behavior. It is easy to find behavior that has become routine and lacks the original, genuine meaning especially in the service business. Bateson (1990) says that many service businesses, with good intentions, have seen people change into "brainwashed robots" when they try to follow the stipulated manuscript for correct behavior. The "have-a-good-day syndrome" has ironically become counterproductive. The stereotype has become associated with something negative; therefore, there is a need to design education and reward systems in such a way that employees can better handle customer needs, rather than just follow a communication model. It is not the model itself that creates the excitement: it is the change, surprise, and improvisation, of the moment that does. This is the heart of improvisation, and it requires familiarity with different roles and procedures, a genuine competence, and knowledge of proper use and timing. Familiarity with different ways of communication and different modes of expression are essential components of improvisation, which in turn will stimulate innovation (Echeverri, 2002).

10.5.   Situational Retrospection as a Path to Issues Beyond Perception

The driver–passenger study showed that many travellers remember a lot of details from a trip, especially infrequent travellers. Almost all refer to non-verbal behavior such as posture, eye movements, and facial expressions. These non-verbal categories were used by the respondents to explain their experiences. They pointed to issues beyond superficial meanings. A discussion will follow about what we already know about the non-verbal behavior of human beings. We will later describe some findings that contribute to our understanding of quality in the service encounter which are issues beyond simple perceptions.

First of all, it has been proven that non-verbal expressions play a major part in communication. Mehrabian (1981) measured, in an early study of *emotional* interaction the verbal part of communication as 7%, the vocal (intonation, pitch, etc.) as 38%, and facial expression as 55%. These figures can be argued when comparing with other contexts, but they indicate something that can become significant. They point to a much broader behavior arsenal than ever imagined. They also confirm the necessity of concordance between our words and our gestures. If they do not match, the other party tends to notice and remembers the gesture at the expense of the verbal. What does one perceive when the driver, red in the face, turns around and yells, "I am not mad at you but can you please step off the bus?" From his words, it seems as though the driver would appreciate if the passenger would choose another way to travel. But from his body language, there probably is an indignant feeling in the driver's mind. The comment is more of a strong order than a humble request, which is evident by what is said not with words but with intonation, accentuation, and fluctuation in voice.

There are also differences in non-verbal communication between different cultures and even within a culture for example between different professions, sexes, and social strata. Professional and company specific differences, together with the actual situation, determine the meaning of a non-verbal behavior. There is a fine line between being perceived as competent or as incompetent. In service businesses, it is important to remember that a customers' perception does not always coincide with that of the provider.

It has been proven that body movements, postures, and gestures are given meanings whether they are intended to or not. "That chauffeur is cute" said one person when asked in an interview what she had seen. Of course, it was not the looks that we referred to but his expression and personality. "That's how nice chauffeurs should be" another passenger said. The study also showed that the customers ascribe different meanings to the chauffeur's behavior, for example, "he is nice, he seems candid, he does not sit there and slouch, or he has a nice posture." Another significant factor was the variation in intonation. The respondents said that "his voice fluctuated" or that he sounded very monotonous, strained, shy, or happy. Behavioral components such as these had different functions in the communication. One result was that through his behavior, the chauffeur "saw" the passenger; he signalled to the passenger that he was an important human being. There seemed to be a desire to be seen in a deeper sense than through mere physical eye contact. This does not have to be interpreted in a deep psychological perspective but more as an expression of an attitude or standpoint toward the passengers.

The driver expressing something verbally, even if it just was a nice mumble, was perceived by the customer as good treatment. It was not always necessary to hear exactly what the driver said, but that he said something at all was appreciated. The videotapes showed how drivers sometimes accompanied their movements with diffuse small talk or filled the space in their own sentences with a variety of sounds (ah, hmm, mm etc.). One interpretation is that the mumbling or small talk confirms what the chauffeur is doing, for instance when he charges the bus card, reads the timetable, or looks for change in his wallet.

This form of feedback to the passenger can instil a comforting feeling that everything is under control and all is well. The facial expression was, not surprisingly, something that was mentioned in the interviews. The chauffeur had eye contact with the passenger several times even if during a much shorter time than the passenger expected. Smiles were by far the most appreciated. Several respondents noted that the drivers did not smile very much at all. Several said that it was nice if his face was "open." Nice treatment was further associated with variation in the voice and intonation. Variation in pitch in different parts of the conversation could be seen as expressions of emotion and empathy. Body positions also proved to be important. The upper body's position was often noted and was given certain meanings, for example, how the driver was sitting and if he was sitting upright facing the passenger. Not all drivers swivelled their chairs to face the customer, which was interpreted as a disinterest in the passenger. The positioning of arms and hands was also given positive or negative meanings. To receive bus cards and payment with both hands actually seemed better than only with one hand.

One aspect, which was not significant in the bus study but has been reported in other service businesses, is when the front person in some way touches the customer. This is a part of the non-verbal arsenal and can be a strong communicative signal in service encounters. Some research that has attracted attention shows that a light touch can be very effective under certain conditions. There is a fine line, however, between what is acceptable and what is not, since touch is direct and physically perceptible and in most cultures associated with very specific meanings (obviously an unacceptable touch could be disastrous). In a study by Hornik (1992), the effect of a gentle touch on the customer's shoulder was studied. In an experiment with 268 regular customers he measured that the time spent in a store increased from an average of 13–22 minutes. The customers' experience of quality increased, and their spending went up by approximately 24%. For a bus driver to touch customers physically, however, can be risky and should definitely be avoided by chauffeurs who are partly separated from the customers by Plexiglas dividers!

If we believe that good demeanor toward customers and the specific communication performed is important, we might consider how this is reflected internally in the service organization. Which organizational structures can support its employees' performance toward customers? How should co-workers communicate to foster good support? How should supervisors and managers communicate to encourage the employees to adopt the company's common goals?

10.6.   Implications for Supporting Structures

It is easy to dwell on words such as customer orientation, empowerment, learning organization, and other jargon that is popular in management discourse, but we seldom ask for a systematic evaluation of the difficulty in implementing the vision of a more profound customer-oriented organization which these concepts want to convey. It seems to be more problematic than one might think. Analogous with the idea of involving customers in developing the core service process by listening to, reflecting on, and discussing customer's perceptions is the idea of involving co-workers and developing internal support systems. The logic of involvement as a mutual two part communication procedure could be addressed throughout the service organization, not only in the specific customer interface but also toward other groups in the organization. Often the gap between vision and reality is caused by a lack of understanding of the human social nature and the myriad of activities to be coordinated and developed within the organization to support customer involvement activities. Internal communication is a central issue in involving personnel and other organizational resources.

10.7.   To Develop the Business through Internal Mutual Communication

In various organizational studies, we find companies having internal problems or a lack of efficiency. In many service organizations, including public transport companies, there is a natural resistance to change. It would be possible, however, to handle these problems by giving more attention to internal communication which is the primary instrument for human interaction. The basic idea in the customer involvement approach is built on communication which is a mutual process of moving toward shared meaning. It could be used as a guiding principle for internal support systems as well. Developing support and involving people is often made difficult because of problems with internal mutual communication. Zeithaml and Bitner (2003) have noted a number of reasons for such communication problems and in the extension and sluggishness in the organization. Choice of language, non-verbal behavior, sets of values, and differences in decision making are important factors. These are examples of communicative aspects that are rarely explored in organizations. If the company leaders do not consider these factors or make efforts to encourage a good dialog within the intra-organizational procedures, there is a risk that co-workers become passive and refrain from actively developing their own organization.

This passive behavior can be seen in a masters' thesis about group processes in a quality circle. The purpose of the quality circle was to develop the service system, partly based on the results from the driver-passenger study. Two students were given the opportunity to observe a newly started quality circle for bus drivers in a Swedish bus company. Their task was to study the internal pattern of communication and the group's non-verbal behavior in detail. In the group process which was oriented toward developing the service business, the students became aware of the company's internal tensions and problems. The tensions became obvious by the way people seated themselves, how they communicated, and by their non-verbal behavior. Different perspectives and asymmetric relations were reflected by the way the participants communicated. Under a sense of agreement and commitment to develop the business, different organizational tactics were used to (discretely) avoid change in attitudes and concrete implementation before, during, and after the group process. In the midst of this, the students observed a number of inspired participants who, with a relatively generous authorization, passionately engaged in developing the company. Co-workers initiated a dialog with their superiors which was something they had never done before. Stimulated by this opportunity they listed a number of problems that they categorized, processed, and suggested solutions to. The group met six or seven times and all the work was documented and compiled in a neat report, which was distributed to a number of involved parties. The report was ignored.

Where the inspiration and enthusiasm went is unknown. It would probably be difficult to rekindle the inspiration. This illustration is neither typical nor a "worst case" scenario for service companies, but if managers are not careful, co-workers' passivity and frustration can shift into cynicism. It is not an easy task to recruit supervisors to companies with cynical "opposing workers" attitudes.

10.7.1. *Why is it so difficult?*

In back offices, there are many subtle organizational mechanisms. Some support, whereas others hinder service development processes. Some conditions that perhaps more indirectly contribute to communication problems are built-in antagonism, locked power positions, lack of participation in the internal dialog, poor contact surfaces between co-workers (formal as well as informal), unclear goals and visions in the organization, and weak or invisible leadership. All of this is part of an organization's work environment that determines to what degree the employees can and want to work on improving the service system. There are obvious connections between work conditions and internal communication; one does not control the other in a deterministic way, but that they are mutually dependent.

Given our assumption that the primary instrument for co-ordination of human activities is communication raises questions about internal support systems in companies. How is backing and support communicated? Can the method of expression itself influence the effectiveness of the support? Researchers have searched for answers to such questions by studying successful service companies. A number of theories have been expressed throughout the years about what characterizes "the good service company." The concepts for success come and go but have been difficult to generalize. One specific characteristic that seems to reappear is when companies focus on their co-workers (Pfeffer, 1994). Grönroos (1990) has on a general level pointed out the need to differentiate between the handling of communication and the handling of attitudes.

He considers both tasks important in order to realize a service culture that will enhance the company's chances to survive and develop. Attitudes concern values and norms which in turn influence many other actions in the business.

Communication is the means by which a common dialog is initiated in the company. One popular theory is that management has a responsibility to communicate the right attitudes and then it is up to the co-workers to adopt the company's ideas. Research has shown that it is not always easy to influence co-workers' attitudes. Some believe that the importance of the management in a service company is exaggerated. Many efforts to change a company have failed. Service culture is not created by internal "campaigns."

On an interpersonal level, we know that a relationship is strengthened when we treat a fellow being respectfully and communicate in such a way that he/she senses the extra effort. Studies in communication theories have maintained this claim, and the idea still exists under different labels. A common denominator in creating mutual understanding is the display of a genuine respect for the other person.

A search for good co-worker care could easily include a great number of aspects, and the list of measurement methods could be very long (for a review of the literature on successful organization, see Pfeffer, 1994). All are related to what normally is called human resource management. In all aspects, communication plays a central role since it is both the means and the goal for the common efforts. There is a reason, therefore, to evaluate visible as well as invisible communication patterns in an organization knowing that not everything can be changed. Just keeping the question on the employees' agenda can be valuable for the internal company spirit.

10.8. To Communicate Norms for Good Customer Treatment

Many attempts at organizational development have come to nothing because those responsible for the changes have not taken the organizational prerequisites into consideration. One such aspect is to consider the conditions that surround the concrete dialog within the organization. Even in those cases where a forum for internal discussions has been created, for example, for common treatment of new ideas, the ambition can capsize if the underlying values and rules are not considered. The organization's former history and how it is presented is a part of what sometimes is called the communication context. The physical surroundings, how the dialog is organized, and acknowledgement of the actors are other important aspects to consider. It is also important to consider how the information is spread in a systematic way and which co-workers receive what information. Is there a policy for how information is spread in the company? What formal and informal contact opportunities exist in the organization?

An organizational corner stone which management must consider is that service to customers, as well as to co-workers, requires more than technical and procedural perfection. It entails such considerations as personal treatment, politeness, and empathy. These aspects are most decisive. Lovelock (1995) discusses the concept of "emotional labor" taken from Hochschild (1983). The concept stands for the action with which someone (a contact person) expresses socially desirable feelings during the service production. Hochschild means that for many, attempts to adjust to the organizational expectations in this dimension is something that is occasionally experienced as a psychological strain. This is true in situations when service personnel are expected to express feelings that they do not honestly feel at the time. Some researchers who have modulated the problem claim that personnel are expected to follow certain norms for expressing themselves ("display rules") (Ashforth and Humphrey, 1993). It is expected to happen in "surface acting" as well as in "deep acting" and in expressions of spontaneous and genuine feelings. Display rules reflect social norms, but are given professional and organizational norms, which are also specific in certain situations. Surface acting means simulation of unaccustomed emotions accompanied by verbal and non-verbal signals (cues) such as facial expressions, gestures, and voice pitch which are capacities that are innate or learned. Deep acting, on the contrary, is a psychological attempt to imagine the desired emotion. Some can experience the expected emotion naturally and express it spontaneously.

10.8.1. *Empowerment through communication*

It can be extremely stressful to put on emotional expressions day after day, especially if the feelings are not genuine. Still, emotional expressions are important and necessary both in customer contacts and in contact with colleagues (external as well as internal). People with boundary exceeding positions are expected to carry out a task efficiently in a polite and helpful way; therefore, the theory that empathy cannot be learned should put high and different demands on hiring personnel. The wrong type of personality in such positions would be counterproductive and unnecessarily burdening for the employee. This awareness has made the concept of empowerment quite appreciated and widespread lately. The idea is to give the employees a greater measure of power to let them depend on their own judgement to a greater extent. This ideology, which tends to look at man as the owner and practiser of a free will (voluntaristic) and equipped with an unselfish attitude vis-à-vis other people (altruistic), stresses commitment to the employer and involvement in company projects. The employees are expected to contribute to company improvement if they are socialized in the right way, are well trained, and kept informed. Likewise, they are expected to work effectively and be capable of self-control and self-direction. Such qualities and conduct that is expected of leaders and management is also anticipated on lower levels in the organization, even in the front lines.

Bowen and Lawler (1992) support empowerment but also point to the fact that all people do not foresee personal development in their jobs. Neither is there a best way to create empowerment — it is context specific. Any co-worker, however, knows if he or she experiences empowerment, and if not can arrive at reasonable ambitions to fulfil the objective through discussions with management.

For a broader understanding of values that are important for a good service performance, aspects on a more social character should be included. In addition to salary and social benefits, a suitable profession for an individual can mean the possibility to raise one's competence and add valuable work experience. It can provide status, stimulation, new acquaintances, better self-esteem and dignity, and the satisfaction of contributing something valuable. Such positive feelings have a bearing on service performances and can, through the individual's communicative behavior, lift customers' quality experience to higher levels. Bearing in mind that people act and react in different ways, it would be wise to partly individualize company policy and support systems. One person may feel psychologically and mentally burdened to feel forced to do something special for the customer, whereas another can feel psychologically and mentally satisfied. Lovelock talks about "a positive working climate" and writes that "employees who enjoy their work are more likely than unhappy ones to give good service to customers" (Lovelock, 1995).

10.9. Concluding Remarks

We have indicated some aspects that will be worth while keeping in mind if an organization wants to improve. We have stressed the need to involve the customer in a more profound way. This chapter described an example of how to use the customer more intensively for *in situ* research, identifying what variables are relevant for study, what concrete elements are important, and how to interpret actions in service encounter interactions. We discussed some internal communication system issues such as how it is designed, its effectiveness, distribution pattern, policy foundation, and authorization. We proposed that such issues should be based on a profound understanding of the customer-service interaction. We have also stressed the need to create arenas for communication and to actively encourage feedback from co-workers on a continuous basis. If this privilege is taken away, a breeding ground is created for misunderstandings, misinterpretation and indifference, uncertainty toward authority, and role behavior. Attempts to cultivate cooperation in terms of being entrusted with responsibility as "a process owner", for example, have proven to be successful.

Genuine customer satisfaction is not created by stereotypical behavior but of genuinely committed co-workers. The attitude of the management and of other co-workers contributes to a naturally positive work climate. How physical surroundings affect the way of communication has been discussed. We have shown examples of how bus drivers, in normal service encounters, can dramatize the every-day conversation with the help of different techniques, thus encouraging dialog. In connection with this, we have pointed out a number of non-verbal conducts such as body language and intonation, which can actively contribute to the feeling that front personnel create a positive service attitude. This in turn strengthens the customers' overall evaluation of the service given. It is worth considering the customer as a development resource.

References

Allwood, J (1995). An activity based approach to pragmatics. Gothenburg Papers in Theoretical Linguistics 76, Göteborg University, Department of Linguistics.

Ashforth, BE and RW Humphrey (1993). Emotional labour in service roles: The influence of identity. *Academy of Management Review*, 18(1), 88–115.

Bateson, JEG (1983). The self-service customer — Empirical findings. In *Emerging Perspectives on Services Marketing*. L Berry, LG Shostack and GD Upah (eds.), pp. 50–53. Chicago, IL: American Marketing Association.

Bateson, JEG (1990). Evaluating the role and place of marketing in service firms. In *Service Management Effectiveness*. DE Bowen, RB Chase and TG Cummings (eds.). San Francisco: Jossey Bass.

Berry, L and A Parasuraman (1991). *Marketing Services*. New York: The Free Press.

Bitner, MJ (1990). Evaluating service encounters: The effect of physical surroundings and employee responses. *Journal of Marketing*, 54(April), 69–82.

Bitner, MJ, BH Booms and MS Tetrault (1990). The service encounter: Diagnosing favorable and unfavorable incidents. *Journal of Marketing*, 54(1), 71–84.

Bitner, MJ (1992). Servicescapes: The impact of physical surroundings on customers and employees. *Journal of Marketing*, 56(2), 57–71.

Bowen, D and E Lawler (1992). The empowerment of service workers. *Sloan Management Review*, 33, 31–39.

Brown, SW, RP Fisk and MJ Bitner (1994). The development and emerge of services marketing thought. *International Journal of Service Industry Management*, 5(1), 21–48.

Czepiel, JA (1990). Managing relationships with customers: A differentiating philosophy of marketing. In *Service Management Effectiveness*. DE Bowen, RB Chase and TG Cummings (eds.). San Francisco: Jossey Bass.

Deighton, J (1994). Managing services when the service is a performance. In *Service Quality — New Directions in Theory and Practice*, RT Trust and RL Oliver (eds.). Beverly Hills, CA: Sase Publications.

Echeverri, P (2002). Methodological issues in researching service encounters — A video-based analysis of communication. Paper presented at the *7th International Research Seminar in Service Management*, La Londe les Maures, France.

Fromm B and L Schlesinger (1994). *The Real Heroes of Business*. New York: Currency Doubleday.

Goodwin, CF (1990). I can do it myself: Training the service consumer to contribute to service productivity. *Journal of Services Marketing*, 2, 71–78.

Gummesson, E (1994). Service management: An evaluation and the future. *International Journal of Service Industry Management*, 5(1), 77–96.

Grönroos, C (1982). An applied service marketing theory. *European Journal of Marketing*, 7.

Grönroos, C (1990). *Service Management and Marketing. Managing the Moments of Truth in Service Competition*. Lexington, MA: Lexington Books.

Heskett, JL (1995). Strategic service management: Examining and understanding it. In *Understanding Services Management*. WJ Glynn and JG Barnes (eds.). Chicester: John Wiley.

Hochschild AR (1983). *The Managed Heart: Commercialization of Human Feeling*. Berkely CA: University of California Press.

Hornik, J (1992). Tactile stimulation and consumer response. *Journal of Consumer Research*, 19(December), 449–458.

Kelly, SW, JH Donnelly Jr. and SJ Skinner (1990). Customer participation in service production and delivery. *Journal of Retailing*, 66(Fall), 315–335.

Kingman-Brundage, J (1995). Service mapping: Back to basics. In *Understanding Services Management*. WJ Glynn and JG Barnes (eds.). Chicester: John Wiley.

Larsson, R and D Bowen (1989). Organization and customer: Managing design and coordination of services. *Academy of Management Review*, 14(2), 213–233.

Lewis, BR and TW Entwistle (1990). Managing the service encounter: A focus on the employee. *International Journal of Service Industry Management*, 3.

Lovelock CH (1995). Managing services: The human factor. In *Understanding Services Management*. WJ Glynn and JG Barnes (eds.). Chicester: John Wiley.

Mehrabian, A (1981). *Silent Messages*, 2nd Ed., Belmont, CA: Wadsworth.

Parasuraman, A, VA Zeithaml and LL Berry (1988). SERVQUAL: A multiple-item scale for measuring customer perceptions of service quality. *Journal of Retailing*, 64(Spring), 12–40.

Patterson, ML, JL Powell and MG Lenihan (1986). Touch compliance and interpersonal affects. *Journal of Non-Verbal Behavior*, 10(1), 41–50.

Pfeffer J (1994). *Competitive Advantage Through People*. Boston, MA: Harvard Business School Press.

Schneider, B (1994). HRM — A service perspective: Toward a customer-focused HRM. *International Journal of Service Industry Management*, 5(1), 64–76.

Schneider, B (1990). Alternative strategies for creating service-oriented organizations. In *Service Management Effectiveness*. D Bowen, RB Chase and TG Cummings (eds.). San Francisco: Jossey Bass.

Surprenant, CF and M Solomon (1987). Predictability and personalization in the service encounter. *Journal of Marketing*, 51(April), 86–96.

Sutton, R and A Rafaeli (1988). Untangling the relationship between displayed emotions and organizational sales: The case of convenience stores. *Academy of Management Journal*, 31(3), 461–87.

Zeithaml, V and MJ Bitner (2003). *Services Marketing. Integrating Customer Focus Across the Firm*, 3rd Ed. McGraw Hill.

11

How to Better Learn from Users

Hans Björkman

Stockholm School of Economics, Sweden
hans.bjorkman@sif.se

11.1. Introduction

This Chapter addresses the issue of managing user ideas. The initial emphasis lies in a problematization of the utilization of knowledge acquired from users. This includes a criticism of the existing market orientation literature as mainly describing the benefits of (often poorly described) market orientation combined with learning orientation. Market orientation literature is often merely describing and analyzing factors behind utilization of market knowledge. Thus, there is a need for prescriptive models and methods — and empirical testing of these models and methods — for enhancing the organizational utilization of knowledge attained from users. The tool box for listening to users is more developed than the tool box for using what is learnt. The need for new, and actionable, knowledge is evident.

The chapter describes the utilization of information acquired from users as a managerial challenge involving a set of specific capabilities. It is based upon evaluations of the role played by task forces/project groups in the Sif setting, where they have been responsible for organizing Design Dialog Groups (with similarities to focus groups) with members/users. The chapter aims at contributing academic and practical knowledge concerning methodological issues for utilization of knowledge acquired from users.

11.2.   User Involvement in Innovation Processes

User participation in product or service development has become an important practical issue and research topic. It is commonly considered that end users or customers are able to contribute to the development of new products or new services in different ways. Since they have other experiences than professional staff do, who participate in the innovation process more or less on a daily basis, they bring with them other experiences and other priorities which enable them to see different service and quality dimensions of new products or services (Magnusson, 2003; Iansiti and MacCormack, 1997; von Hippel, 1977; Hatchuel, 2001).

11.2.1.   *Market orientation and learning orientation*

Reliable market information has been described as a necessary, but not always sufficient, factor for facilitating innovations required for long-term competitive advantage (Baker and Sinkula, 1999, 2002; Dickson, 1996; Han *et al.*, 1998; Slater and Narver, 1995). Research has also suggested that abilities to engage in higher order learning must accompany a strong market orientation before a firm is likely to achieve long-term competitive advantage. Thus, Slater and Narver (1995) as well as Baker and Sinkula (2002) argue that there is a synergistic effect between market orientation and learning orientation on organizational performance — market orientation is only likely to significantly enhance performance when it is combined with a strong learning orientation (*ibid*, p. 8). Baker and Sinkula have thus defined market orientation as the degree to which a firm's analysis of the external marketing environment (outcome of market information acquisition, dissemination, and interpretation activities about customers, competitors, channel members and strategic partners) influences the strategic planning process, while a learning orientation was defined as the degree to which firm's proactively question whether their existing beliefs and practices actually maximize organizational performance (Argyris and Schön, 1978). In this chapter, it will be argued that learning should focus on managerial capabilities enabling a better understanding and commitment in relation to acquired information, and hence a more accurate utilization of the information.

11.2.2. *The missing link in customer orientation theory*

The use of market knowledge within firm's is discussed in an article by Menon and Varadarajan (1992). They provide a review of different approaches to measurement of market knowledge utilization, but conclude the article with a call for a clear identification and definition of market knowledge utilization. Menon and Varadarajan (1992, p. 62), develop a new knowledge utilization typology, conceptualized along three dimensions:

- *Action-oriented use*: demonstrated in changes in the users activities, practices or policies that can be linked to the findings in the study;
- *Knowledge-enhancing use*: results in changes in the users knowledge and understanding of the issues and themes of the study;
- *Affective use*: related to general levels of satisfaction, confidence, and trust. This could be expressed as the use of research with the intent (italics from original) of "feeling good."

Menon and Varadarajan (1992) discuss a variety of factors influencing market knowledge utilization. A factor of specific interest is *perceived credibility and usefulness of the information*. Underlying credibility dimensions are realism of research, accuracy, level of specificity of the problem addressed, consistency of the research output and implications, comprehensiveness and completeness of the research, and validity of research from both theoretical and methodological standpoints. Underlying usefulness dimensions are meaningfulness (of personal interest and making sense to users), goal relevance (relating to the tasks facing the users), operational validity (action-oriented and such that something can be done with it), and innovativeness (degree of non-obviousness).

The utilization of market research has been discussed by Deshpande and Zaltman in a series of articles (Deshpande and Zaltman, 1982, 1984, 1987). They have identified variables affecting the managerial use of market information. Arising from their research (Deshpande and Zaltman, 1982), organizational structure, technical quality, surprise, actionability, and researcher–manager interaction were found to be the most important variables.

Piercy (1995) argues that customer satisfaction has been in focus over the past few decades as a means to reach high market performance, but that virtually no serious attention has been given to the use of customer satisfaction studies to improve performance. In his study, Piercy (1995) finds internal barriers that can hamper the proper use of customer satisfaction survey results. Survey findings included many internal barriers in companies. Among these are internal politics (that customer satisfaction measures become part of the "politicking" between departments and groups), market simplification (that people make assumptions about the market and customers that make customer satisfaction issues appear unimportant), and corporate culture (that evaluating and using customer satisfaction measurements is believed to be "inappropriate"). Other hindering factors are market complacency (that people believe they know what customers think and that they have the best product, which is what really matters), resources/capability (problems in getting resources and expertise), and cost barriers (that finance is not available). Finally, credibility (that the results are seen to be ignored) is identified as a key factor.

To conclude, the value of listening to customers or users has not been neglected in the literature. There is even some literature describing causes behind a lacking utilization of market information. However, there is a lack of prescriptive models for an enhanced utilization of market information. An exception is Johnson and Gustafsson (2000), who describe the production of strategy matrices out of customer satisfaction data as a means for enhancing managerial decision making based upon acquired information. A recent study in Sif concludes that lacking methodological knowledge among managers and staff is an important factor behind a poor utilization of market information (Björkman, 2005). In this chapter, I will argue that specific managerial abilities are required for a meaningful utilization of market information. More specific, empirical data and analyses from an ongoing action research project will be used in order to suggest a model for enhancing the utilization of qualitative customer data.

11.2.3. *Utilization of market information — A managerial challenge*

Market information is produced with a number of purposes. The information may be acquired in order to be utilized instrategic positioning processes, for evaluation and development on operational levels and for assessment of specific activities. Specific service, product, or process performance may also be assessed. Moreover, market information — derived not least from customers or users — may be essential in product or service innovation processes.

A number of methods for producing market information have been developed and are described in the literature (see, e.g., Edvardsson and Gustafsson, 1999). While methods supporting strategic positioning and performance evaluations often are of an aggregate or quantitative nature, qualitative methods — often involving user participation — may be more useful in innovation processes (Björkman, 2005). Thus, information from customer satisfaction surveys can provide strategic information concerning strengths and weaknesses in the product or service portfolio and information useful for product/service improvement activities, whereas a deeper involvement of users enables a creation of innovative ideas. Moreover, the deeper user involvement can be used for the creation of a stronger user/customer focus in the organization.

I have referred to research indicating that learning orientation is a critical factor for utilization of market information, and I have moreover, presented factors hindering a proper utilization of acquired information. Henceforth, the chapter will concentrate on customer/user information and not on information on competitors. Furthermore, the chapter describes user involvement of some depth, what Alam (2002, p. 255) has termed *extensive consultation with users*. In order to operationalize the utilization of user information, it is possible to formulate a managerial challenge.

The managerial capability to initialize and conduct research is critical for the value and utilization of the acquired results. Thus, it is a managerial issue to ensure that the organization gathers and processes reliable information on the intended topics in a format emphasizing enhanced organizational understanding and actionability. This calls for capabilities to

- prepare for the research to be conducted;
- acquire the needed information;
- document, analyze, and further elaborate the acquired information;
- diffusing and using (and re-using) the information for decision making;
- infusing a customer-oriented focus in the organization.

I will now delve into the utilization of a specific method for user involvement — the Design Dialog Methodology — in order to describe its capabilities in respect of the managerial challenge stated above. From the description to follow, some prescriptive principles for managerial actions for a better utilization of user information will be elaborated.

11.3. Background and Setting

The setting studied is Sif, a major white-collar industrial trade union in Sweden. Sif — the Swedish Trade Union for White-Collar Workers in Industry — is a politically independent trade union that organizes white-collar employees in the manufacturing, construction, computer and consulting industries. The organization is among the leading unions in Sweden with over 300,000 members. This figure has been on the increase until recently, and the union can boast a strong financial base. The study is a partial account of a large-scale modernization project, and as action research, is an input to that project. This project has highlighted that a modern union needs to develop services that correspond to a variety of individual needs. In a trade union context, services can consist of new methods for advice on wage levels, competence development, and career planning, etc. The development of the Sif service portfolio of individual and collective services has been described in some detail by Björkman and Huzzard (2005).

The organization has recognized a closer relationship to its members as a critical factor for the development of services and articulation of positions before negotiations. The administrative organization — the staff — has to develop its capability to handle, refine and organize its service portfolio in a continuous and ongoing dialog with its members.

A specific methodology, Design Dialog Groups (DDGs), has been developed in order to enhance learning from members in different projects aimed at developing a more attractive membership package. The methodology is still emerging and shortcomings are continuously detected.

The chapter is based upon four years of continuous research and development of the organization's capability to listen to and learn from members (Björkman, 2005). In total, about 60 Design Dialog Group sessions have been held, engaging about 350 members and non-members and more than 30 Sif employees. Methodologically, the study is an ongoing insider action research project, in which I have hade the role as employed by Sif as service developer simultaneously as I have conducted my doctoral studies. More thorough descriptions of the used research methodology can be found in Björkman (2005).

11.3.1. *The design dialog process*

In short, the Design Dialog Group (DDG) methodology is a systematic process that connects members' demands directly to the strategic development of the organization. Fully developed and implemented, it is meant to be a powerful instrument, linking members, their preferences and needs with services, developed within the organization and offered to members. Members should regularly be invited to take part in a discussion around the services and support that they could expect from their membership. The dialog between the administrative staff is considered to be an institutionalized process, included in their job descriptions.

The DDG methodology includes three different activities, idea generation, idea transformation to possible action programs and confirmed strategic decisions. A more thorough description of evaluation results from one particular set of sessions aiming at developing activities for managers has been published elsewhere (Björkman, 2003). The components of the DDG process are rather conventional. What makes the methodology different is the conscious and systematic combination of procedures used during the process.

11.3.2. *The task force*

Beer and Eisenstadt (2000) have specifically addressed the problems concerning strategy implementation and learning. They discuss positive experiences from a method in which task forces play a substantial role. In brief, the method starts with the top team of the business unit or corporation defining its strategy. A cross-functional team (task force) of lower-level managers is then commissioned to collect data concerning strengths and barriers to implementing the strategy. The task force then conducts interviews with organizational members and customers and finally reports to the managers and researchers.

In the Sif study, the task forces have had roles resembling those given in the study conducted by Beer and Eisenstadt (2000). The task forces have been assigned to be in charge of major development projects. Their role has been to listen to members and then report findings in terms of new ideas, concepts and cultural knowledge. They are important actors in the development of new services.

A typical process starts with a decision to establish a project team (task force) recruited within the organization, commissioned to present solutions to important issues, as they are identified by the management board. The outcome of a task force consists of reports, describing a set of organizational measures, descriptions of new alternatives or propositions on the re-orientation of existing activities and services. Up to now, the DDG methodology has been applied with a wide array of purposes, developing services and activities for managers, the mapping of competencies and skills required by members in the engineering and consultancy industry, shaping a virtual community platform for members, development of web based learning tools and the preparation of national negotiation rounds. A typical task force consists of three to eight middle managers and experts from departments that are affected by the issue.

11.3.3. *The design dialog group*

One of the main responsibilities for each task force is to organize a dialog, directly with members, who are willing to participate with their ideas in a design process. A DDG has some superficial similarities with a focus group. The focus group methodology has become popular in market research due to its ability to produce rapid results with high face validity and involve many participants at a comparably low cost. The method is friendly and respectful (Frey and Fontana, 1993; Kreuger, 1994). The focus group methodology originates from sociological and mass media research during the 1940s. Merton used the notion "focused interview" for this qualitative method for studies of attitudes, values and complex phenomena that occurred in social interactions in the 1950s (Merton *et al.*, 1990). Some properties are common to most definitions of focus groups (Bormann, 1972): The purpose is to collect qualitative data, the participants have something in common, and the discussions are held from a specific focus, for example, a film, a specific event, a scenario, a specific notion, or an imaginative theme.

A typical focus group consists of 4–12 participants and a moderator. The group interview duration may vary with one and a half to four hours being normal (Edmunds, 1999). Frey and Fontana (1993) define focus groups as structured and formal, while brainstorming groups are unstructured with the leaders non-directing. Others claim that the role of the moderator in a focus group may vary from non-directing to strongly directing. Millward (1995) believes that the moderator controls *what is discussed and the process*. What is discussed should not be strongly controlled in a focus group. The control over the process normally varies during the focus group meeting. In the DDG setting, the role of the moderator is to achieve an open and creative context rather than impose a dialog scheme that is given beforehand. He/she is supposed to act mainly to control undesired behavior among participants (like people talking too much, not allowing other participants to have divergent opinions, clarify the arguments rather than taking up a definite position). The guidelines for the coordinator are strongly inspired by the dialog criteria, defined by Gustavsen (1985).

While the majority of focus groups are organized by market research consultants as assignments from the organizations that will use the results, DDGs are organized by the organization to use the collected data *in its own developmental processes*. Furthermore, the specific properties that distinguish DDGs from traditional focus groups are the following:

- Participants are invited to a session by the organization in which they are members (or potential members).
- The sessions are moderated by an organizational member (in this case a Sif employee).
- The sessions are generally held on the organization's premises.
- The sessions not only have the purpose of bringing experiences and ideas to the organization, but they also create relations among the participants and between the participants and the organization.
- The sessions are video recorded and followed on a TV screen by the task force and sometimes other organizational employees in order to enhance learning in the organization.
- All sessions are evaluated by the participants.

11.3.4. *Organizing and utilizing DDGs*

The task force assignment contains three distinctive phases: (1) recruitment of DDG participants, (2) execution of the group session, and (3) evaluation, elaboration, and documentation of the process results in order to produce utilizable information for the organization. In most cases, the recruitment has been conducted by an external market research firm, from directives concerning the participants professional occupation and other factors. In principle, each group session covers the following topics:

- clarifying the present situation — based on stories from participants' own experiences,
- identifying action that is needed to overcome or improve existing shortcomings and problems,

- finding activities that can be organized by the union,
- an example of a typical group session (in this case targeting managers) is given to illustrate its work procedures:

> The dialog group meeting was held as a two-hour session, mediated by the author. The discussions focused on three aspects:
>
> - "Being a manager" — situation, role, opportunities, threats,
> - "How can the managers' role and situation be improved" — what kind of knowledge and skills needed to be developed?
> - "What can external parties (such as trade unions) do to enhance the managers' situation?"
>
> Each of these aspects were described by each participant after a short time for individual reflection and discussed in the group. Documentation by the dialog groups and analysis of the video recordings were used to produce a list of service ideas that had been discussed. This service idea list was then used in the evaluation process.

Sixteen DDGs have been specifically assessed by the assigned task forces. Their assessments have resulted in the following:

- Some ideas are assessed as creative.
- Many ideas are expressed at a systems level rather than at a detailed level.
- Many ideas are reproducible.
- Ideas assessed as creative are evaluated as less reproducible than other ideas.
- The capacity of the organization to use newly obtained ideas is a problem.

11.3.5. *The interplay between the DDG and the task force*

Usually, the session moderators are members of the task force and will become well informed about what happens during a group session. Every session in a design dialog group is observed by members of the task force in real time, since the discussions are followed on a TV screen in an adjacent room. The moderator and observer task after each session also involves writing a report on important impressions. All sessions have also been video recorded, to enable content analysis afterward.

The idea generation process in the DDGs provides important input into the work of the task force. By real time observing the activities in the groups, members of the task force have, during breaks, the opportunity to communicate with group coordinators and ask them to clarify or sometimes also change the focus of the ongoing discussion. Most important, however, is that the task force members have an opportunity among themselves to reflect upon and discuss the ongoing dialog in the room next door. In most cases, a rather informal reflection, idea selection, and idea refinement process takes place in the task force.

The interplay with the DDG includes elements that challenge the prevalent thinking in the organization. Members participating in the dialog carry with them different working backgrounds, experiences and pictures of the world that at times will bring up suggestions for services that hardly fit into established practices. The role of the task force is to scrutinize them, search for the important design aspects, examine how they could fit into existing organizational practices and add to preparation of organizational changes. The task force compiles documentation, consisting of all information in writing from the DDG session and brief individual reflections from the task force members. The documentation from a set of DDGs is then processed by the task force. The results from this filtering through the internal knowledge system may then be used in the further development of new concepts in terms of services or trade union positions/opinions.

However, results have been translated into action in terms of new activities or services to a lesser extent than expected. Thus, it is important to further develop the role and working procedures of the task force.

11.3.6. *Outcomes from the DDG process*

The DDG process has so far been successful and has ended in several contributions to services offered to members. Since we focus our attention on the process itself, we only briefly illustrate their range. Some examples will show that concepts and ideas have been converted and implemented as new services. One hundred and forty service ideas originating from 12 group sessions have contributed to the development of the Sif website. Concepts and knowledge obtained from the groups concerned, for example, search engines for an easy access to relevant legislation and collective agreements, information on individual rights and responsibilities, advice on salaries and contractual issues for managers and tools for the creation of networks between managers. The DDG process has also been used in a strategy formation context in a project on strategic positioning aiming at an attractive membership for managers. DDGs have been used to identify conceptual platforms for development of questionnaires or to find important bargaining objectives.

Evaluations have indicated that the methodology had been relatively successful in terms of newly acquired concepts and knowledge. However, three specific problems or challenges have been identified:

- organizing user involvement to obtain high levels of creativity in group settings,
- organizing learning from users: Improvements of the utilization of new concepts and knowledge,
- improving the dissemination of results outside the project groups involved.

Returning to the managerial capabilities previously described, the Design Dialog Methodology has proven to enable the organization to

- prepare for the research to be conducted;
- acquire the needed information to a rather high extent, while additional and unforeseen information simultaneously has been collected;
- develop work procedures to document, analyze, and further elaborate the acquired information;
- infuse a customer-oriented focus in the organization.

One managerial capability — *diffusing and using (and re-using) the information for decision making* — has thus far been the least developed. Suggestions for improvement of this specific capability will be proposed.

11.4.   A Model For Learning from Users

From the experiences gained through development, utilization and evaluations of the DDG methodology described, I propose a prescriptive model for organizing learning from user groups (Table 1). The model is based upon rather intense user involvement (Alam, 2002).

11.4.1.   *Preparations*

The task force — as previously described — is a working group, whose active involvement is critical for the outcome of the entire process. Thus, it is essential that the task force is involved in the preparations, including choice of qualitative method, choice of topics and preparation of discussion

Table 1:   A model for organizing learning from users.

Activity	Critical factors
1. Preparations	Timeliness, project group participation, choice of users
2. Idea generation by users	Group creativity (domain-related skills, creativity-relevant processes, task motivation)
3. Documentation and elaboration	Group creativity, documentation formats and responsibilities
4. Decision making and diffusion	Clarity, re-use, access and storage

guides, choice of participating users, and design of the process for documentation and further elaboration of attained ideas. If internal interviewers or group moderators will be used in the research — and I strongly advise these options to be considered (Björkman, 2005) — it is important that they develop a considerable expertise in the research methodology chosen. Careful preparations are essential for the results and the propensities for active participation by the task force members are strengthened through their early involvement.

Another issue to consider early is during which phase of a product or service innovation process users should be involved. I argue that, in many cases, a very early participation is preferential. The advantages are obvious, as the organizational capability to adopt and utilize ideas or concepts on an overall/structural/architectural level in the actual innovation project depends on an early introduction of such ideas. Simultaneously, more specific or detailed ideas can be collected in early phases and utilized later in the process. Moreover, if acquisition of more detailed user input is deemed to be needed, further customer involvement can be organized during following developmental stages.

11.4.2. *Idea generation by users: A basic model for group creativity*

The focus in this chapter is on utilization of ideas, concepts, and experiences acquired from users and not on the interaction with users itself. Thus, the description of the specific interaction with users will be brief. A more thorough discussion on creativity in Design Dialog Groups can be found in Björkman (2004). In my research, I have chosen to use Amabiles (1996) components of creative performance as a basic group creativity model. Her model consists of three creative components: domain-relevant skills, creativity-relevant processes, and task motivation.

11.4.2.1. Domain-relevant skills

The role of domain-relevant skills in the production of creative work has received scant attention from researchers, but there is some evidence that exposure to a wide array of information in a domain can enhance creativity (Amabile, 1996).

11.4.2.2. Creativity-related processes

In brief, the outcome of creativity-related processes in a group context depend on group size, the design of the group sessions, the skills and actions taken by the moderator and on the work style in the group. Knowledge and the use of heuristics is one important creativity-relevant component (Amabile, 1996, p. 89). A heuristic can be defined as "any principle or device that contributes to a reduction in the average search to solution" (Newell et al., 1962, p. 78). The use of heuristics/methods enabling creative performance may be explicit (the overt application of a specific method) or implicit (embedded in the moderating activities). Brainstorming techniques (Osborn, 1963) and other specific techniques aiming at enhancing creativity (see de Bono, 1992) may be examples of usable heuristics as well as more general problem-solving methodologies, such as SWOT analyses.

There are, however, also several factors related to group interaction and work style that may be detrimental to creativity, such as evaluation apprehension, free riding/social loafing, production blocking, compliance, and pressure for cognitive uniformity/conformity. Evaluation apprehension relates to the risk that productivity is impaired when members fear expressing ideas because of potential retaliation, (Amabile, 1996; Paulus, 2000; Pinsonneault et al., 1999). Free-riding refers to the motivated, intentional withdrawal of efforts. Production blocking occurs in groups as only one can talk at a time, and ideas may be forgotten while people wait for the moment to express their ideas (Paulus, 2000). Compliance occurs when participants give the answers the moderator is assumed to want (Albrect et al., 1993; Kelman, 1961). Finally, pressure for cognitive uniformity/conformity indicates that members may feel pressure to remain within group or social norms (Pinsonneault et al., 1999).

11.4.2.3. *Task motivation*

Intrinsic motivation arises from the individual's positive reaction to qualities of the task itself: interest, involvement, curiosity, satisfaction, and positive challenge (Amabile, 1996). A person is said to be intrinsically motivated to engage in an activity if that person views such engagement as an end in itself and not as a means to some extrinsic goals (deCharms, 1968; Deci, 1975; Lepper and Greene, 1978). Extrinsic motivation arises from sources outside the task itself: evaluation, contracted-for rewards, external directives, etc. (Amabile, 1996). The importance of intrinsic motivation and a freedom from extrinsic constraints has been expressed by theorists working within philosophy, humanistic psychology, and social psychology (Amabile, 1996; Crutchfield, 1962; Koestler, 1964; Rogers, 1954).

Amabile (1996, p. 119) has formulated "The Intrinsic Motivation Principle of Creativity": Intrinsic motivation is conducive to creativity; controlling extrinsic motivation is detrimental to creativity, but informational or enabling extrinsic motivation can be conducive, particularly if initial levels of intrinsic motivation are high.

To summarize, our research has indicated that group sessions gain from being carefully designed in respect of choice of participants, preparation of discussion guide (including heuristics), and avoidance of negative factors hampering group creativity, such as evaluation apprehension, free riding and production blocking. Thus, I propose the following:

- Try to avoid evaluation apprehension through guarantees that ideas and discussions are carefully followed by the task force, but that no-one outside of the task force will have opportunities to trace concepts, ideas, experiences, or opinions to a specific group or individual.
- See that all participants are addressed in the discussion on each topic.
- Control the effects of groupthink and production blocking through a mix of individual assignments and group discussions.

11.4.3. *Documentation and elaboration*

User group sessions provide the innovation process with fresh suggestions for potential service commitments. Consequently, the sessions, the discussions and the ideas formulated, need to be carefully and exactly documented. Video recordings are good instruments. However, they may be a bit practically inconvenient. In our studies, they have been mainly used for clarification. Evaluations of early DDGs indicated a strong need for rigorous documentation methods. This documentation problem has been treated in different ways. Before starting a new round of dialog groups, the purpose of the design dialog and its expected outcomes are discussed within the task force and the moderators. A detailed agenda to be used to structure the dialog session is prepared. The task to document what happens in the dialog sessions is distributed among participants in the control room so that every individual records some specific aspects of the dialog. Even more important is the task force summary and revision of events during the dialog sessions.

11.4.3.1. Concept elaboration

In evaluations of early Design Dialog Group sessions, a strong belief in the task force members' abilities to play a role in concept generation, departing from a closer observation of the DDG session, has been indicated. The task force could thus organize its own "post-DDG" session in order to develop further concepts. Theory suggests that such a session should be free from evaluative work (Amabile, 1996).

In an emerging and enhanced model, the task force members assume four distinctive roles. First, they are responsible for the preparations. Second, they are responsible for the DDG documentation. Third, they use their knowledge to elaborate concepts. The external stimuli (input from the DDG session) and work procedures could then provide an "incubator climate." Fourth, they use their knowledge and former experiences in order to find original and viable concepts/ideas. This final process should be separated from the creative process. Thus, I propose the following: the task force shall be given specified assignments concerning documentation of user group sessions, further elaboration on attained ideas and concepts, and a role for selecting original and viable concepts/ideas.

11.4.4. Decision making and diffusion

In the context studied, the organization's poor capability of utilizing concepts emanating from user groups for decision making has been an evident problem. This has partially been due to imperfections in the stages described above. For example, the task force has lacked in ability to find concepts useful in its own decision making or to present decision alternatives for the management in an appropriate moment. Other factors include that the management has not been properly informed about the utilized methods and their properties.

Thus, in order to enhance the decision-making processes based upon information acquired through user involvement, I suggest that the critical deliverable from the task force should be formulated as a proposition for decision making, and to inform the management about the utilized user involvement method and its properties.

Idea creation sessions often result in ideas, which are original, but not useful under the current circumstances. These ideas may be either useless or impossible to develop into viable services or products. However, they may be useful under other circumstances, such as in other projects or when technologies have been further developed or more cost efficient. It is also a part of the creative process to take care of ideas that are not converging with the prevalent conceptions in the organization. Divergence must be accepted and organized, the horizon must be contingent, as many new concepts will not be immediately used, and the re-use of excess knowledge must be managed (Hatchuel *et al.*, 2001).

Hence, the issue of diffusion of creative ideas is not only related to the moment the ideas are acquired and initially presented — it has also aspects concerning storage and exhibition. A concrete and practical proposition is that the task force should deliver a document describing each idea/concept and a recommendation for its further "life." An example is shown in Table 2.

Using a metaphor, the ideas saved for later will be kept deep frozen until needed. The importance of an updated freezer inventory, easily accessed by all internal service or product developers, is evident. Moreover, during regular defrosting activities hidden and forgotten delicacies may show up.

11.4.5. *A customer-oriented focus in the organization*

One of the major properties of the DDG methodology is that it brings "users' voice" into the organization, as organizational members (the task

Table 2: Suggested documentation table for ideas attained from users.

Ideas/concepts	Accepted	Saved for later	Refused
Idea # 1 (description)	(description of its utilization, incl. timeline)		(often information or ideas already known or used)
Idea # 2			
Idea # n			

force) are assigned to prepare for listening, to listen and to utilize ideas and experiences gained. It is a considerable difference between real persons and statistics. Aggregate measures are often poorly used when unexpected or challenging results are presented. It is easy to conclude that the respondents did not understand what was asked, and thus, their answers cannot be taken seriously. The distance between the organization and the users has hence not decreased through the quantitative study. On the other hand, when listening to personal experiences from users, given the opportunity to delve a bit deeper into the ideas and experiences expressed, it is most likely that a respectful relation to the user is established. As a task force member, you soon realize that there is no "average user", and that all users are unique individuals with individual needs. Bringing the user into the organization in order to listen to him or her has in the DDG case proven to create "a rucksack of commitment" among the task force members — the users are perceived as very important. The diffusion of the methodology in the organization is interesting, as it has not followed from managerial decisions. Instead, people who previously have been involved in task forces have initialized the utilization of the methodology in new development projects. Their preference of the methodology is most likely to be explained as following from their experiences that users' contributions are important — something they realized after previous DDG sessions. Some quotations from interviews with involved internal service developers indicate how Design Dialog Group sessions are perceived:

> "The members are a huge mass; here I could listen to individual narratives that developed my knowledge." (Jenny, concerning managers)

> "What you learn from the DDGs is that when we (those employed by Sif, authors comment) talk, we talk about big issues and with our words on everything, and then, when listening to the members, they express themselves totally differently and the issues are more everyday nature." (Anna)

> "We have lots of contact with our members, but looking closer at them, it is a kind of membership contact that is not very deep or reflective, it is more like mass communication, and then it may be we who have contact with them, but they don't have contact with us." (Mathias)

"(We learn about) typically basic needs, which we tend to overlook in our daily work, because they are so difficult to satisfy . . . We need to adapt to different member groups. Otherwise it doesn't matter how much information you send them." (Mathias)

" . . . I think I have got used to something I always have known, but have had problems internalizing, that the members do not define their problems as we do." (Mathias)

"Some have their first contact with Sif and perceive this in a way as a means of entry to Sif. "I have been a member for 100 years and now at last I have the opportunity to put forward my opinions. Now I really have the opportunity to talk" . . . It is interesting, as it indicates that their liaisons with Sif are rather limited." (Jenny)

" To really listen, take a step back, try to see things from the outside, not be blinded by what you bring into the project, but to take a step back and listen to the expressed opinions." (Eva)

" . . . I noticed that, emotionally, I brought my experiences from the DDGs all the way to the negotiation table . . . I know that we referred as often to experiences in the DDGs as to decisions made by our National Negotiation Conference." (Mathias)

One important experience from the DDG setting is that the cross-functionality of the assigned task forces has been an important factor behind the diffusion of the methodology and, hence, in a process toward a stronger user focus. Thus, in order to enhance the customer focus in the organization, I suggest recognizing and utilizing the user involvement processes as a means for a strengthened customer focus in the organization.

11.5. A Final Conclusion

Based upon an examination of the learning capabilities deployed in the projects where DDGs have been used, a model for organizing learning from user involvement has been suggested in this chapter. The aim has been to provide simple and useful advice for practitioners — as well as for researchers involved in learning from users. Even though the model is a result of thorough research and experiences gained during several years, the model may be incomplete or difficult to use outside of the setting in which it has been developed. Nevertheless, I presage that organizations of many different types will find that the model provides a useful basis for enhanced learning from users.

I have argued that a better learning from users is strongly connected with a set of managerial capabilities, enabling the organization to

- prepare for the research to be conducted;
- acquire the needed information;
- document, analyze, and further elaborate the acquired information;
- diffuse and use (and re-use) the information for decision making;
- infuse a customer-oriented focus in the organization.

The presented study concerns user interaction in developmental processes. However, my previous research (Björkman, 2005) has also included studies on the utilization of an annual quantitative member satisfaction study with strategic and operational purposes. My conclusion is that the managerial capabilities presented above are equally important in respect of user information of such character. Important prerequisites for a successful development of the required managerial capabilities have in my previous studies been proposed. Three specific propositions (adapted from Björkman, 2005, pp. 106–107) are strongly relevant to expose:

- Knowledge enhances learning: the utilization of market information requires knowledge among managers and employees about the instruments used to ensure accurate interpretations and utilization of the results acquired. Knowledge thus has a role in breaking down the barriers preventing accurate utilization of market information.
- Task alignment (Beer et al., 1990) is a viable strategy for the creation of learning micro-climates: Learning through the change of work behaviors is the core element of a task alignment strategy. Task alignment is a strategy targeting learning capabilities in the organization that is not only an approach for solving problems in the long term, but also an immediate response to tangible business problems.
- Various political behaviors hampering learning processes may often be traced. Senior management has a specific responsibility to scrutinize both its own behaviors and organizational practices. A broad level of participation and involvement of managers and employees during the development and adaptation of the market orientation instrument can enable open and trustful discussions for enhancing organizational learning from users.

To conclude, the managerial capabilities discussed in this chapter comprise of both knowledge-related aspects and cultural aspects. There is a need to bring the user into the organization, to establish a customer focus among service developers. In this chapter, I have discussed some managerial capabilities needed for the creation of user knowledge and commitment.

The lack of prescriptive models for learning from users was the starting point of this chapter. This problem is not solved through the introduction of one model. More models need to be developed and tested — and this is an issue of huge academic and practical importance. The users deserve not only to be listened to, but also to be learnt from.

References

Alam, I (2002). An exploratory investigation of user involvement in new service development. *Journal of the Academy of Marketing Sciences*, 30, 250–261.

Albrect, TL, MG Johnsson and JB Walther (1993). Understanding communication processes in focus groups. In DL Morgan (ed.), *Successful Focus Groups. Advancing the State of the Art*: 51–64. Newbury Park: Sage Publications.

Amabile, TM (1996). *Creativity in Context*. Boulder, Colorado: Westview Press.

Argyris, C and DA Schön (1978). *Organizational Learning: A Theory of Action Perspective*. Reading, MA: Addison-Wesley.

Baker, WE and JM Sinkula (1999). The synergistic effect of market orientation and product innovation on organizational performance. *Journal of the Academy of Marketing Science*, 27, 411–427.

Baker, WE and JM Sinkula (2002). Market orientation, learning orientation, and product innovation: Delving into the organization's black box. *Journal of Market Focused Management*, 5, 5–23.

Beer, M and RA Eisenstat (2000). The silent killers of strategy implementation and learning. *Sloan Management Review*, 41(4), 29–40.

Beer, M, RA Eisenstat and B Spector (1990). *The Critical Path to Corporate Renewal*. Boston, MA: Harvard Business School Press.

Björkman, H (2003). Service innovation — A collaborative approach. In Adler N, A Shani and A Styhre (eds.), *Collaborative Research in Organizations*. Thousand Oaks, CA: Sage.

Björkman, H (2004). Design dialog groups as a source of innovation: Factors behind group creativity. *Creativity and Innovation Management*, 13(2), 97–108.

Björkman, H (2005). Learning from members. Tools for strategic positioning and service innovation in trade unions. Stockholm: Stockholm School of Economics, The Economic Research Institute.

Björkman, H and T Huzzard (2005). Membership interface unionism: A Swedish white-collar union in transition. *Economic and Industrial Democracy*, 26 (February) (1).

Bormann, EG (1972). Fantasy and rhetorical vision: The rhetorical criticism of social reality. *Quarterly Journal of Speech*, 68, 396–407.

Crutchfield, R (1962). Conformity and creative thinking. In Gruber H, G Terrell and M Wertheimer (eds.), *Contemporary Approaches to Creative Thinking*. New York: Atherton Press.

de Bono, E (1992). *Serious Creativity*. New York/London: Harper Business.

deCharms, R (1968). *Personal Causation*. New York: Academic Press.

Deci, E (1975). *Intrinsic Motivation*. New York: Plenum.

Deshpande, R and G Zaltman (1982). Factors affecting the use of market research information: A path analysis. *Journal of Marketing Research*, 19, 14–31.

Deshpande, R and G Zaltman (1984). A comparison of factors affecting researcher and manager perception of market research use. *Journal of Marketing Research*, 21, 32–38.

Deshpande, R and Zaltman, G (1987). A comparison of factors affecting use of marketing information in consumer and industrial firms. *Journal of Marketing Research*, 24, 114–118.

Dickson, PR (1996). The static and dynamic mechanics of competition: A comment on Hunt and Morgan's comparative advantage theory. *Journal of Marketing*, 60, 102–106.

Edmunds, H (1999). *The Focus Group Research Handbook*. Lincolnwood, Ill: American Marketing Association/NTC Business Books.

Edvardsson, B and A Gustafsson (1999). Quality in the development of new products and services. In Edvardsson, B and A Gustafsson (eds.), *The Nordic School of Quality Management*: 189–225. Lund, Sweden: Studentlitteratur.

Frey, JH and A Fontana (1993). The group interview in social research. In Morgan, J DL (ed.), *Successful Focus Groups. Advancing the State of the Art*: 20–34. Newbury Park, CA. Sage.

Gustavsen, B (1985). Workplace reform and democratic dialog. *Economic and Industrial Democracy*, 6, 461–479.

Han, JK, N Kim and RK Srivastava (1998). Market orientation and organizational performance: Is innovation a missing link? *Journal of Marketing*, 62, 30–45.

Hatchuel, A (2001). Toward design theory and expandable rationality: The unfinished program of Herbert Simon. *Journal of Management & Governance*, 5(3–4), 260–273.

Hatchuel A, P Le Masson and B Weil (2001). From R&D to R-I-D: Design strategies and the management of 'innovation fields.' Conference paper presented at the *8th International Product Development Management Conference*, Enchede, June.

Iansiti, M and A MacCormack (1997). Developing products on internet time. *Harvard Business Review*, 75 (5), 108–117.

Johnson, MD and A Gustafsson (2000). *Improving Customer Satisfaction, Loyalty, and Profit: An Integrated Measurement and Management System*. San Francisco, CA: Jossey-Bass.

Kelman, H (1961). Processes of opinion change. *Public Opinion Quarterly*, 25, 57–78.

Koestler, A (1964). *The Act of Creation*. New York: Dell.

Kreuger, RA (1994). *Focus Groups: A Practical Guide for Applied Research* (2nd Ed.). Thousand Oaks, CA: Sage.

Lepper, M and D Greene. Over justification research and beyond: Toward a means-end analysis of intrinsic and extrinsic motivation. In Lepper, M and D Greene (eds.), *The Hidden Costs of Reward*. Hillsdale, NJ: Lawrence Erlbaum Associates.

Magnusson, PM (2003). Customer-oriented product development. Experiments involving users in service innovation. Stockholm: Stockholm School of Economics.

Menon, A and PR Varadarajan (1992). A model of marketing knowledge use within firms. *Journal of Marketing*, 58, 53–71.

Merton, RK, M Fiske and P Kendall (1990). *The Focused Interview. A Manual of Problems and Procedures* (2nd Ed.). New York: The Free Press.

Millward, L (1995). Focus groups. In Breakwell, GM, S Hammond and C Fife-Shaw (eds.), *Research Methods in Psychology*: 274–292. London: Sage.

Newell, A, J Shaw and H Simon (1962). The processes of creative thinking. In Gruber, H, G Terell and M Wertheimer (eds.), *Contemporary Approaches to Creative Thinking*. New York: Atherton Press.

Osborn, AF (1963). *Applied Imagination* (2nd Ed.). New York: Scribner.

Paulus, PB (2000). Groups, teams, and creativity: The creative potential of idea-generating groups. *Applied Psychology: An International Review*, 49(2), 237–262.

Piercy, NF (1995). Customer satisfaction and the internal market. Marketing our customers to our employees. *Journal of Marketing Practice: Applied Marketing Science*, 1(1), 22–44.

Pinsonneault, A, H Barki, RB Gallupe and N Hoppen (1999). Electronic brainstorming: The illusion of productivity. *Information Systems Research*, 10(2), 110–133.

Rogers, C (1954). Towards a theory of creativity. *ETC: A Review of General Semantics*, 11, 249–260.

Slater, SF and JC Narver (1995). Market orientation and the learning organization. *Journal of Marketing*, 59(3), 63–74.

von Hippel, E (1977). Has a customer already developed your next product? *Sloan Management Review*, 18(2), 63–74.

12

Video-Based Methodology: Capturing Real-Time Perceptions of Customer Processes

Per Echeverri

Service Research Center, Karlstad University, Sweden
per.echeverri@kau.se

12.1. Introduction

For decades, researchers in service management have perceived service as being something different from products. The dynamic, interactive, and somewhat fuzzy nature of the service concept has been stressed, and it is apparent that the processual and interactive nature of services is difficult to investigate, measure, and analyze. Indeed, Gummesson (1996) questioned whether the concepts, categories, models, theories, statistical data, and statements provided by research actually capture reality.

These problems have not always been addressed and discussed in mainstream service research (Menor *et al.*, 2002; Thomke, 2003; Vargo and Lusch, 2004a); although the problems are often alluded to when questions are raised about data-collection methodology. The question of *when* to collect data, that is, before, during, or after the customer's experience, is especially relevant when assessing customer perceptions of the service experience. The question of *what* to collect involves an assessment of the relevant factors and social mechanisms to explore. The question of *how* to collect empirical data involves assessments of methods that provide a realistic representation of what really happens "out there." Shortcomings at the level of data collection also raise questions about the results of advanced techniques of data analysis, and therefore about the overall validity of conclusions concerning service quality (Dahlsten, 2003; Matthing, 2004). Data collection clearly has implications for the development of theory and for the practical insights it provides. Research on user involvement (Alam, 2002; Magnusson *et al.*, 2003) has focused on some of these critical empirical and methodological issues affecting the foundation of existing research.

The present chapter illustrates some of these problems through a study of passengers using a public-transport service. In particular, the interactive process aspects of the service are examined. The chapter also uses the case study to comment on some theoretical problems in understanding customer satisfaction and perceived service quality. Finally, some methodological problems are discussed such as the need for more accurate methods of data collection in service research and service industry.

12.2. Practical Problems

According to government policy, the Swedish public-transport system should be "accessible for all" by 2010 (SOU 1995:70). Having a handicap or a functional disorder should not be a hindrance to accessibility. Participating in everyday activities is an important determinant of health and well being and the opportunities to participate in societal life should be equal for all people (U N, 1993). Corporate and governmental research and development (R&D) has therefore set out to identify problems for passengers in managing the "landscape" of transportation services. In traffic planning, the expression "the entire travel chain" has been introduced to emphasize the scope of a trip (Rikstrafiken *et al.*, 2003). Travelling from "door to door" in a multimodal transport system is not an easy task, especially at the nodes between different transport modes where travellers can experience problems in navigating the system. Physical infrastructure and communication symbols (such as signs and artefacts) are not always in accordance with customer thinking (cognition) and physical movements (spatial layout). Such shortcomings have an effect on customers, perceptions of quality.

These problems are exacerbated for disabled people with various handicaps. Travelling is more difficult for a person with functional limitations than it is for a person without such limitations (Ståhl, 1987). If a trip on the transportation service is perceived to be a "high-risk" project, some will not even consider using the system. This is a challenge to service developers and calls for a profound understanding of what really happens "out there." Management needs to understand the driving factors for perceptions of bad quality, customer complaints, and low levels of usage of public-transport services.

12.3. Theoretical Problems

Problems such as those previously outlined are faced by customers and practitioners in various service sectors. They imply a gap between the intended experience of service-process quality and the actual experience. In theory, the problem is how to identify the relevant factors that provide an adequate explanation of what creates perceptions of quality for customers. Research on service quality has proposed various determinants of this experience based on a perception of service phenomena as objects or entities, rather than as processes (Parasuraman *et al.*, 1988; Oliver, 1997). In perceptual and cognitive research, several studies have aimed at deriving categories of critical incidents (Bejou *et al.*, 1996; Bitner *et al.*, 1990; Friman *et al.*, 1998) that have then been used to analyze perceived service quality. Research on emotional and affective appraisals has focused on the relationship of perception with satisfaction (Friman, 2000).

These research traditions rely on perceptual categories as determinants of service quality — but they do not address the question of behavioral data. This makes for a shallow empirical foundation that depends on data from memory-based cognition and emotions. Moreover, the research often has a limited view of the service phenomenon and lacks sufficient recognition of the processual and interactive aspects of behavior. Finally, research traditionally is based on retrospection which limits data to what could be stored in memory. Capturing customer data in natural settings *during* service experiences renders alternative conclusions which are important factors for the user in the specific interaction. Other results might be obtained from studies based on (i) behavioral data, (ii) alternative methods of data collection, or (iii) alternative forms of data analysis. The results of research using such alternative approaches might have implications for future theory development.

12.3.1. *Service systems*

In the literature, a service has often been defined as something that becomes "real" when a customer interacts with some specific prerequisites such as organizational structures, activities, people, and other customers (Lovelock *et al.*, 1996). This can be referred to as a "service-system approach." Because a service becomes "real" during personal interaction, it is not easy for the customer to obtain a clear understanding of what he or she will receive until the actual interaction takes place. During this interaction, there are many factors that affect the customer's experience. The service interaction is surrounded by physical and communication elements that provide information on the nature of the service and give clues as to its quality.

The previous discussion has relevance to public transport in that various kinds of passengers need to use the system which could include different modes of transport during a single trip. For disabled passengers, it is important that they can have trust in each specific link in the chain. If one link is missing, the whole trip could be an unsatisfactory experience. A lack of trust in a transport system can be a significant problem.

12.3.2. *Service environments*

In American literature on service management, the "service environment" has been referred to as the "servicescape" (Bitner, 1992) with design, esthetics, functional quality, and service logic all playing a part. This servicescape affects customers by altering behavior at the customer level. Aubert-Gamet (1997) divided the environment into a physical aspect and a psychological aspect, with the psychological aspect being created in the customer's mind. Situational factors have an effect on customers' perceptions, and hence on their behavior (Grace and O'Cass, 2004). Questions, however, remain unanswered about what (cues) and how (interactions) the environment affects perception and behavior. The empirical foundation is too shallow to provide adequate answers.

Consumer-behavior theory approaches the environment in terms of (i) its social aspects and (ii) its physical aspects (Peter *et al.*, 1999).

The first of these, the *social environment*, can be further subdivided into a macro-environment (culture, subculture, social class) and a micro-environment (social psychology, social interaction). For passengers on a public-transport system, both are relevant. *Macro-social factors* affect the attitudes, emotions, and behavior of customers. Using public-transport is, in some strata of society, associated with specific values and norms (which are not always positive). For those who use private vehicles, public transport can even be perceived as a "necessary evil." In contrast, for disabled people, public-transport is associated with social well being and quality of life. For these people, the individual ability to access public-transport is associated with having a "normal" life. The *micro-social* environment includes social interactions among people (including other customers) in the environment. Other passengers can be transformed from "just being there" to being an "audience" to being "involved co-passengers", to being "helpers", and so on. Other passengers can, in fact, become co-producers in the service system.

According to consumer-behavior theory, the second element, the *physical environment*, includes all non-human physical aspects. This can be divided into spatial and non-spatial elements. Spatial elements include physical objects, architecture, layout, and so on. Non-spatial elements include such factors as temperature, noise, light, odor, and so on. Questions remain about how such cues affect the behavior and perceptions of users.

Research on services has shown that these factors have a substantial effect on customer satisfaction. Bitner (1992) identified three aspects at the individual level: cognitive, emotional, and physiological. These spatial features influence customer perceptions of reliability, security, comfort, and so on. The servicescape "talks" to the customer which is a concept referred to as "object language" by Ruesch and Kees (1956). Bitner (1992) identified three types of services: self-service, interpersonal service, and distance service. All three are relevant to the management of transport services. For example, infrequent and disabled customers need to negotiate various aspects of an information system, including the following:

- ordering and using the telephone or the Internet (distance service);
- managing personal interaction and talking to service persons before, during, and after the trip (interpersonal services);
- using equipment, elevators, and so on (self-service).

Categorizations such as that of Bitner (1992), however, are not helpful when it comes to more enduring and complex customer processes because the spatial environment needs to be organized in a way that customer mobility is possible for different customer segments.

Wakefield and Blodgett (1994) observed that the service environment (or servicescape) assumes greater importance when a service is time consuming and when a service is associated with pleasure activities. In coming to this conclusion, they distinguished between functional services and experience-based services. Moreover, in their study of leisure services (Wakefield and Blodgett, 1996), they identified five factors as having a major effect on quality perceptions: (i) accessibility, (ii) esthetics, (iii) sitting comfort, (iv) electronic equipment, and (v) cleanliness. Factors such as these are certainly relevant in certain service settings, but they are too general to be of assistance in assessments of public-transport requirements.

It is apparent that the servicescape needs to be organized in a way that facilitates mobility for all customers. What is easy and logical for able-bodied and frequent passengers is not necessarily easy and logical for disabled and infrequent passengers.

12.4. User Oriented Research Design and Methodology

From the previous discussion, it is apparent that mainstream methods for data collection (surveys and personal interviews) lack validity when it comes to assessment of certain aspects of service processes. Traditional surveys have fixed and *a priori* concepts which lack flexibility in collecting relevant data on the subjective personal experience of service processes. There will always be a substantial gap between the collected data and the experience of what happened in the real situation. Personal interviews are closer to the phenomenon and provide a better indication of the subjective experience of customers. Moreover, the verbal exchange between the respondent and the interviewer can attempt to manage the retrospective problems of a complex experience. This kind of data, however, remains retrospective by its very nature, and the collected data always represent an experience of a *past situation* — with the possibility of error when relying on memory during an interview. Retrospective methods make it difficult to identify what *really* had an effect on customer perception.

For these reasons, various authors have noted that researchers need to go beyond retrospective psychological perception as the ultimate resource for obtaining data on customer perceptions of quality (Silverman, 1993;

Den Haring, 1997; Heath, 1997; Echeverri, 2002). To overcome validity problems, researchers need to develop different kinds of observational methods to get closer to the phenomenon being studied. Researchers could, for example, participate in real situations taking field notes and documenting environmental details through the use of cameras. The present study therefore argues that there is a need for approaches that are capable of collecting naturally occurring data during the actual experience. This kind of data is the best representation of what people really perceive. Therefore, we should investigate the use of methodologies that are closer to the phenomenon, such as video-based data collection. Using video linked to customer perceptions we might obtain more valid information and we might proceed in assessing customers' experiences as a resource for developing different kinds of services.

In a study of public-transport customers aiming at creating a more accessible, safe, and functional public-transport environment, two samples were included. Both groups were to complete a "well-known" travel chain and an "unknown" travel chain. The first group consisted of eight individuals with functional disorders. These included (i) complete loss of sight, (ii) complete loss of sight with hearing aid, (iii) severe visual impairment, (iv) inability to use lower extremities (wheelchair user), (v) reliance of walking aid ("rollator"), (vi) complete loss of hearing, (vii) a parent with a child in a baby carriage, and (viii) cognitive limitations).

The second sample consisted of people without any functional limitations. Six of them were defined (for the purposes of the study) as "infrequent travellers." The other six were defined as "frequent travellers." The customers were equipped with a mobile microphone to document customer cognition, emotions, and behavior. They did this during a trip from their homes to a chosen destination. During the trip, a second person (a researcher) used a mobile video camera. This person followed the traveller to document the physical and communication environment as perceived by the customer. The passengers were instructed to contribute by a "think-aloud" methodology which is a psychological method for documenting spontaneous perceptions of the travel experience.

The data consisted of video recordings of several hours for each of the passengers. Although the majority of the recordings were of limited value, especially those when the passenger was merely sitting in a transport mode waiting to be transported, many sequences were of greater value for the research purpose. These included recordings of the passenger leaving one mode, passing a transit hall, and then continuing by another transport mode. In the videos, researchers were able to observe the passengers' mobility, behavior, and gestures as well as the various physical objects that formed elements of the process. Researchers could observe the respondent pointing, asking, touching, and smelling different aspects of the environment. If something in the service environment was of significance, the respondent was able to comment on it using the mobile microphone. This enabled the researchers to understand the contextual setting by having the respondent point out the important aspect and provide his or her interpretation of it.

Following the *in situ* research approach based on open coding of data (used in conversation analysis, discourse analysis, ethno methodology, grounded theory), the investigation uncovered what determinants/factors are relevant for the customers/participants/respondents. In that sense, the customers are utilized (by introspection) to collect data, to sort out what is relevant, and to interpret data. As a theoretical frame, usability is a sensitizing concept to guide analysis since this concept includes functional capacity, environmental demands, and customer activity (Carlsson, 2002). The empirical material was then categorized with the help of the respondent's comments. From each sequence, the researchers identified the most significant aspects. These were then categorized into more general concepts and variables. This enabled the identification of cues and concepts, the relationships between such concepts, general variables, and new elements for theory building. Because the data collection was close to the actual perceptions of the customers, it can be argued that the methodology had high face validity.

12.5. Complex Issues Beyond Expectations

The study documented 33 trips (13 with functional limitations and 20 without functional limitations). Respondents commented on their previous travel experiences as well as their present experience.

In particular, respondents reported on their problems in managing nodes between different transport modes (transit areas, walking passages, layout, and so on). The final link (from final transport mode, via transit halls, and further on to the final destination) was especially problematic. Electronic information systems were not always working, and some of them were difficult to use. It is apparent that the outcome of the service process is dependent on the links between its parts.

Handling telephone "menus" (to obtain special help during or before the actual trip) was difficult (even for frequent passengers). The overcrowded and noisy environment made it more difficult for respondents to hear what the automated voices were saying. Some new services (such as turning on footlights for the subway and using the telephone) suffered from malfunction.

In addition, there was a lack of informative signs and tactile references in the physical layout. The information placed at the travellers' disposal (signs, timetables, and so on) was not always helpful in supporting the processual dimension of the trip. The study reveals a wide range of contextual and processual factors influencing customers' quality perceptions. Unexpected matters, that might form a new ground for explanatory theory are the *possibility* to interact with different elements of the service system and the *guiding* communicative elements (physical lay-out) simplifying the navigation within the transportation system (environment). Disabled passengers reported a sense of being stigmatized (Preiser and Ostroff, 2001); however, they also reported a positive experience of having access to public space and an extended mobility. If possible, the environment should initially be designed for equal use for all citizens — and not merely adapted later.

12.6. Discussion of Methodology and Empirical Issues

As previously described, the purpose of this study was to explore the dynamic and interactive aspects of services by using an advanced qualitative method based on a video-recording procedure as respondents actually experienced the service process. This is a way of conducting self-reporting of cognitive processing during a performance (a task such as to "think loud" during a trip). Although the researchers expected the procedure to be time consuming, difficult to manage, and somewhat difficult for the passengers to use most of the respondents found the procedure enjoyable, engaging, and worthwhile in providing valid data. Even though much of the recordings were redundant, the "think-aloud" procedure did allow the identification of important relevant factors in the process.

The methodology is in line with psychological theories of priming and implicit memory, since it uses particular cues and stimuli that seem to activate mental associations at the respondent level. Priming occurs in data collection when recognition of certain stimuli is affected by prior presentation of the same or similar stimuli (Neely, 2003). We obviously need to consider the priming effect in this kind of observational research. It is clear that mental pathways induced by the empirical context are oriented into a specific direction due to former experiences in customer's minds. This implies both strengths and weaknesses. Some of them will be commented on in the following section.

In studying complex cognitive processes such as problem solving or decision making, we could apply more developed methodologies. As shown in this paper, advances could be obtained by combining video documentation with verbal protocols. In such a documentation, the participants describe aloud all of their thoughts and ideas during the performance of a given cognitive task (for instance using public-transport). We found, however, that even such a method has limitations. Cognitive process may be altered by the act of giving the report, or outside of conscious awareness, or take place so rapidly that we or the respondent fail to notice it.

In the methodological approach, there is a semantic priming effect, due to the problem of hiding the purpose of the specific study. Prior presentation always has a bias to perception. In one way or another, respondents find out the purpose or create a purpose by using fragments of information from researchers, the context, the items, or other communicating elements in the study settings. The very presence of the researcher partly influences the respondent's perception. This problem, however, could be found in almost all data collecting methods. The proposed video-based methodology limits such information to a minimum.

The priming effect could be a problem if other stimuli (for instance former and irrelevant experiences in memory) give distortion. Stimuli could be priming in a misleading way, giving too much scope for pre-understanding, such as favorite memories, specific opinions, etc. The methodology, however, could be said to limit the area of possible associations which would minimize any negative priming effects due to specific pre-understanding.

Normally, priming simplifies recognition. Priming is the very mechanism when the respondent recognizes specific limitations or opportunities of relevance. By putting respondents into real situations, priming stimulates cognitive functions beyond conscious awareness. By being confronted with a specific and relevant context in a real time situation the respondent make correct associations. The methodology limits the priming effect to stimuli in real time contexts, not former experiences or memory based experiences irrelevant in the given context. This is an important strength since priming is caused by meaningful context or by meaningful information in the study setting. Specific real time context provides rich information which normally is not at hand in traditional data collection. Elements in the context prime the respondent to mental pathways relevant for the respondent rather than the researcher. Giving priority to the respondent's (or informant) uninfluenced perception, we have better guaranties that *a priori* perceptions, concepts, and vocabulary in the researcher's mind and language are not biased to empirical data.

The respondents used the "think-aloud" methodology quite easily and found it convenient to report on various aspects of the environment. Although the data were authentic and concrete, there were some problems in getting the respondents (or informants) to provide accurate information. To "think-aloud" is not an easy task for everyone. It became apparent that the researchers need to develop more explicit instructions so that respondents provide more detailed descriptions of their experiences — especially with respect to assessments of value/quality ("this is bad" or "this is good") and explanatory comments. As with all information gathering, there is a need for "triggers" to guide the informants. In a search for what really matters in the service process, such guidance should be relatively "open" ensuring that the voice of the customer is heard. Any guidance that leads to structuring customer perceptions using a set of *a priori* concepts (to be "measured") will decrease validity.

At a customer level, it was apparent that physical attributes, spatial factors, self-service machines, guiding sounds, communication signs (or lack thereof), and transport noise are important cues. If these are inappropriate, the travel process is perceived as difficult, less accessible, and somewhat insecure. Because of these problems, passengers with functional limitations hesitate to use public-transport — with resulting social segregation and high community cost. Able-bodied travellers, especially in the "infrequent traveller" group, showed similar perceptions. People who are not used to the environment find it difficult to navigate the transit environment.

12.7. Conclusions and Implications

The present study tested an advanced methodology for capturing customer perceptions and provided new insights into what really happens within dynamic and interactive customer processes. The method gives rise to new ideas on how to develop research into services. In particular, the development and testing of a video-based methodology provides a tool for getting close to the essence of the service phenomenon. Such advanced observational methods are especially promising for investigating the contextual and processual aspects of service provision.

Theoretically, there is a possibility that such new methods of data collection, and the empirical results that they provide, might raise questions about existing service theories. Some findings from the present study indicate that respondents report on unexpected issues when confronted with the actual real-time service experience. Such issues, cues, and factors can form new ground for explanatory theory and a more profound understanding of what really matters. The theoretical implication is that better (more grounded) theory might emerge in the future.

Finally, the study reported on some empirical findings. There is a need for change in the perception of what constitutes "quality" in public-transport. Quality assessments could be oriented toward the introspective or retrospective aspect of perceived quality. Usability contains more of the processual dimension of quality. Sometimes, we need to pay more attention to the introspective, real-time based experience of process quality than to the retrospective, memory-based experience of perceived quality. More emphasis should be placed on customer experiences than on specific features of the actual service. Service processes need to be developed more from a customer perspective if management wishes to create a more accessible and non-discriminating transport system. The wide range of findings from the empirical study indicates potential areas for quality development. Information should be designed with a practical view of optimizing the flow of travellers. Customers are in constant motion and need reference points to direct their moves to their chosen destination.

Procedural (processual) capacity is needed to simplify navigation in a given surrounding. The more developed the procedural memory is, the more likely it is for the individual person to be able to navigate in a particular system. Two resources need to be at hand. Internally, the individual needs a capacity, or opportunity, to imagine a way through different communicative elements. Externally, there is a need for giving relevant and helpful information when it is needed.

The present study was conducted in the specific context of public-transport services. It is therefore problematic to generalize the results to other contexts. The results of the study and the exploration of this methodology, however, provide valuable input to the discussion on advanced qualitative observational methods. The method used provided cues that have not been reported in other studies of accessibility in public-transport. The processual aspect of signs and lay-out, for example, has not been reported elsewhere.

In summary, the study contributes to the existing literature on observational research, and provides alternative research paths for qualitative data collection and analysis. Environmental designers could benefit from using this type of data on customer behavior — paying particular attention to the communication environment from a processual perspective. Marketing personnel could provide more accurate information to passengers during, before, and after trips. The study also has implications for obtaining market information. Using the sort of naturally occurring data presented in the present study, marketers could have a tool for obtaining more detailed information on the actual purchase and consumption of service processes. The research methodology promises data that are more authentic and dynamic. Armed with a more profound knowledge of customers' real-time perceptions, service operators would be better placed to design effective services. This, in turn, could have a substantial impact in inducing customers to switch from specially designed and costly, road-based transport vehicles (such as various kinds of taxis for disabled customers) to public-transport.

The data also provide a new opportunity to manage inter-organizational service development. Customers' real-time perceptions could also be an alternative starting-point for service design-especially in integrating various responsible organizations. The data provide a new opportunity to manage inter-organizational service development. In the case of public transport, there are many actors including the operators of various transport modes (bus, train, and tram), the various community authorities, different regional authorities, and various customer representatives. All of these parties could use this kind of information as a platform for a more profound dialogu that promotes a long-term, accessible, and sustainable service system.

References

Alam, I (2002). An exploratory investigation of user involvement in new service development. *Journal of the Academy of Marketing Science*, 30(3), 250–261.

Aubert-Gamet, V (1997). Twisting servicescapes: Diversion of the physical environment in a re-appropriation process. *International Journal of Service Industry Management*, 8(1), 26–41.

Bejou, D, B Edvardsson and JM Rakowski (1996). A critical incident approach to examining the effects of service failures on customer relationships: The case of Swedish and US airlines. *Journal of Travel Research*, 35, 35–40.

Bitner, MJ, B Booms and MS Teatrault (1990). The service encounter: Diagnosing favorable and unfavorable incidents. *Journal of Marketing*, 54, 71–84.

Bitner, MJ (1992). Servicescapes: The impact of physical surroundings on customers and employees. *Journal of Marketing*, 56(2), 57–71.

Carlsson, G (2002). Catching the bus in old age. Methodological aspects of accessibility assessments in public-transport. Dissertation, Lund University, Sweden.

Dahlsten, F (2003). Avoiding the customer satisfaction rut. *Sloan Management Review*, 44(4), 73–77.

Den Haring, MJ (1997). Psycho-social dynamics of service encounters: Exploring quality in face-to-face communication. Dissertation, Roskilde University, Denmark.

Echeverri, P (2002). Methodological issues in researching service encounters — A video-based analysis of communication. Paper presented at the *7th International Research Seminar in Service Management*, La Londe les Maures, France.

Echeverri, P (2003). Customer driven development of the service landscape — A video-based analysis of non-frequent travellers and travellers with functional limitations handling the seamless multimodal door-to-door experience. Paper presented at the *ECOMM 2003 Conference on Mobility Management*, Karlstad.

Friman, M (2000). Effects of critical incidents on customer satisfaction. Dissertation, Göteborg University, Sweden.

Friman, M, B Edvardsson and T Gärling (1998). Perceived quality of public-transport service: Inferences from complaints and negative critical incidents. *Journal of Public Transportation*, 2, 69–91.

Grace, D, A O'Cass (2004). Examining service experience and post-consumption evaluations. *Journal of Services Marketing*, 18(6), 450–461.

Gummesson, E (1996). Service management: An evaluation and the future. In *Service Management: Interdisciplinary Perspectives*, Edvardsson and Modell (eds.), pp. 249–273, Stockholm: Nerenius & Santérus.

Heath, C (1997). The analysis of activities in face to face interaction using video. In *Qualitative Research, Theory, Method and Practice*, Silverman (ed.), Sage Publications.

Lovelock, CH, S Vandermerwe and B Lewis (1996). *Services Marketing — A European Perspective*. London: Prentice Hall Europe.

Magnusson, P, J Matthing and P Kristensson (2003). Managing user involvement for service innovation: Experiments with innovating end-users. *Journal of Service Research*, 6(2), 111–124.

Matthing, J (2004). Customer-involvement in new service development. Dissertation, Karlstad University.

Menor, LJ, MV Tatikonda and SE Sampson (2002). New service development: Areas for exploitation and exploration. *Journal of Operations Management*, 20, 135–157.

Neely, JH (2003). Priming. In *Encyclopedia of Cognitive Science*, Vol 3, L Nadel (ed.), pp. 721–724. London, England: Nature Publishing Group.

Oliver, RL (1997). *Satisfaction: A Behavioural Perspective on the Consumer*. New York: McGraw-Hill.

Parasuraman, A, VA Zeithaml and LL Berry (1988). SERVQUAL: A multiple-item scale for measuring customer perceptions of service quality. *Journal of Retailing*, 64, (Spring), 12–40.

Peter, P, J Olson, J and K Grunert (1999). *Consumer Behavior and Marketing Strategy* (European Edition). McGraw Hill.

Preiser, WFE and E Ostroff (eds.) (2001). *Universal Design Handbook*. New York: McGraw-Hill.

Rikstrafiken *et al.* (2003). Hela resan (English. The entire travel chain).

Ruesch, J and W Kees (1956). *Nonverbal communication*. Berkely and Los Angeles University: California Press.

SOU (1995:70). Allmänna kommunikationer — för alla?

Silverman, D (1993). *Interpreting Qualitative Data. Methods for Analyzing Talk, Text and Interaction*. London: Sage Publications.

Ståhl, A (1987). Changing mobility patterns and the aging population in sweden. *Transport Research Record*, 1135, 37–41.

Thomke, S (2003). R&D comes to services: Bank of America's path breaking experiments. *Harvard Business Review* 81, (April), 71–79.

United Nations (UN) (1993). *Standard Rules on the Equalisation of Opportunities for Persons with Disabilities*. New York: UN.

Vargo, SL and RF Lusch (2004a). Evolving to a new dominant logic for marketing, *Journal of Marketing*, 68(1), 1–17.

Wakefield, K and J Blodgett (1994). The importance of servicescape in leisure service settings. *Journal of Services Marketing*, 8(3), 66–76.

Wakefield, K and J Blodgett (1996). The effect of the servicescape on customers behavioural Intentions in leisure service settings. *Journal of Services Marketing*, 10(6), 45–61.

13

Customer-Oriented Service Engineering As a Success Factor — Findings of Case Studies of Customer Integration in the Service Development Process

Rainer Nägele

Fraunhofer Institute for Industrial Engineering (IAO)
Stuttgart, Germany
rainer.naegele@iao.fraunhofer.de

13.1. Introduction

Recent studies and publications provide convincing evidence that customer orientation plays a pivotal role in the service development activities of best practice companies. It is obvious to assume that customer-involvement in service development gives companies the potential to be more professional and successful in fulfilling the customers' expectations and needs.

It is not clear, however, in which phase of the service development and performance process that customer-oriented service engineering procedures and methods will offer promising potential and competitive advantages. This uncertainty has been analyzed in a case study. This paper presents and draws on the findings of this case study. Based on these findings, the paper describes the first draft of a maturity model of customer orientation during the service development process. This draft will actually be evaluated and specified in a broader empirical survey among 5.050 German companies.

13.2.   Case Studies in the Field of Service Research

13.2.1.   *Case studies undertaken in the framework of "CoRSE"*

Current service research relies heavily on case studies carried out on their own as well as in combination with other methods of empirical research. This is partly due to the fact that case studies enable non-quantifiable fields of study to be approached in the context of an explorative, iterative research process (Tomczak, 1992).

The case studies undertaken within the framework of "CoRSE" — Customer Related Service Engineering (http://www.corse-projekt.de) (Bullinger *et al.*, 2002; Scheer *et al.*, 2004) which is supported by the German Federal Ministry of Education and Research (BMBF) — are perhaps best described as problem finding studies or case studies based on the incident method (see Appendix A for an overview of the companies involved in this survey).

13.2.1.1.   *Focus of "CoRSE"*

The aim of the case studies undertaken within the framework of the "CoRSE" project is to analyze how companies develop services and integrate their customers in the process. This involves identifying, in consultation with companies themselves, a service development which is both new and of major importance for the company or industry. In this context, a total of eight companies and one public service provider were studied, including both conglomerates as well as small and medium-sized enterprises from both "new" and "old" markets (1 see Appendix A). Project participants were interviewed in person and asked for detailed information about the service development process. The individual perspectives illustrated by these interviews were subsequently compiled into a case study by the interviewers. An appropriate interview structure was established in advance, and this ensured that the interviews themselves were conducted effectively and were focused on the relevant subject. "Customer orientation" should be considered as an integral aspect of all phases of service development. From the initial impulse through to the market launch of the service, companies nonetheless question the nature of "customer orientation" throughout this entire process. The interviews dealt with nine different aspects. The first step was to define the object of study, include documentation of the most important company data, and describe the service which had been developed. Another general topic was the customer orientation of the organization itself and, in particular, the importance of the customer for the company. This was followed by an analysis of the service development process. Development projects were evaluated in terms of the degree to which management of the development process was systematic and underpinned by a specific methodology. The benefits, success factors, and challenges associated with customer-oriented service development were identified from the company's point of view and the relevance of appropriate procedure models, methods, and tools for the future were discussed.

13.2.1.2. *Findings of the "CoRSE" case studies*

The service providers, who were surveyed, primarily understand customer orientation as the ability to offer the customer the very best in individualized services. In many cases, individual service packages are created by compiling a number of standardized service modules. Service companies also appear to have a particular understanding of customer orientation as the integration of customers in the service creation and provision process. There is a wide spectrum of views about what optimum integration actually entails. Differences occurred from one company in the survey to the next with some of them identifying the sensitive recognition of customer requirements as a key factor of customer integration. Others stress cooperation and a collaborative partnership with the customer. Many companies regard customer orientation as a way of retaining customers and as an instrument which includes the professional documentation of customer information. Some companies go a step further by defining customer orientation in terms of an orientation toward their customers' own customers. In other words, it is not only the company's business customer, but also the business customer's own customer who is analyzed and integrated into the service development process. This is an example of the way in which the competitiveness of business customers may be supported and promoted by service providers.

13.2.1.3. *Type and intensity of customer integration*

Almost all of the companies in which interviews were conducted perform customer surveys themselves which are designed to identify the requirements, expectations, and needs of their customers and to take these into account in the service development process. Most companies use quantitative and qualitative market research methods.

Approximately half of the companies studied supplement their customer information with evaluations of reported problems and complaints. The companies studied exploit their own customer care and service that is, call centers or customer calls, to garner information about changes affecting the customer as well as their wishes and requirements. Customer suggestions are evaluated and used in the development of services. Most of the activities undertaken by companies to sustain their customer orientation are focused on information gathering. There are only a few companies who endeavor to engage customers as "players with a proactive role." Workshops and prototype evaluations are used by the surveyed companies to retain customers.

The service development process can be divided into five phases, from the generation of the original idea to market launch (see Fig. 1). New ideas are collected and evaluated during the definition phase. Numerous proposals are evaluated primarily in terms of how they correspond with the corporate strategy, the company's strengths and weaknesses, as well as with the present and future market environment. It is possible in this process to integrate the customer as the triggering factor — whether existing information is evaluated in the company or new ideas are elaborated in customer workshops.

After the idea has been refined and the customer requirements have been specified, work begins on conceptualizing the individual components of the service itself. Process and product models can be jointly developed

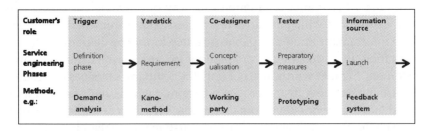

Figure 1:   Generic phase model of a customer-oriented development process.

with the business customer, and it is possible to ensure, at a very early stage, that processes are geared toward customers and that all modules are designed in a way which complies with the customer's requirements.

The service must be tested before it is launched on the market. Critical elements must be rectified prior to market launch, whereas important but non-critical complaints are taken into account in a later revision phase. The customer therefore tests and helps to optimize prototype services.

In the final phase, the customer with whom the service has been developed can play a supporting role during its market launch. As an "innovator" or "early adapter", the customer is in a position to help the product make deeper inroads into the market. Surveys of a broader base of customers, as well as documentation of customer responses recorded in the call center or by customer advisers, reflect the degree of acceptance enjoyed by the service in the market. This information can be used in turn to make adaptations to the service or can be used in the development of entirely new services.

Based on the stylized service development phase model described here, it is apparent that most companies integrate their customers in the first two phases. The results of the customer surveys are mainly used as a spur to service design or to identify customer requirements. In contrast, customer surveys or a design role in the conceptualization phase for customers themselves are seldom implemented. A few of the companies surveyed cited the testing of a prototype by selected customers as a preparatory measure on the way to market launch. Most companies maintain contact with their customers even after the service has been launched. The information they are able to gather from their customers in this way is systematically prepared, however, and used by a relatively small number of companies.

The case studies show that services are the outcome of fairly unsystematic processes in a lot of companies, many of which fail either to design product models or to plan systematic service provision processes.

In contrast to everyday business practice, considerably more companies believe that a structured, systematic, and method-based approach represents a decisive success factor in terms of customer-oriented service development. Those speaking on behalf of the surveyed companies also cited organizational issues as relevant factors which influence the success of outcomes. These organizational issues include the importance of rapid and flexible decision making, planning, and communication processes which can be best achieved by coordinating within small project teams or in the context of flat corporate hierarchies. It is crucial that projects pursued by service developers are supported by the company management. Companies also cited factors relating to corporate culture such as mutual trust, leeway to act on one's initiative, and willingness to take risks. Most companies stressed the importance of regular contact with customers if market opportunities are to be identified at an early stage.

In addition to these success factors, the companies were also faced with a series of challenges that were similar in many cases. Almost all companies cited that motivating and convincing their executives and employees to develop original new services was one of their key challenges. Some companies have first needed to build the skills and qualifications in their workforce which new services and customer integration demand and in many cases employees have had to be persuaded of the need to acquire new expertise before work could actually begin. Other problems cited by companies which are closely related to these workforce-based issues include difficulties associated with people's tendency to think within departmental boundaries, internal competition for budget resources, conflicting views among employees, and a lack of readiness to engage in continuous improvement processes. Another challenge, in addition to those previously mentioned which principally concern personnel management issues, is that of service development itself. Service development concerns the planning and provision of service provision resources, getting across the customer benefits of an original new service, assessing service ideas, determining customers' willingness to pay, and estimating costs. This list shows that most of the presenting challenges are associated with internal conditions. Only a few companies report difficulties with external collaborative partners, public authorities, or statutory constraints. These internal problems illustrate the importance of professional service management, and particularly service management which is able to deliver in terms of personnel management issues and method-based, customer-oriented service development. An institutionalized, well structured service development process with clearly defined working packages, milestones, and go or no-go-decisions for each phase, could help to face the challenges mentioned and to convince executives and employees to strive for a targeted customer-oriented service development. The case studies also reveal that customer orientation is already a powerful reality in corporate practice. They also show, however, the potential that still remains to be exploited in most companies if the service development process is to be even more consistently geared toward the customer.

13.3. Development of a Maturity Model of Customer Orientation During the Service Development Process

13.3.1. *The importance of customer-oriented service development*

For a long time, "customer orientation" was understood as an orientation toward consumers. Studies initially focused on issues relating to the recording of customer satisfaction, customer loyalty, and quality assurance in the field of mass production (Haischer, 1996). At a later stage, the concept of customer orientation was expanded to include aspects of service management and extended to the internal business processes of the providing companies. Since the mid-1990s, concepts relating to customer orientation have also been expanded to include business customers (Burghard and Kleinalthenkamp, 1996). In the business-to-business field in particular, customer orientation provides opportunities for developing and offering market-driven products and services. The relevance of transferring the concept of customer orientation to the business-to-business sector is confirmed and supported by an empirical study where 76% of 282 German companies surveyed provide most of their services for business customers (Fähnrich *et al.*, 1999). These business customers increasingly demand and expect to be offered additional, individualized services as Ehret and Glogowsky (1996), for example, have demonstrated in the plant engineering and construction industry. Kleinaltenkamp (Haischer, 1996; Kleinaltenkamp, 2000) points out that the customization of services in business-to-business markets has necessarily led to the integration of the customer and thus to an intensive form of customer orientation. Kleinaltenkamp highlights the links between supplier and customer value adding processes which arise, for example, when services that were previously supplied internally are replaced by outsourced services and supporting enterprise processes are altered as a result. The supplier's influence is not therefore restricted to the business customer's value chain; the supplier is also able to influence its customer's ability to achieve competitive advantages (Haischer, 1996). The supplier has an enormous opportunity in this context to increase the value of its services by providing individual, custom-tailored service packages which help the buyer to become more competitive. In the business-to-business field, consistent customer orientation which supports the customer's market positioning offers a means of strengthening business customers' loyalty to the supplier.

In order to create custom-tailored services, it is essential to discover the buyer's precise requirements and to ensure that these are taken into account directly during the service development process (Haischer, 1996). While standardized service packages often fail to address customers' requirements, suppliers cannot possibly afford to develop tailored solutions for every buyer. In order to be able to act in this area of conflict of standardization vs. individualization economically, more and more enterprises are modularizing their services.

Services are broken down into separate items which can then be bundled into packages for business customers. Customer integration should not, however, only develop once tangible support begins to be provided to specific customers, nor should it be regarded as an instrument to develop customized services. Customer integration must be implemented unilaterally when a company is building up its service offering. Only if they are consistently geared toward the customer will companies be able to provide an appropriate response to the growing needs of well-informed buyers and survive in rapidly evolving markets in the long term.

How, though, can companies develop services in a customer-oriented way? Based on the case studies described in this paper, a first draft of a maturity model was developed which is designed to help companies evaluate their corporate processes and customer orientation. This draft is evaluated and specified in a broader empirical survey among 5.050 German companies.

13.3.2. *Quality assurance based on maturity models*

To date, maturity models have been seen mainly as quality management methods in the field of software development where they are used to guarantee a high standard of software quality during the product development process. To this end, process-oriented measures for continuous improvements in quality are formulated in the model. These measures relate to the entire product development and life cycle and provide guidance on how the development process can be improved, from the innovation itself through to the development, marketing, and maintenance phases. The best known maturity models are the Capability Maturity Model, Bootstrap and ISO 15504 Software Process Improvement and Capability Determination Model (Pivka and Javornik, 1998). One of the first maturity models to be designed for the purpose of evaluating the software development process was the Capability Maturity Model (CMM) (Paulk *et al.*, 1995). The model defines five levels that distinguish different levels of development maturity (Schmelzer and Sesselmann, 1998):

- *Maturity level 1* — Initial: ad hoc and chaotic development,
- *Maturity level 2* — Repeatable: orderly, organized development,
- *Maturity level 3* — Defined: defined and documented development processes,
- *Maturity level 4* — Managed: quantitative development objectives,
- *Maturity level 5* — Optimized: development focuses on continually improving process performance.

CMM enables assessments to be performed to determine the current maturity level. Process improvement measures which enable software development to be organized at a progressively higher level are also described for each level.

Maturity models have proven to be effective instruments for achieving continuous, successive, and long-term effective improvement processes because based on comprehensive assessments they generate a clear picture of the current level of quality and facilitate the formulation of recommendations for action and improvement measures.

13.3.3. *A maturity model of customer-oriented service development*

Qualitative and quantitative empirical studies reveal that, in practice, the extent to which the customer is integrated in the development of services differs widely and interactions with business customers are organized at varying levels of intensity (Spath and Azhn, 2003). The case studies presented in this paper also suggest similar results. In most cases, customers appear to be involved in the development process by, for example, surveys of their needs or requirements. In other cases, the business partner is integrated in the development as co-designer. Competence alliances are either forged or individual customers are integrated in the engineering process. The range of integration encountered in practice extends from superficial forms, such as standardized surveys, to more intensive forms of supplier–customer partnerships geared toward service development and marketing (Pfeifer, 1996). These empirical findings are used to propose a first draft of a maturity model of customer-oriented service development. The model and the elaborated assessments will be differentiated and validated in the course of current and future research.

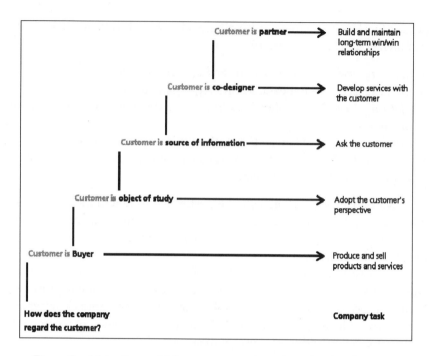

Figure 2:   Maturity model for customer-oriented service development.

Drawing on the Capability Maturity Model, five levels are defined which describe varying degrees of customer integration in the service development process.

The higher the level, the more intensive is the interaction and the stronger the degree of customer integration. The levels thus defined are not independent of each other, but build on each other progressively. This means that a company which is classified as having achieved a higher level of maturity has mastered and makes selective use of all the procedures and methods of customer integration used by companies at lower levels of maturity.

The image of the customer held by the company and the patterns of action derived from this image are descriptive elements in the maturity model. Perceptions of the customer by company employees determine the actions taken in the course of developing new services.

At the lowest level of the maturity model, the customer is primarily regarded as a consumer of products and services. The customer continues to be seen in the passive user or beneficiary role which was assigned to customers until well into the 1990s (Prahalad and Ramaswamy, 2000).

Company employees think and act in terms of selling and competing. They assume to know exactly what their customers want out of their market research and data, but they do not ask the customer for their explicit needs and ideas for new services. Services are designed to customer needs, requirements, and wishes without explicit reference during the development process. As a result, companies do not take the opportunity to assess the service idea and optimize the conceptualization with the support of the customer. The company reacts to the response of the market after the service itself has been launched. Only then does it become clear whether the service, as developed, will be accepted or rejected on the market. The risk that the development may be inappropriate and costly, are compensated for by the short time-to-market cycle which can be kept to a minimum by excluding the customer from the development process. Most services are developed at this lowest level in an ad hoc and unsystematic way, and this is an additional factor which can exercise a negative impact on the quality of the service. Many companies have not defined standardized processes for the development of services and approach this task in a highly unsystematic fashion (Haischer, 1996). This approach contrasts dramatically with the systematic concepts and procedure models used in product development where high levels of product quality are guaranteed by suitable methods and subject to ongoing controls (e.g., via Quality Function Deployment, Failure Mode, and Effects Analysis).

Development projects performed at the first level of maturity are associated with many business risks including, in the worst case, the danger that the customer may be lost as a result of poor service quality. The importance in terms of customer retention of service quality was demonstrated by a study undertaken in 1988. The results of this study show that the most common reason for customer defection is poor service quality (Fonvielle *et al.*, 1988). Poor product quality plays a much less important role. At the same time, it is becoming increasingly difficult to stand out from the competition simply on the basis of the quality characteristics of physical products (Benkenstein, 1993). Service quality is therefore enormously important for sustained business success.

Customers adopt a far more critical attitude toward the quality of services as these tend to be rendered in a non-material, interactive way. Customers who purchase physical goods retain permanent possession of a material object. In contrast, customers who purchase services do not possess anything at all — they experience a service. Although most services also include a material component, the importance of this element is usually subordinate to the part of the service which is rendered interactively. Customers' inconsistent critical attitudes are mainly oriented toward the two poles of tangibility/intangibility. It is precisely these two characteristics (tangible and intangible deliverables) which give rise to the challenges of controlling and ensuring service quality (Fonvielle et al., 1988).

At the second level of maturity, the service provider takes the first steps toward the explicit inclusion of customer needs in the service development process. The point of departure for service development is to consider which of the customer's problems and challenges can be competently solved by the company. Customer needs and company requirements are weighed and evaluated; the feasibility of the service development and the benefits offered by the planned service are assessed. Although customer needs are systematically analyzed at level two, customers are still not asked directly about the situation in which they find themselves. As a result, the company is only able to elicit customer needs indirectly from its external perspective. There is consequently a risk that the service provider may only have a limited and distorted view of the customer's situation given the supplier's own intention to offer services. This tendency can lead to an overly optimistic assessment of the market potential of the service.

Despite these initial moves toward a systematic approach, companies which operate at this maturity level are just as much dependent on post-launch market responses as the companies operating at level 1.

At maturity level 3, the supplier not only endeavors to see the world through the eyes of the customer, but the customer also sheds his passive role and is discovered to be an expert and source of information for the service which is intended to solve the customer's business problems. The customer is now the yardstick against which the conceptualization and design of the service modules of the company are measured and is integrated in the service development process for the first time at this maturity level.

The supplier questions the customer through interviews or questionnaires and measures internal company perceptions against the perspective and views of the buyer. The case studies presented reveal that many German companies already perform surveys designed to integrate the customer in the service development process. This tendency is also confirmed by quantitative studies where 70% of all companies which develop customer-oriented services carry out surveys. Popular techniques include interviewing key accounts or undertaking questionnaire-based surveys geared toward a large customer group (for an overview of survey methods, refer to Stauss, 1999).

At maturity level 3, the company takes a highly efficient route toward reaching the customer. Surveys are both time and cost effective. This approach, however, is not entirely without risks. Discrepancies frequently arise between the benefits which a customer anticipates from a projected service and those which the customer actually experiences. The predictive power of survey results is seldom overwhelming in terms of assessed benefits, acceptable price range, needs, and requirements. There are a number of reasons for these discrepancies. In the context of surveys, customers usually consider the service in superficial terms. The lack of critical engagement of surveyed customers, which Köcher (1997) identified in relation to the evaluation of product characteristics during the early stages of development, is equally relevant to the assessment of services. At the onset of a service development process, the customer is not yet in a concrete situation in which he wishes to have the service or use the offer to solve his problems. The customer must regard the service creation situation from the inside. Usually he is likely to overlook the conditions which are decisive for demand and provision of the service, as these influencing factors are complex and lack transparency. The customer is therefore only partially able to evaluate the service idea or to formulate its requirements. Customers will probably overlook critical conditions.

This situation is compounded by the tendency of the customer to evaluate the service too positively. The customer remains optimistic that a service package could be put together which is tailored precisely to his needs and requirements. It should come as no surprise if surveys of this sort generate positive responses and therefore inaccuracies of this nature can make it considerably more difficult to interpret the findings of customer surveys. Forecasting the acceptance and market potential of a service is always subject to residual risk.

Companies which develop their services at maturity level 4 minimize the risk of misinterpreting customer requirements and acceptance. At this level, the customer is integrated as a co-designer in the service development process. It is important to contact and integrate the customer as early as possible (Spath and Zahn, 2003). The one dimensional exchange of information via surveys and interviews which takes place at maturity level 3 is superseded at level 4 by open dialog which may be initiated in the framework of working parties. The customer is no longer regarded solely as a source of information, but is now involved as a tester and active co-designer. During prototyping, for example, the buyer tests the innovative service or individual service modules over a lengthy period of time and provides the supplier with feedback at a number of intervals about how the prototype could be modified (Bullinger and Meiren, 2001; Rau et al., 2002). The service provider continually improves the service throughout this test phase and makes use of the improvements proposed by the customer in order to be able to offer a mature solution in the market. The customer who is integrated in working groups and workshops now takes a much more serious approach to the pros and cons of particular service modules. The customer makes resources of its own available, such as personnel. The customer's own contribution enhances the importance of the service to the customer who consequently adopts a more critical and committed role in the development process. The development of services in partnership with one or several customers is an ideal basis for inter-organizational learning and for the accumulation and exchange of know-how. The integration of the customer as co-designer enhances the ability to ensure a high level of service and process quality which profits from the input made by the customer. The risk of inappropriate development can be reduced and high costs avoided. At the same time, maturity level 4 is also linked to the challenge of organizing interfaces to the customer in a more transparent way. This is the only way in which the buyer can build up the confidence needed if collaborative work is to take place (Spath and Zahn, 2003).

Maturity level 5 includes the planning of long-term development partnerships of this nature. Permanent and intensive relationships exist between companies and business customers. Although company relationships established in the context of maturity level 4 are dissolved once service development work is complete, partnerships and networks established at maturity level 5 are long term in nature. Customer integration extends beyond individual development processes in terms of time and content. Dialog between companies and business customers is permanently implemented by establishing user groups, business customer clubs, or customer forums (Prahalad and Ramaswamy, 2000; Schildhauer, 1996). Knowledge accumulated during the development process is not lost but can be added to in new projects. Joint campaigns and events are organized to reinforce the relationship between companies and customers, particularly on the basis of the informal exchange of company representatives from both sides. The main advantage, however, is that the company itself is able to arrive at a better understanding of customer requirements. Partnerships of this type need not only be built on isolated relationships between suppliers and buyers, but can also be organized as networks between supplier companies and selected customers.

The active integration of and proximity to the customer not only ensures the service and process quality of individual services or service modules but also eases the identification of changes affecting the customer, business, and industry trends in the future. Thus, customer-oriented modifications to the company's own service portfolio or the launch of new developments can be optimized. This type of partnership also reinforces the customer's emotional loyalty and stimulates the customer's interest, commitment, and active involvement. Customers who are involved in this way are not only more loyal, they are also more effective propagandists for the company. Bayón and von Wangenheim (2002) assume that, thanks to their experience and the knowledge they have about the supplier, customers who have been loyal to a company for a long period of time effectively and successively recommend the supplier to other potential customers. As a result, long-term professional customer relationship management can also enhance the company's image among potential new customers (Bullinger, 2002).

13.4. Conclusions

The findings presented in this paper show that customer orientation in service management plays an important role in every phase. Customer orientation is indispensable during service development. The customer, however, should not only be seen as spurring on the company's development activities, but also as a co-designer and ongoing source of information and benefits for the company. The maturity model presented in this paper illustrates the progressive integration of the customer in the company.

The presented draft of a maturity model of customer-oriented service development reflects the incremental integration of the customer in the service provider's development processes. The nature of customer orientation is manifested in the model and made tangible for the service development process. An assessment procedure enables the status quo in the company with regard to customer integration to be captured, and the degree of customer integration assigned to the maturity levels has to be developed. Evaluation criteria have to be defined for this purpose which maps the requirements and success factors governing customer-oriented service development. A first draft of these criteria includes aspects of customer interface management, employee qualification, corporate culture, quality management, service engineering, and so on. The potential benefits and weaknesses of each category have to be analyzed in an audit framework. Instructions on how to achieve improvements and reach a higher maturity level have to be described. As a result, the maturity model could meet the practical need for assessment results which can be implemented directly in specific measures. Prior to the assessment, the company specifies which maturity level it believes it would be appropriate to aim for in the relevant category, bearing in mind that it is not always worthwhile developing a service at the highest maturity level. The work and expense as well as the benefits must always be precisely weighed before a decision is reached. In terms of the maturity model presented, the customer only begins to be effectively integrated in the service development process from level three upwards when the customer is involved as a source of information and expertise. A service which is already highly attractive to the market and has an excellent springboard position should, however, be developed at a higher level of integration. The assessment of these two fundamental conditions is supported by a portfolio analysis (Schreiner *et al.*, 2001) which draws on evaluation criteria for market attractiveness such as market volume, market growth, customer situation, and customer potential. The company's own starting point can be assessed by looking at competence/employee qualification, project management, knowledge of the market, etc. Equally relevant, however, is customer segmentation. The customer structure can thus be evaluated in terms of turnover, potential, or profitability, for example, on the basis of an ABC analysis. However, in the service sector, equal importance must also be attached to behavior and process-oriented segmentation based on perceived benefits and other purchase decision criteria, type of use, or the intensity with which the customer wishes to exercise influence on the service creation process. These interactive criteria are also the decisive influencing factors which will enable a service provider to differentiate from competitors.

Appropriate forward-looking service development requires that long-term skills and expertise are built with the customer in the framework of development partnerships. In collaboration with selected customers, innovations and modifications can be elaborated and the supplier's service portfolio designed in a customer focused way. A high level of enduring customer loyalty will only be achieved by means of such customer and thus quality-oriented services.

References

Bayón, T and F von Wangenheim (2002). Valuation of customers' word-of-mouth referrals: Approach and first result. Working paper 10, International University in Germany GmbH, Bruchsal.

Benkenstein, M (1993). Dienstleistungsqualität: Ansätze zur Messung und Implikationen für die Steuerung. *Zeitschrift für Betriebswirtschaft*, 11, 1095–1116.

Bullinger HJ (2002). Technologiemanagement, Forschen und Arbeiten in *einer vernetzten Welt*, Berlin *et al.*

Bullinger, HJ, AW Scheer and E Zahn (eds.) (2002). Vom Kunden zur Dienstleistung; Fallstudien zur kundenorientierten Dienstleistungsentwicklung. In *deutschen Unternehmen*, Stuttgart.

Bullinger, HJ and T Meiren (2001). Service engineering — Entwicklung und Gestaltung von Dienstleistungen. In *Handbuch Dienstleistungsmanagement*, M Bruhn and H Meffert (eds.), pp. 149–175. Wiesbaden.

Burghard, W and M Kleinaltenkamp (1996). Standardisierung und Individualisierung — Gestaltung der Schnittstelle zum Kunden. In *Customer Integration*, M. Kleinaltenkamp, S Fließ and F Jacob (eds.), pp. 163–176, Wiesbaden.

Ehret, M and A Glogowsky (1996). Customer Integration im industriellen Dienstleistungsmanagement. In *Customer Integration*. M Kleinaltenkamp, S Fließ and F Jacob (eds.), pp. 203–218, Wiesbaden.

Fähnrich, KP *et al.* (1999). Service Engineering, Ergebnisse einer empirischen Studie zum Stand der Dienstleistungsentwicklung. In *Deutschland*, Stuttgart.

Fonvielle *et al.* (1988). Customer focus research study — Preliminary report of overall findings, Boston.

Haischer, M (1996), Dienstleistungsqualität — Herausforderung. In *Service Management in Theorie und Praxis der Wirtschaftsinformatik*. 187, 35–48.

Kleinaltenkamp, M (2000), Kundenbindung durch Kundenintegration. In *Handbuch Kundenbindungsmanagement*, M Bruhn and C Homburg (eds.), pp. 337–354 Wiesbaden.

Köcher, W (1997). Präferenzen von zukünftigen Nutzern entdecken. In *Bedürfnisse entdecken, Gestalten zukünftiger Märkte und Produkte*. AM Frankfurt. *et al.*, pp. 97–124.

Paulk, M *et al.* (1995). *The Capability Maturity Model — Guidelines for Improving the Software Development Process*. New York.

Pfeifer, K (1996). Praktische Ansatzpunkte der Customer Integration auf Basis der Kundenorientierung. In *Customer Integration*, M Kleinaltenkamp, S Fließ and F Jacob (eds.), pp. 123–135 Wiesbaden.

Pivka, M and B Javornik (1998). Die Softwarequalität reifen lassen. *Qualität und Zuverlässigkeit*, 43, 280–282.

Prahalad, CK and V Ramaswamy (2000). Wenn Kundenkompetenz das Geschäftsmodell mitbestimmt. *Harvard Business Manager*, 4, 64–75.

Rau, J, P Lienhard and M Opitz, (2002). Prototypische Entwicklung der Dienstleistung TÜV CERT Excellence Audit. In *Vom Kunden zur Dienstleistung,* HJ Bullinger, AW Scheer and E Zahn (eds.) pp. 43–48, Stuttgart.

Scheer, AW, D Spath and E Zahn (eds.) (2004). Vom Kunden zur Dienstleistung — Methoden, Instrumente und Strategien zum *Customer related Service Engineering,* Stuttgart.

Schildhauer, T (1996). Borderless organization — Instrument der customer Integration am Beispiel der Lufthansa Systems Berlin GmbH. In *Customer Integration,* M Kleinaltenkamp, S Fließ and F Jacob (eds.), pp. 137–148, Wiesbaden.

Schmelzer, HJ and W Sesselmann (1998). Assessment von Geschäftsprozessen. *Qualität und Zuverlässigkeit,* 43, 39–42.

Schreiner, P, L Klein and C Seemann (2001). Dienstleistungen im Griff — Erfolgreich gründen mit System, Stuttgart.

Spath, D and E Zahn (2003). Kundenorientierte Dienstleistungsentwicklung. *deutschen Unternehmen,* Berlin.

Stauss, B (1999). Kundenzufriedenheit. *Marketing,* 21(1), 5–24.

Tomczak, T (1992). Forschungsmethoden in der Marketingwissenschaft: Ein Plädoyer für den qualitativen Forschungsansatz. *Marketing,* 2, 77–87.

Tomczak, T and S Dittrich (1997). *Erfolgreich Kunden binden.* Zürich.

Appendix A: Companies Involved in the Case-Study Survey

Schenker Logistics

Name	Schenker Deutschland AG, Geschäftsstelle Berlin
Industry	Transport & Logistics
Employees	250
Turnover	41 Mio. Euros
Address	Schwanenfeldstr. 11, 13627 Berlin
Internet	http://www.schenker.de

PLAN.Net media

Name	PLAN.NET media GmbH
Industry	Advertising and Media agency
Employees	30
Turnover	10 Mio. Euros
Address	Augustenstr. 22, 80333 München
Internet	http://www.plan-net.de

Bilger-Schwenk GmbH & Co. KG

Name	Bilger-Schwenk GmbH&Co. KG
Industry	Facility Management
Employees	700
Turnover	46 Mio. Euros
Address	Christian-Messner-Str. 44-50, 78647 Trossingen
Internet	http://www.bilger-schwenk.de

IDS Scheer AG

Name	IDS Scheer AG
Industry	Consulting and Software Engineering
Employees	1.500
Turnover	125 Mio. Euros
Address	Altenkesseler Str. 17, Building C2, 66115 Saarbrücken
Internet	http://www.ids-scheer.de

RWTÜV

Name	RWTÜV Anlagentechnik GmbH
Industry	High-level technical services
Employees	600
Turnover	90 Mio. Euros
Address	Steubenstr. 53, 45138 Essen
Internet	http://www.rwtuev-at.de

Gemeinde Eppelborn

Name	Gemeinde Eppelborn
Industry	Local Government
Employees	130
Turnover	25 Mio. Euros
Address	Rathausstr. 27, 66571 Eppelborn
Internet	http://www.eppelborn.de

Daimler Chrysler AG

Name	DaimlerChrysler AG
Industry	Automobile industry
Employees	416.500
Turnover	162,4 Billion Euros
Address	Mercedesstr. 120, 70546 Stuttgart
Internet	http://www.daimlerchrysler.de

JET Online GmbH

Name	JET Online GmbH
Industry	Consulting and Software Engineering
Employees	30
Turnover	2 Mio. Euros
Address	Altenkesseler Str. 17, Building B5, 66115 Saarbrücken
Internet	http://www.jet-online.de

Siemens AG Medical Solutions

Name	Siemens AG Medical Solutions
Industry	Medical Engineering
Employees	28000
Turnover	5.1 Billion Euros
Address	Henkestr. 127, 91052 Erlangen
Internet	http://www.SiemensMedical.com

14

Service Innovation, User Involvement, and Intellectual Property Management

Christiane Hipp and Cornelius Herstatt

Brandenburg University of Technology Cottbus, Germany
Hamburg University of Technology, Germany
hipp@tu-cottbus.de
c.herstatt@tu-harburg.de

14.1. Introduction

Because of the interactive nature of services, it has become more important that services are co-developed by the producer and the intended user or customer. Consequently, some issues may arise such as the intellectual property issue where two parties could claim the ownership of the resulting service. This important issue, however, is completely neglected in the literature. Instead, a "win–win" situation is often expected where both parties benefit from the joint effort. At least, Herstatt and von Hippel (1992) highlighted that lead users should sign a contract that they do not claim intellectual property before they are invited to take part in the co-development process.

When involving users in the development process, knowledge spillovers are of major importance and necessary. Appropriating knowledge that is produced and developed by a firm is called a "knowledge spillover" (Grupp, 1996). Unwanted or uncontrolled knowledge spillovers emerge due to the imperfect protection system of the innovating firm (Kaiser, 2002). Technology based companies may apply formal intellectual property rights; yet, service firms face specific problems of protecting their innovations, as it is not possible to protect intangibles with a wide range of intellectual property rights. That means the co-development increases the risk of customers gaining strategic supplier knowledge (Nambisan, 2002) and also vice versa. Both directions of unwanted knowledge spillovers help to increase bargaining power for the particular parties involved.

This chapter will analyze the following five protection strategies within service innovation which have been derived from Blind *et al.* (2003): (1) formal intellectual property rights strategy, (2) secrecy and first-to-market strategy, (3) external lock-in strategy, (4) complex design strategy, and (5) internal lock-in strategy. Special focus is placed on user involvement and co-development processes. Empirical material from a German study on service-intensive companies will highlight aspects of the conceptual findings.

14.2. Principles of Intellectual Property Rights

Few researchers have pragmatically addressed the major new challenges that arise from the increasing dominance of the service economy, such as the protection of new forms of knowledge based output and the prevention of uncontrolled knowledge spillovers. Granstrand (2000), Teece (2001), as well as Miles *et al.* (2000) were some of the first authors to describe the new intellectual capital paradigm along with the new difficulties of intellectual property protection. These new challenges require, for example, the understanding of the nature of knowledge and the manner in which it can or cannot be bought and sold.

Wider relations in the context of intellectual property regimes of services and regulatory framework have been explored both in terms of how they may influence and shape service innovation, and as an indicator of service innovation (Andersen and Howells, 2000; Miles *et al.*, 2000). It has often been noted that services have much weaker intellectual property regimes and this might impede and restrict their innovative progress. Whereas manufacturing and science-based firms have patents, service firms have lacked an effective intellectual property regime to protect more intangible innovations.

Recent evidence suggests that service firms do not rate the lack of effective intellectual property rights as a major hurdle in innovation (Tether, 2003). Evidence from European surveys indicates that at least in terms of barriers, service firms rated "ease of copying" as only their seventh most important barrier (Howells and Tether, 2004). But, it could also reflect the fact that they use other mechanisms, such as secrecy, short service cycle times, complex designs, and tacit forms of work organization (Andersen and Howells, 2000). This may also explain why — although trademark and copyright data for service enterprises may have some usefulness as indicators for innovative activity in services — their applicability and wider utility have remained limited (Hipp and Grupp, 2005).

Before providing detailed analysis of intellectual property protection mechanisms, it is useful to briefly define and describe the term "property." Property as a generic notion, and intellectual property as a particular species of it, is in the first place a notion developed by legal science. Therefore, the traditional understanding and history of property rights are mostly based on legal or "formal" frameworks (Bouckaert, 1990).

Property rights are different from other rights such as contractual claims, easements, personal rights, and rights within the family. The legal tradition is a "store" of centuries-old experience and provides a diverse range of practical claims that occur in daily life. Even with these kinds of formal rights, however, legal experts cannot explain why there are preferences for particular rules of acquisition, nor can they completely clarify why different property solutions reach into different problem areas, or whether or not life is better and easier with property solutions. People in business administration, economics, politics, and ethics can debate and search for answers to such questions in which the institutional question is linked with the aims of business or moral life.

Granstrand (2000) chose a slightly different approach and focused on business and economic factors. For him, property is primarily defined as a resource or asset, such as a physical, tangible, material good, or a good over which somebody can exercise some justified control. If someone has the right to exclude others from using the good or asset and/or they can derive benefits from the underlying resource, the term "property" can be applied. Consequently, property rights allow the enforcement of this definition of property, ensuring benefits to the property holder. Property rights may be transferable and are, therefore, treated as a property or resource itself. Today, in Western societies, intellectual formal property rights typically comprise patent rights, copyrights, design rights, trademark rights, trade secrets, and a few other special property rights.

When discussing intellectual property rights in services, it is often a discussion about the protection of ideas such as new business concepts, new services, new processes, or customer integration. At the center of all these discussions lies one fundamental question — who owns the idea and who is allowed to profit from the idea (Garmon, 2002)?

14.3.   Instruments of Intellectual Property Management in Services

In all developed countries and regions, similar intellectual property instruments have been established (Andersen and Howells, 1998) such as the following:

- *Patents:* provide exclusive rights to make, use, import, sell, and offer for sale a product and process invention for up to 20-years,
- *Trademarks:* protect words, names, symbols, sounds, or colors that distinguish goods and services. Trademarks, unlike patents, can be renewed forever while they are being used in business. The shape of a Coca-Cola bottle is one such familiar trademark,
- *Utility and design patents:* protect useful processes, machines, and compositions, or guard the unauthorized use of new, original, ornamental designs for articles and products. Examples include fiber optics, computer hardware, medications, and shoes. A test of "degree of newness" such as that used in patent applications is not necessary. In case of use, the protection is valid for up to 25-years,
- *Copyrights:* protect works of authorship, such as writings, music, and works of art that have been tangibly expressed. The Library of Congress (in the US) registers copyrights, which last for the life of the author plus 50-years, and
- *Trade secrets:* There are no special requirements or registration rules. Trade secrets are kept secret in order to gain or maintain an advantage over competitors. Secrecy is especially important if the institutionalization of property rights is not possible, too expensive, or ineffective. The formula for Coca-Cola is the most famous trade secret.

Miles *et al.* (2000) point out that intellectual property and knowledge management strategies used in the service sector differ from those of manufacturing companies. The authors also argue that service companies have grown up without a formal protection culture and, therefore, most innovations are not protected in the traditional sense. Andersen and Howells (2000) present a number of explanations which support the notion that intellectual property strategies are different and more complex for service firms than they are for manufacturing firms. Blind *et al.* (2003) have summarized the main findings as the following:

- Intellectual property protection is much weaker in most service innovation contexts (i.e., the protection of intangibles) than for manufacturing innovations (as represented by artifacts and physical systems).
- Intellectual property is not only weaker but also more difficult to monitor and enforce in services than in manufacturing systems.
- Although the copyright system has significant historical roots (in terms of published works), its history of application to innovative activity is much more recent, less developed and, most importantly, less defined than the patent system. For example, in the US, the 1976 Copyright Act only provided partially effective cover for software programs and only became fully effective with an amendment in 1980 to make explicit the applicability of copyright to such offerings (Braunstein, 1989). Similarly in the UK (although copyright law had been flexible in its approach), the first specifically targeted piece of legislation which dealt with computer software was the Copyright (Computer Software) Amendment Act, which emerged as late as 1985 and was soon followed by the Copyright, Designs, and Patent Act of 1988.

The challenges of such complex systems may be surmounted by a complex response on the part of innovating service firms through the use of multiple intellectual property instruments. Alternatively, the challenge may be so daunting as to make real strategic intellectual property activity more or less non-existent. Complicating this context yet further is the argument that innovative service companies have traditionally matured within regimes that have not adequately protected their creations and innovations. Innovative service firms are arguably more likely to be driven to utilize informal protection mechanisms, instruments, and strategies to protect their intellectual property and core knowledge.

This analysis indicates that alternative methods, which step outside of the traditional protection system, might be of major importance for service firms, alongside the more or less appropriate formal protection mechanisms previously mentioned. Miles *et al.* (2000) and Jennewein (2005) discuss this salient issue, claiming the importance of informal mechanisms such as the following:

- Secrecy and secret know-how can involve different procedures, such as preventing employees from disclosing important information and knowledge, as well as the strict government of knowledge spillovers to co-operation partners, suppliers, and customers. An overemphasis on secrecy can, however, limit the possibilities for collaboration and knowledge trading. In today's networked economy, it is probably impossible to have and sustain secret knowledge for a long time.
- Short innovation cycles and following a first-mover or short lead-time strategy can also help to overcome the negative impact of competitor's imitations. In this case, by the time a potential competitor does copy or imitate the innovation, it is too late because the next service or product generation is being developed. This strategy, however, requires an enormous innovation investment, which has to be amortized over a short time period.
- Intangible products can be protected by making them more tangible via a physical technology. This strategy enables companies to partly rely on the more "concrete" patent application and allows them to hide the intangible part of the customer offering inside hardware. In the 1980s, many IT firms hid and embedded their software within microchips, naming them "firmware." There are a variety of methods for incorporating software in electronic circuits and it was the ease of software copying and piracy that encouraged such strategies. Today, similar strategies are used, bundling software with other hard-to-reproduce tangible goods. Other mechanisms such as "dongles" or customer helpdesks, which monitor user status and therefore diminish illegal software copying, are moving in the same direction.
- Lock-in effects can also help to reduce the danger of imitation and uncontrolled knowledge spillovers, and there is a range of different strategies applied. One example is the creation of complex designs and interrelated services that provide maximum value when using the whole offering from just one supplier. Lock-in also arises when specific customer relationship programs are successfully implemented or specific standards or protocols are necessary (these approaches appear to be especially popular in software, IT, and telecommunication services).

Whereas the formal intellectual property mechanisms of technology based companies can be analyzed by evaluating their patent applications, there also exist many companies which are either primarily technology users or providers of low technology intensive services (Blind *et al.*, 2003). Thus, it seems obvious and sensible to extend the analysis of intellectual property rights, and protection strategies in general, beyond the traditional view of patents. This will generate more valid results and insights into the relative importance and effects of intellectual property protection. Many of the alternative protection mechanisms described in this section, however, do not legally require the registration of the property that is to be protected; this creates severe obstacles for quantitative analysis.

14.4. Intellectual Property Management and Co-Development of Services

The flexibility and value creation potential of inter-firm collaboration has accelerated a growing number of alliances during the past decade (e.g., Hansen and Nohira, 2004). Benefits in terms of innovation through collaboration have encouraged increasing numbers of R&D partnerships in diverse sectors (Chakravorti, 2004). The literature to date has analyzed co-development between networks of high-tech firms, start-ups and incumbents, suppliers and clients, and more unusually between competitors (Miotti and Sachwald, 2003). Additionally, for the purpose of improved innovativeness, firms also ally with universities, public research institutes, and private research institutes (e.g., Teece, 1989).

It is often stated that the intangibility of the service sector and the lack of formal protection mechanisms (e.g., patents) might hamper collaborative service innovation arrangements, as firms are confronted with increased risks from knowledge spillovers and opportunism (Helm and Kloyer, 2004; Jordan and Lowe, 2004). Thus, firms face a dilemma: collaborative innovation offers great potential to gain access to specialized human, technical, and financial resources. Those involved, however, cannot always predict in advance the exact requirements, costs, and benefits involved in the overall process.

14.5. Service Innovation, User Involvement, and Intellectual Property Management: Some Empirical Evidence

A significant insight from the empirical study undertaken by Blind *et al.* (2003) shows that customers are the preferred partners for collaborative innovation activities within the service sector. This hints that innovation

Table 1:   Linear regression analysis of relationship between protection activities and customer involvement.[a]

Dependent variable $N = 59$	Independent variable: co-operation activities with .... customers	
	Coefficient	SE
Patents	0.206*	0.064
Trademarks		Not significant
Copyrights	0.141*	0.065
Secrecy		Not significant
Long-term labor contracts	0.131*	0.062
Lead-time advantage	0.169*	0.068
Customer relationship management	0.176*	0.062
Exclusive contracts (e.g., with suppliers)	9.636E-02[+]	0.057
Complex product design	–	Not significant
Embodying intangibles in products	–	Not significant

Data source: Blind *et al.* (2003), own calculations.
[a]Note: $+p < .10$; $*p < .05$; $**p < .01$.

in service firms is strongly customer and market driven; collaboration with clients ensures the transfer of market-relevant knowledge. Here, the informal and formal protection instruments like patents, long-term labor-contracts, lead-time advantage, and customer relationship management are of major importance (see Table 1).

The Department of Technology and Innovation Management of the Harburg Technical University initiated the "Harburg Study" of service-intensive companies in 2004. The purpose of this study was to get a better understanding of protection activities of service-intensive companies. The questionnaire contained sections on intellectual property protection and innovation activities as well as questions to probe the different knowledge assets required to deliver the competitive advantage of the companies involved.

Of the 99 companies that participated in the survey, almost half focused their protection activities on an internal lock-in strategy, followed by activities relating to secrecy and first-to-market strategies. Twenty-nine per cent of the firms concentrated on a complex design strategy while 27% of the corporations lock-in their customers and suppliers. Only 6% of the firms adopt a formal protection strategy (see Table 2).

Innovation activities themselves can also influence the way in which companies handle the protection topic. When looking at service companies

Table 2:   Overview of the indicator concept used in the Harburg Study.

Measurement object	Attributes, variables used	Strategy	Percentage ($N = 99$)
Use of protection mechanisms	• Patents • Trademarks • Copyrights	*Formal intellectual property rights (IPR) strategy*	6
	• Secrecy • First-mover advantage (being first in the market with new products and services)	*Secrecy and first-to-market strategy*	34
	• Long-term labor contracts	*Internal lock-in strategy*	48
	• Customer relationship management • Exclusive contracts with suppliers, external experts	*External lock-in strategy*	27
	• Complex product design • Integration and combination of tangible and intangible parts in new products and services	*Complex design strategy*	29

Data Source: Harburg Study, own calculation and illustration.

following an external lock-in strategy (integration of customers and suppliers), the acquisition of machines and supplies, as well as the takeover of smaller service companies, are the dominating innovation activities. This is congruent with the network orientation of this grouping and it can be assumed that the knowledge-sourcing strategy of these firms revolves more around bringing knowledge in, rather than building knowledge internally. The low importance of in-house training and education supports this assumption.

The Harburg Study also shows that the search for knowledge about consumers and the market place is highly interconnected with protection mechanisms such as trade marking. A strong knowledge of the market also supports a functioning customer relationship management system, which can enable the integration of customers into the development process of complex products and services. In such circumstances, protecting internal process knowledge, particularly how to extract and incorporate customer requirements, is a major competitive strategy with close links to a variety of different protection mechanisms.

Table 3:   Regression analysis showing the interrelation between protection mechanisms and company result.[a]

	Proportion of service turnover in relation to total turnover	Proportion of turnover with services new to the market (1–2 years)	Proportion of turnover with services older than 2 years (3–6 years)
Patents	22.227	−13.825	−3.175
Trademarks	−22.088	13.913	3.226
Copyrights	−.055*	.687**	.712**
Secrecy	−.197+	−.388*	−.401*
Long-term labor contracts	−14.785	−3.641	−1.551
First mover advantage	−.025	−.415*	−.386+
CRM	−.062	.746**	.779**
Exclusive contracts with suppliers/experts	24.003	27.141	17.321
Complex design	−.054	.780**	.806**
Combination of tangibles and intangibles	−8.983	−24.312	−16.668
Constant	160.818**	246.406**	212.512**
Number of observations	98	98	98
Probability > F	0.0020	0.0000	0.0000
R^2	0.0636	0.1672	0.1602

Data source: Harburg Study, own calculation and illustration.
[a]Note: $^{+}p < .10$; $^{*}p < .05$; $^{**}p < .01$.

In addition, the survey shows that successful service innovators are more likely to focus on locking-in their customers and following a complex design strategy, rather than maintaining secrets or being first on the market (see Table 3). This would suggest that some service-intensive companies recognize that being first on the market is not always the best approach, even if traditional theories state that a monopolistic situation will create the best returns on investment for a certain time.

14.6. Conclusions

Discussions regarding intellectual property rights in services often revolve around the protection of ideas such as new business concepts, new services, new processes, or customer integrations. Unlike most manufacturing innovations, many service innovations have to deal with characteristics such as network structures or a high degree of customer involvement. Thus, service companies not only have to solve the problem of making their new offerings visible, attractive, and trustworthy but they do so whilst also preventing the externalization of knowledge to competitors and imitators.

Business managers and researchers are informed by theory that service innovations include threats of uncontrolled knowledge spillovers. However, the empirical results provide protection guidelines for decision makers within companies for a number of scenarios, for example, whether they are highly dependent on internally or cooperatively generated knowledge. In particular, the combination and integration of tangible and intangible assets can deliver service products that are difficult to imitate due to the unique combination of tacit and explicit knowledge. The analysis clearly indicates that informal mechanisms that can hinder imitation from the early phases of development are both highly valued and used in practice.

This analysis provides, for the first time, a deeper insight for policy managers into innovation and protection activities of service firms. The results indicate that the lack of formal protection rights utilized by most service companies is not a significant barrier to innovation. Managers should be wary of investing excessive effort into debates on intellectual property mechanisms for service innovators. Instead, it appears that competition and the danger of imitations has forced improved innovation output and performance, because firms have reacted by enhancing their fulfilment of customer needs, accelerating innovation cycles, and reducing time-to-market. The heterogeneity of the innovation activities and the implementation of strategies to protect company-specific knowledge and technologies inside the service sectors, require further differentiation.

References

Andersen, B and J Howells (2000). Intellectual property rights shaping innovation in services. In *Knowledge and Innovation in the New Service Economy*, B Andersen, J Howells, R Hull, I Miles and J Roberts (eds.), pp. 229–247. Cheltenham: Edward Elgar.

Andersen, B and J Howells (1998). Innovation dynamics in services: Intellectual property rights as indicators and shaping systems in innovation. CRIC Discussion Paper No. 8, University of Manchester.

Blind, K, J Edler, U Schmoch, B Andersen, J Howells, I Miles *et al.* (2003). Patents in the service industries. Final report prepared for the European Commission. Fraunhofer-ISI, EC Contract No ERBHPV2-CT-1999-06.

Bouckaert, B (1990). What is property?. *Harvard Journal of Law and Public Policy*, 13(3), 775–816.

Braunstein, YM (1989). Economics of intellectual property rights in the international arena. *Journal of the American Society for Information Science*, 40(1), 12–16.

Chakravorti, B (2004). The role of adoption networks in the success of innovations: A strategic perspective. *Technology in Society*, 26(2–3), 469–482.

Garmon, CW (2002). Intellectual property rights — Protecting the creation of new knowledge across cultural boundaries. *American Behavioral Scientist*, 45(7), 1145–1158.

Granstrand, O (2000). *The Economics and Management of Intellectual Property*. Cheltenham, UK: Edward Elgar.

Grupp, H (1996). Spillover effects and the science base of innovations reconsidered — An empirical approach. *Journal of Evolutionary Economics*, 6(2), 175–197.

Hansen, MT and N Nohira (2004). How to build collaborative advantage. *MIT Sloan Management Review*, 46(1), 22–30.

Helm, R and M Kloyer (2004). Controlling contractual exchange risks in R&D interfirm cooperation: An empirical study. *Research Policy*, 33(8), 1103–1122.

Herstatt, C and E von Hippel (1992). From experience: Developing new product concepts via the lead user method: A case study in a "low-tech" field. *Journal of Product Innovation Management*, 9(3), 213–221.

Hipp, C and H Grupp (2005). Innovation in the service sector: The demand for service-specific innovation measurement concepts and typologies. *Research Policy*, 34(4), 517–535.

Howells, J and B Tether (2004). Innovation in services: Issues at stake and trends. Final report to the European Commission, INNO-Studies 2001: Lot 3, Contract No. INNO-03-01, University of Manchester.

Jennewein, K (2005). *Intellectual Property Management*. Heidelberg: Physica-Verlag.

Jordan, J and J Lowe (2004). Protecting strategic knowledge: Insights from collaborative agreements in the aerospace sector. *Technology Analysis & Strategic Management*, 16(2), 241–259.

Kaiser, U (2002). Measuring knowledge spillovers in manufacturing and services: An empirical assessment of alternatives approaches. *Research Policy*, 31(1), 125–144.

Miles, I, B Andersen, M Boden and J Howells (2000). Service production and intellectual property. *International Journal of Technology Management*, 20(1–2), 95–115.

Miotti, L and F Sachwald (2003). Co-operative R&D: why and with whom? An integrated framework of analysis. *Research Policy*, 32(8), 1481–1499.

Nambisan, S (2002). Designing virtual customer environments for new product development: Toward a theory. *Academy of Management Review*, 27(3), 392–413.

Teece, DJ (2001). *Managing Intellectual Capital*. New York: Oxford University Press.

Teece, DJ (1989). Inter-organizational requirements of the innovation process. *Managerial and Decision Economics*. Special Issue, 35–42.

Tether, BS (2003). The sources and aims of innovation in services: variety between and within sectors. *Economics of Innovation and New Technology*, 16, 481–506.

15

Customer and Supplier Involvement in New Service Development

Frank Hull*, Bo Edvardsson† and Chris Storey‡

Service Research Center, Karlstad University, Sweden
*Frank.Hull@asu.edu
†boedvard@kau.se
‡C.D.Storey@city.ac.uk

15.1. Introduction

This chapter enlarges upon a model of concurrent product development that has been tested in two goods studies. The present paper elaborates upon the initial model by testing the extent to which external involvement by customers and suppliers/partners in new service development (NSD) explains additional variance in performance. The added concept is the horizontal integration of the value chain — from suppliers to customers via the internal organization.

The model builds on the discipline of concurrent engineering, which is a managerial approach to product development that engages diverse functions simultaneously rather than serially in decision making (Susman and Dean, 1992; Hartley, 1992). Its cornerstone is the reorganization of product development by transforming functional hierarchies into a project-based approach, or what is often termed, an "organic" organization (Burns and Stalker, 1961). This is achieved by empowering cross-functional teams with responsibility for specific product development projects within predefined boundary conditions. This concurrent approach has proven to be successful in goods industries (Nevins and Whitney, 1989; Zirger *et al.*, 1990; Slade, 1993; Gatenby *et al.*, 1994; Liker *et al.*, 1999; Hull *et al.*, 1996; Zirger and Hartley, 1996; Fleischer and Liker, 1997). Companies deploying concurrent methods of product development are more cost effective and innovative than others.

The flattening of external relationships is a logical extension of concurrency principals from intra-organizational to inter-organizational relationships in the value chain. The inter-organization analog to organic, cross-functional teaming is "partnering", which implies reciprocity in relationships. Outsourcing has increased in recent years, not only in goods industries, but also in services. This requires an enlargement of the notion of concurrent product development systems to include integration of the value chain from upstream suppliers to downstream customers, both of which are external to the core company.

The "Voice of the Customer" is a central tenant of total quality management and considerable research has documented the benefit of co-involving end users in goods industries (e.g., Griffin and Hauser, 1993). Much less literature has focused on co-involving customers in NSD despite the fact that customers are often directly involved in service production (i.e., co-production). Recently, however, the literature has focused on involving customers or consumers in NSD in order to learn from and with them in new ways (e.g., Alam, 2002; Kristensson *et al.*, 2003, 2004; Magnusson *et al.*, 2003; Matthing *et al.*, 2004; Tomke, 2003). The literature suggests that involving customers in NSD reduces cycle time, results in more innovative services, and forms the basis for customer education. Our point of departure is that services are in time and space linked activities and interactions provided as solutions to customers' problems (Gustafsson and Johnson, 2003; Edvardsson *et al.*, 2005). We argue that to understand the interactive, relational, and process dimensions of services and value creation through services, we need new approaches in NSD. Customer involvement is one approach which may contribute to a more in-depth understanding of customers' latent needs and service value (Edvardsson *et al.*, 2005; Narver *et al.*, 2004; Vargo and Lusch, 2002).

Similarly, supplier involvement has been shown to aid successful innovation in manufacturing industries (e.g., Handfield *et al.*, 1999) while little has been written about supplier and partner involvement in NSD. Yet service companies are increasingly like goods companies in focusing on their core competencies and outsourcing ancillary activities. Even a large service company such as Citigroup bundles products from outside as well as inside its boundaries for sale to customers. Thus, this paper will explore how involvement by external companies in NSD decisions affects innovation performance.

The enlarged model of concurrent product development is tested by analyzing data on 70 large-scale service establishments in the New York metropolitan area. The plan of analysis has three foci: First, how well do *internal* practices of the companies developing service products predict the level of involvement by *external* customers and suppliers/partners? Second, does the involvement of *externals*, such as customers and suppliers/partners, explain additional variance in performance beyond internal product development practices? If so, how much of the impact on performance of internal practices is indirect via the involvement of externals. Third, to what extent do task contingencies moderate relationships between internal and external involvement in product development practices? The two contingencies explored herein are the type of innovation strategy and the type of knowledge strategy that the enterprise pursues.

15.2. Composite Model of NSD

Research on goods companies has shown that core elements of product development operations bond together as a "composite" (Hull *et al.*, 1996; Collins and Hull, 2002, 2003). Moreover, the composite model has been replicated in the same service dataset further analyzed in this paper (Tidd and Hull, 2003; Hull, 2004a,b). Synergistic bonds among these elements explain the success of companies deploying the concurrency model. At the operating core of the model is a troika of elements: Organization, Process, and Tools (OPT). Each of the OPT elements serve a general purpose. Organization provides coordination of people, Process provides control, and Tools provide transformation capabilities.

- O = Organization — OTS (Organic Team Structure), influence exerted by all stakeholders in a cross-functional team throughout the product development cycle.

- **P** = Process — IDC (In-Process Design Controls) for flexible, enabling guidance to team members working on development projects outside of their functional homes.
- **T** = Tools — CIT (Computer Information Technology) for transforming inputs into outputs, supporting communication among team members regardless of time or location, and maintaining continuously updated processes.

Recent research in services has used a similar troika of operational concepts in additive model for predicting product development performance. For example, Meyer and DeTore (1999) argue that three key elements are critical for a platform approach commonly deployed by goods industries (Lutz, 1994) which may also be applied to services. They describe these three elements as (1) multidisciplinary teams, (2) very specific processes, and (3) computer systems technology. Using measures of these three elements, Froehle *et al.* (2000) found that all were predictors of performance in an analysis of 175 service businesses. Moreover, other studies confirm that one or more of these three sets of practices predict statistically significant differences in levels of performance in services (Cooper and Edgett, 1999; Lievens and Monnaert, 2000; Avlonitis *et al.*, 2001). Case studies and prescriptions by consultants also reinforce the importance of these sets of practices (Terrill, 1992; Fruen, 1993; Drew, 1995; Edvardsson and Olsson, 1996).

15.2.1. *Organization*

The "O" is organic team structures (OTS), the cornerstone of the composite model. It enables people to be relatively more creative in the face of new and uncertain tasks (Damanpour, 1991; Katzenbach and Smith, 1993). Large service corporations need to infuse organic practices into their bureaucracy to become more innovative because formalization increases with growth in size (Blau and Shoenheer, 1971). Organic practices involve restructuring to achieve a project-based organization where employees work as cross-functional team members. Sometimes, these team members are physically collocated and rewarded as a group to reinforce collaboration. The key is to include diverse functions from all departments and points on the value chain so that ideas are cross-fertilized (Rochfordt and Rudelius, 1992). Early input by all functions is needed because the bulk of the product design is committed at initial stages even thought the actual costs are expended much later. Correcting faulty decisions at late stages is far more expensive than getting it right up front. The essence of concurrency is that spending the time and energy at the fuzzy front end pays off in faster and more cost effective product realization than the back end (Collins and Hull, 2002; Hull, 2003).

Today, the notion of organic design has been refashioned more proactively than simply removing bureaucratic constraints and hoping that creative people will make something innovative happen. Cross-functional teams (CFTs) evolved as a kind of "provisional organization" within the matrix framework. In their weakest form, members act as liaisons with their functional homes. In stronger forms, "heavy weight" teams enjoy considerable autonomy with significant resources committed to them up-front (Clark and Wheelwright, 1993). According to participants in a Concurrent Engineering user group in the US, a rule of thumb is that practicing concurrency is feasible only if at least 60% of resources are allocated up front to project teams instead of departmental functions. Strong CFTs resolve some of the ambiguities in matrix organizations where employees have two bosses, but are typically controlled more by one in a functional department than by others in professional disciplines (Galbraith, 1977). Purposive CFTs explicitly integrate the work of specialized functions, including that of line and staff. CFTs served as a wedge for horizontally integrating work across the base of the hierarchy by infusing organic practices into bureaucratic hierarchies.

15.2.2. *Process*

The "P" is In-process Design Controls. IDC refashions mechanistic controls so as to provide flexible and adaptive guidance to product development teams instead of rigid rules and inviolate standard operating procedures. IDC refers to a dynamic mode of concurrent processes that are adapted to the contingent needs of project teams. IDC offers alternative methods of control that guides rather than stifles innovation. Process is more flexible and enabling relative to the rigid constraints typical of mechanistic bureaucracies (Adler and Borys, 1996). Processes for managing development projects include charters, model plans, stage-gates with exit and entry criteria, product review criteria, etc. So long as processes are guides rather than inflexible mandates, product development teams may use them to retain focus, reuse knowledge, and track progress toward targets (Melan, 1985; Garvin, 1993; Graessel and Zeidler, 1993; Lovitt, 1996).

The axis of the composite model is a synergistic bond between OTS and IDC. Organic team structure enables people to be relatively more creative while in-process design controls supply focused discipline. Synergy between these two elements results in an increased capability for cost effective innovation because the advantages of both organic and mechanistic forms of organization are melded (Burns and Stalker, 1961; Hull and Hage, 1982; Duncan, 1976; Daft, 1978; Hull, 1988; Hull *et al.*, 1996; Hull, 2004a).

15.2.3. *Tools*

The "T" represents computer information technologies. Many kinds of service business use computer programs to transform symbols. Service sector companies have been even greater consumers of information technology than manufacturing industries (Roach, 1988) and are automating all kinds of transactions, from checks to program trades (Dabholkar, 1994; Rayport and Sviokla, 1995). Increasingly, computer programs are used to analyze human behaviors. Moreover, many kinds of service also involve a physical aspect where transformation of things is part and parcel of the service product. The process of delivering services is increasingly simulated by computer models. Delivery processes are particularly important for many kinds of services in which the exchange is tantamount to the product itself. Although CIT is more difficult to exploit in services with high levels of intangibility, in principle services may involve the transformation of things as well as data and people (Collins *et al.*, 1988).

The recent emergence of soft, programmable automation has revolutionized transformational technologies (Collins *et al.*, 1996). Formerly tools were mechanistic determinants of behaviors not only in manufacturing, but also in many service operations. The rise in computing power coupled with highly capable software applications supports both the discipline of mechanistic practices along with the creativity of organic ones. For example, Computer Information Technology (CIT) enables processes to be more flexible and adaptive, which softens mechanistic constraints. CIT enables team members to communicate information with one another asynchronously as well as simultaneously, which provides mechanistic discipline to the organization via commonly shared knowledge. Software for handling imprecise information with fuzzy logic makes socio-explicit integration in new service development more feasible. Thus, CIT is important not only for transformation in services, but also for augmenting OTS organization and IDC processes, especially to the extent enterprises pursue a strategy of developing novel products (Hull, 2004b).

15.3. Conceptual Model of External Involvement in NSD

The framework proposed herein augments an internal model of new service development by adding the input of customers and suppliers/partners to NSD. As shown in Fig. 1, involvement in NSD decisions by external companies is presumed to be increased by the internal practices of the enterprise. The degree of collaboration with externals presumably predicts performance level. The influence of the externals on performance is contingent on the firm's strategy.

15.3.1. *External involvement and NSD performance*

There is extensive literature linking a firm's market orientation with organizational performance including innovation performance (e.g., Jaworski and Kohli, 1993). This implies that the voice of the customer is central to new product success (e.g., Griffin and Hauser, 1993; Gruner and Homburg, 2000). To ensure that the customer's voice is heard and understood, many companies engage their customers in the different stages of the development process or involve them in a kind of development partnership. They

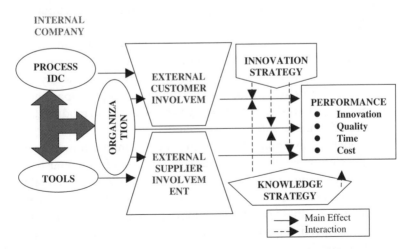

Figure 1:   Composite model of product development with external co-involvement and contingency factors.

are invited to have a say in NSD. However, customers often have trouble expressing their needs in enough depth or giving effective feedback on intangible offerings (e.g., Leonard and Rayport, 1997; Ulwick, 2002). The input from customers in NSD may deal with new service ideas, the design of product features and/or characteristics of delivery processes. This engagement may occur at various stages, from the product concept to modifications of the offering after initial sale (Kristensson *et al.*, 2003). The degree of involvement may range from the feedback on specific issues to formally joining the new service development team (Alam, 2002). One of the key characteristics of services is the inseparability of production and delivery and that services are activities, interactions, and processes often embedded in relationships. Indeed in certain services customers are heavily involved in co-producing the service (Edvardsson *et al.*, 2005). Therefore, it would be expected that service customers may have an even more important role to play in service development than in the development of physical products.

Similarly, the importance of incorporating suppliers into the development process and the development team has been well documented (e.g., Handfield *et al.*, 1999; Petersen, *et al.*, 2005). To date, there has been no research investigating this in the context of service organizations. Increasingly, however, companies create and deliver services in partnership with others. For example, suppliers often link service companies with end use customers, such as independent insurance agents, brokers of financial services, contract nursing care, advertising agents, information technology vendors, call centers. To the extent external companies supply critical components of the service and/or its delivery, their involvement in NSD is potentially important. This input may range from simple consultation on design matters to fully transferring the responsibility of subsystems including delivery processes to suppliers. Suppliers/partners may be engaged at various stages, from the product concept to modifications of the offering after initial sale.

Incorporating external partners (both upstream and downstream) in service development projects produces a number of potential benefits: enhanced information and expertise, early identification of potential problems, provides extra resources, improves communication, and information exchange. In turn, these can result in more positive outcomes in terms of development speed, improved quality, reduced cost of development, and a smoother launch.

Therefore, for service firms, product development performance will be increased by the extent of involvement by external companies in the development process:

Hypothesis 1: The greater the level of involvement by external companies in NSD by Customers (1a) and Suppliers/Partners (1b), the higher the level of service development performance.

15.3.2. *Composite model as a predictor of external involvement*

Petersen *et al.* (2005) argue that additional research is needed into the processes and managerial actions that increase the likelihood of successful integration. Similarly, Walter (2003) suggests that the degree of supplier integration depends strongly on the strategies and capabilities of the "buyer" firm. It is argued that the three dimensions of the composite model each will have an important impact on external involvement in NSD.

Brown and Eisenhardt (1997) introduce the concept of the communication web and stress the importance of extensive task-oriented communication both within the project team and outside the organization. This increases the amount and variety of information generated increasing the performance of the development team. Communication problems, however, have often been identified as key issues in involving partners in NPD (Wynstra *et al.*, 2000; Liker *et al.*, 1996). This occurs as a result of NPD teams defending their own functions and resisting sharing proprietary information (McIver and Humphreys, 2004). What is required is a culture that breaks down the internal barriers that exist within the traditional functional view of the firm that is, an organic team structure. Petersen *et al.* (2003) found that successful supplier integration was achieved by actively including them in the team decision-making process, including supplier representatives as part of the development team to overcome corporate culture issues, and establish open lines dialog. McIvor and Humphreys (2004, p. 196) demonstrated that effective implementation of external "requires a culture permeating the organization hierarchy that encourages and values collaboration." Supporting this, Bonner (2005) found that the use of team-based rewards increases cross-functional integrations and are positively related to the degree of customer interaction during NPD.

Social problems often occur because of a lack of co-coordinating mechanisms (Petersen *et al.*, 2005). McIver and Humphreys (2004) found a lack of clear policy guidelines limiting the involvement of external partners during NPD. It helps reduce uncertainty between the internal and external to have a more formal set of process design controls. Bonner (2005) found that when formal in-process controls (i.e., those directed toward the development process) are coupled with clear process output controls (i.e., setting standards and performance criteria) they are positively related to the degree of customer interaction during NPD. Similarly Petersen *et al.* (2003) identified activities such as re-engineering the NPD process, and using formal tools (e.g., QFD) as aiding supplier integration. However, if controls are too formalized, there is a reduced motivation to experiment and to seek new information affecting the degree of customer interaction.

Similarly, the use of CIT can enhance communication with suppliers during NPD (Petersen *et al.*, 2003) and can enable more effective control mechanism to be put in place. However, CIT goes beyond simple communication tools to sophisticating modeling of new services. Roy *et al.* (2004) argue that greater IT adaptation and system integration between buyer and seller leads to greater innovation performance, though this is likely to be more incremental rather than radical in nature. Recently, these have been extended to the customer and von Hippel (2001) demonstrates that customers can be more involved in the development of new products via user toolkits.

Based on the previous discussion, external involvement will be increased by the OTS, IDC, and CIT.

Hypothesis 2: The greater the level of deployment of service development practices into Organic Team Structure (2a), In-process Design Controls (2b), and Computer Information Technology (2c), the greater the involvement of external enterprises in service development.

15.3.3. *Contingency effects — Innovation and knowledge strategy*

Contingency theory suggests that effective organizational strategies, processes, and structures are not universal but rather are tied to the specific context at hand (Lawrence and Lorsch, 1967; Souder *el al.*, 1999). Situational effects often moderate the relationship between input and output variables.

For example, it is suggested that the importance of supplier involvement in NPD will vary according to the situation (Petersen *et al.*, 2003). An important contingency is the way firms aim to compete in the marketplace. If processes do not fit strategies, the implementation of these strategies can be problematic. Two aspects of a firm's strategy are explored here: innovation strategy and knowledge strategy.

Enterprises vary in their innovation strategy. Some firms try to be first to market with novel and innovative new products and services. Other firms try to be fast followers (sometimes referred to as "analyzers") waiting until there is more certainty in the marketplace before launching new products. Therefore, firms will face different levels of uncertainty or risk. Previous research suggests that the importance of supplier integration in the development process is contingent on the degree of uncertainty faced. When faced with high uncertainty, that is, with radically new technologies or markets, firms will often approach key suppliers to influence their development efforts reducing this uncertainty (Petersen *et al.*, 2003). Primo and Amundson (2002) suggest that during innovative projects, there may be a greater perceived interdependence among suppliers and customers hence increasing the level of external involvement.

However, there is a counter-argument in radical innovation there may be less certainty about which suppliers to link with, and there may be strategic disadvantages of being locked into a particular supplier (Eisenhardt and Tabrizi, 1995; Handfield *et al.*, 1999). Suppliers may also be less inclined toward radical innovation as it may lower the importance of current supplier relationships. Hence, Swink (1999) found a negative interaction between supplier influence and product newness.

Similarly, it has been found that the degree of product newness sought moderates the effect of the customers influence on new product advantage (Bonner and Walker, 2004). Callahan and Lasry (2004) have shown that the importance of customer input increases with product newness. Embedded ties between an organization and its external partners can aid NPD in two ways. It can motivate the open exchange of proprietary information, and it can increase the ability to exchange rich, complex knowledge. Also, the more outside players involved in the NPD process, the greater the variety of perspectives, competencies and experiences will be brought to bare fostering greater creativity in the process. Kristensson *et al.* (2004) found experimentally that users produce more original and more valuable new service ideas than in-house people (though these ideas were not as realizable). Research from involvement of mobile telephony end users indicated that the outcome from customer involvement was heavily dependent on how the users were involved. For instance, the amount of information the customers received negatively affected the originality of the ideas (Kristensson and Magnusson, 2005). Firms can get too close to their customers, however, resulting in unified thought — worlds and incremental rather than radial innovation (Magnusson *et al.*, 2003).

Mechanistic-functional practices are often best for executing improvements in standard operations and existing services. But to the extent the strategy is targeted at producing more innovative new services, the organization needs to more closely integrate NSD decision making by internal people with those in external companies. This requires a more "organic" mode of organization (Burns and Stalker, 1961; Damanpour, 1991). Research in both goods and services has demonstrated the need for more organic organization to the extent that products are novel (Olsen *et al.*, 1995; Collins and Hull, 2002; Hull, 2003).

Consistent with the previous discussion and contingency theory, one may hypothesize that the more novel the service development, the greater the benefit of multi-functional and multi-enterprise involvement. The impact of OTS and involvement by externals is presumably greater if the product development strategy entails novelty as indicated by the dotted lines signifying interaction effects in Fig. 1.

Hypothesis 3: The more novel the service development strategic targets, the greater the impact of external involvement of Customers (3a) and Suppliers/Partners (3b) on service development performance.

A knowledge management perspective is taken to understand how service firms compete in the market. At the heart of knowledge management is the distinction between tacit and explicit knowledge (Polanyi, 1966; Nonaka and Takeuchi, 1995). Companies compete on their relative strengths of tacit and explicit knowledge. It is argued that these two types of knowledge allow organizations to offer and deliver value to customers in different ways and hence form a different basis for competitive advantage. Explicit knowledge-based services deliver value via the creation of a reliable, standardized offering. These are largely impersonal and are often reliant on computer automated delivery processes. By contrast, tacit value added involves interpersonal interchanges and ongoing interactions with customers. Sometimes, the service product is essentially its delivery process. In some respects, it is easier to improve intangible services, their delivery, and consumption processes than physical goods, especially after initial sale. The notion of the "augmented service offering" argues this point (Storey and Easingwood, 1998). Such services imply judgmental decisions by the service provider, and the quality of the service is heavily dependent on the knowledge heard by front-line staff. Sometimes, exchanges between provider and customer continue after sale in ways that involve personal and different kinds of value, including trust.

In general, we presume that the more tacit the knowledge base, the more enterprises should design their product development system in a relatively more organic than mechanistic mode. This tacit knowledge is more difficult to share and is considered sticky (von Hippel, 1994). Therefore, this knowledge needs to be shared by personal interaction or by allowing the holders of this information to make relevant decisions. Conversely, the more explicit the knowledge base, the more the company should design its product development system in a relatively more mechanistic than organic mode. Following this line of reasoning, one may speculate that direct involvement by external companies in NSD is relatively more important to the extent that knowledge is tacit rather than explicit (Roy *et al.*, 2004). External company involvement in NSD is presumed to be moderated by the knowledge strategy of the service firm. Thus, the benefit of external involvement in NSD decisions is possibly contingent upon the degree to which the firm's competitive advantage is based cn tacit knowledge as indicated by the dotted lines in Fig. 1.

Hypothesis 4: The greater the firm's tacit knowledge strategy, the greater the impact of external involvement of Customers (4a) and Suppliers/ Partners (4b) on service development performance.

15.3.4. *Research methods*

A service sector questionnaire on concurrent methods of product development was adapted from a 200-page compendium of best industrial practices, identified during the conduct of case studies of goods companies participating in a concurrent engineering user group. Graduate students in a special topics MBA course helped to shorten the compendium and adapt it to services. Twenty-seven companies participating either in a study of strategic business process improvement and/or a benchmarking user group, helped adapt industrial practices to better suit services. Many industrial practices needed to be recast in more abstract terms to better fit the diverse service establishments under study and some new ones were added focusing on the organization of the service function and service delivery.

15.3.4.1. Sample

Large companies were targeted because growth in size increases bureaucratic structuring and other barriers to innovation. Fifty-eight service companies were identified from the 1996 Crain's New York Directory list of the 100 largest companies in terms of employment. Smaller service businesses ranking in the top 25th percentile of their category were also selected to capture the diversity of enterprises within the region.

Letters were written to either the CEO or other executive if known. The letter requested that the executive refer the questionnaire to either someone in the product development function or persons in business development, TQM (Total Quality Management), BPR (Business Process Reengineering), and Productivity Improvement. Of 223 mailed, only three were returned completed. Over 20 came back "addressee unknown."

To increase responses, priority was placed on the 58 companies originally targeted as the largest in the metro area. We made phone calls to try to identify appropriate respondents. We also contacted members of the American Society of Quality Control and the Association for Quality and Participation for assistance in identifying respondents. More effort was given to financial services and insurance relative to accounting, consulting, and legal firms.

Respondents from 70 businesses in 51 corporations completed questionnaires. Of these, 62 provided detail on multifunctional involvement by 10 functions at three stages of the product development cycle. Lines of business surveyed within a single corporation did not overlap, such as private banking and syndicated banking, which operated as separate companies for almost all practical purposes.

The distribution of categories of the service sector is attached as Appendix A. The largest category was financial services, followed by insurance and health care. Most major categories in the service sector were represented except advertising. With these exceptions, survey respondents appear to be reasonably representative of large service companies in the New York area. The enterprises were almost entirely businesses within large corporations. Participating companies include one or more enterprises from 38 of the 58 corporations in the initial target list. Participants include 11 of the 12 largest publicly held service companies. Only four companies employed less than 500 people.

15.3.4.2. *Measures*

Respondents were asked to describe a "typical service product" with which they were familiar to be used for the purposes of answering the questionnaire. A service product was defined as

> "A service product is something a customer pays for receiving even though it may be intangible (i.e., not a physical object). The service may be attached to a tangible product, e.g., warranty agreement, field repair, insurance, etc. However, a great many service products are intangible even though they may have a physical manifestation, e.g., bank check, an insurance policy, a charge card, etc. Often interpersonal experiences are critical to the delivery of service products, e.g., airline travel where the customer and employees are in relatively constant contact. This is in contrast to an object purchased in a store and used without further contact with the provider (except for any repairs and/or field service)..."

The bulk of the questions asked the respondent to rate the extent of practices or changes during the past five years. Judgments by respondents were recorded on the following scale: (1) Not at All, (2) Just a Little, (3) Somewhat, and (4) A Great Deal.

Following data collection, the measures within each section of the questionnaire were factor analyzed (Varimax method) so that inter-correlated items could be combined in indices for parsimony. The construction of the final scales consisted of the factor items derived from these analyses. Appendix B provides the scales along with αs.

15.3.4.3. *Dependent variable*

Six questions were asked about innovation performance in terms of product features, quality, time, and cost, All items were significantly inter-correlated and are scaled in a single index of product development performance ($\alpha = 0.90$).

15.3.4.4. *External involvement of customers and suppliers/partners (C&SPD)*

Organic practices may be used to integrate people across enterprise boundaries. Therefore, questions were asked regarding the participation of customers and suppliers/partners in two kinds of decisions, development of service products and development of service delivery. The four questions are inter-correlated ($\alpha = 0.85$). Each pair of questions is also added together for customer involvement in product development, CPD ($\alpha = 0.79$) and suppliers/partners, SPD ($\alpha = 0.85$). In the analysis, we look at customer and supplier involvement separately as well as in totality.

15.3.4.5. *Organic team structure (OTS)*

Organic organization design was measured as the average of six items from a page of the questionnaire dedicated to this topic. The items are unified by the theme of organic organization design that includes diverse practices, for example, restructuring from a functional to a project-based organization that minimizes hierarchy, CFT — cross-functional teaming, physical collocation, etc. ($\alpha = 0.89$).

15.3.4.6. *In-process design controls (IDC)*

A page on process included items measuring IDC. These items are unified by the theme of process control, for example, benchmarking, Quality Function Deployment, product reviews, conformance with process, etc. ($\alpha = 0.84$).

15.3.4.7. *Computer information technology (CIT)*

A page on tools/technology included nine items summed to measure CIT. These items are unified by the theme of computer usage, information management, and computer-based communications ($\alpha = 0.83$). Most of these items loaded in a single factor. However, two dealt with electronic communications with external customers and suppliers. As the two factors are significantly inter-correlated (0.47), they are combined in a single index with a better α coefficient than either separately.

15.3.4.8. *Innovation strategy (NEW)*

A page on strategy included several items used to assess the strategic intent of the company during the past five years. One item, "Developing novel service products" is used to indicate the innovation strategy of the enterprise.

15.3.4.9. *Tacit knowledge strategy (TKV)*

Due to the lack of research into the distinction between tacit and explicit knowledge strategies, an operationalization was needed. Participants in a user group of service companies were asked how their typical service products provided value for their customers. These were then grouped into those based on tacit knowledge and those based on explicit knowledge. The dimension connoting aspects of tacit knowledge based services included four items ($\alpha = 0.67$)[1]: personal service, convenience, guarantees, and transactional changes. Personal service implies interpersonal exchanges, which are likely to involve dealing with human idiosyncrasies requiring ad hoc improvisations, for example, consulting. Convenience implies adaptation to unique customer needs and local conditions, for example, luxury retail services. Guarantees imply some degree of trust, an inherently subjective as well as possibly objective assessment of probabilities, for example, insurance. Transactional changes involve alterations that have risks and benefits requiring judgmental decisions, for example, private banking, loans, etc. To the extent these changes recur, the relationship between the service provider and customer may be ongoing.

15.3.4.10. *Correlation matrix and descriptive statistics*

The components of the OPT model all have significant correlations with performance as well as with each other.

Organization measured as internal practices of organic team structure (OTS) is correlated 0.69 with involvement by customers and suppliers in decisions about the development of service products and delivery processes (C&S). OTS is positively correlated with both contingency variables, a strategy of novel product development, and tacit value added.

---

[1] The other grouping deals with relatively more explicit knowledge than inter-personal knowledge. It included five aspects ($\alpha = 0.79$) of professional-technical knowledge pertinent to their service products: professional knowledge, knowledge bases/research, software, hardware, and communications. The knowledge could be more easily codified for applications in conformance with pre-defined standards, for example, medical diagnostics, pharmaceutical dispensation, etc. Hardware is often necessary for supporting the delivery of many kinds of services, for example, ATMs and construction tools. Software is essential for developing many kinds of service products, for example, hazard analyses for life insurance, discounted cash flow analyses, simulations of returns from new derivative products, econometric modeling, etc. It is also required for many kinds of service delivery, for example, credit cards. Many communication technologies require both hardware and software.

Table 1:   Correlations and descriptive statistics.

	PDP	C&SPD	CPD	SPD	OTS	IDC	CIT	NEW	TKV
Performance (PER)	1.00								
Customer & supplier Involvement (C&SPD)	0.60	1.00							
Customer involvement (CPD)	0.52	0.90	1.00						
Supplier involvement (SPD)	0.58	0.91	0.63	1.00					
Organization (OTS)	0.60	0.69	0.61	0.65	1.00				
Process (IDC)	0.59	0.73	0.59	0.75	0.76	1.00			
Tools/technology (CIT)	0.45	0.22	0.23	0.16	0.38	0.38	1.00		
Innovation strategy (NEW)	0.49	0.43	0.34	0.42	0.51	0.56	0.31	1.00	
Tacit knowledge strategy (TKV)	0.18	0.16	0.19	0.10	0.33	0.19	0.13	0.15	1.00
Mean	2.70	2.52	2.66	2.35	2.81	2.86	2.83	2.86	3.07
SD	0.77	0.87	0.92	0.99	0.83	0.74	0.69	1.13	0.71

Coefficients greater than 0.25 are significant at the 0.05 level of confidence.

However, C&S is positively correlated only with a strategy of product novelty (Table 1).

15.4.   Results

15.4.1.   *Predicting external involvement*

Table 2 examines how the components of the OPT model predict external involvement by customers and suppliers/partners in development decisions about service products and delivery processes. The table is divided into three parts: First, the effects of OPT on both customer and supplier involvement are examined (C&SPD). The effect of OPT on customer involvement (CPD) and supplier involvement (SPD) is then examined in Models 2 and 3, respectively.

Organic team structure (OTS) has significant main effects on the external involvement of both customers and suppliers/partners in the development of service products. This effect is stronger for customers than it is for suppliers/partners.

In-process Design Controls (IDC) has significant main effects on the external involvement of both customers and suppliers/partners in the

Table 2:   Regression of customer and supplier involvement on predictors.

	Customer & supplier M1	Customer M2	Supplier M3
OTS	0.45**	0.47**	0.35**
IDC	0.46**	0.29*	0.54**
CIT	−0.11	−0.03	−0.17*
NEW	−0.01	−0.06	0.03
TKV	−0.10	−0.05	−0.13t
R2	0.63	0.43	0.61
R^2 Adj	0.59	0.37	0.57
F-ratio	17.4**	7.7**	16.4

**$p = 0.01$, *$p = 0.05$, $t = 0.10$.

development of service products. This effect is stronger for suppliers/ partners than it is for customers.

Computer Information Technologies (CIT) has a slightly negative effect on the involvement of suppliers in product development, SPD.[2] TKV also has a slightly negative effect on SPD. Perhaps uncertainty and lack of specificity make supplier/partner involvement relatively more difficult.

Two of the three elements of the composite model explain appreciable variance in the level of external involvement, OTS and IDC. Moreover, they have an interaction effect on C&SPD that is significant at the 0.05 level of confidence (not shown in the table). These results support Hypotheses 2a and 2b, but not Hypothesis 2c.

15.4.2.   *Effects of external involvement on performance*

The effects of each of the OPT components on performance are shown in Table 3, Model 1. Each component has at least a modestly significant main effect and over 40% of variance is explained in product development performance.

In Table 3, Model 2, the index of external involvement (C&SPD) is added to the equation. The reduction in the strength of the impact of any of the OPT elements may be considered as an indirect effect via the involvement of customers and/or suppliers/partners. OTS and IDC have main

---

[2]If the two items in the CIT index dealing with computer exchange with customer and suppliers are examined separately, their effect is still negative, but less than significant.

Table 3: Regression of NSD performance on internal practices and index of customer and supplier involvement.

	M1	M2	M3	M4
C&SPD	—	0.44**	0.40**	0.42**
OTS	0.26**	0.06	−0.35	−0.60t
IDC	0.22t	0.01	0.04	−0.01
CIT	0.24*	0.29**	0.25**	0.32**
NEW	0.15	0.16	−0.43	0.17t
TKV	0.00	0.05	0.06	−0.54t
OTS × NEW	—	—	0.90t	—
OTS × TKV	—	—	—	1.04*
R2	0.46	0.53	0.55	0.56
R^2 Adj	0.41	0.47	0.49	0.50
F-ratio	8.8**	9.6**	8.7**	9.0**
F-ratio Δ		7.0**	2.3t	3.0*
ΔR^2		0.07	0.02	0.03

$**p = 0.01$, $*p = 0.05$, $t = 0.10$.

effects that are reduced to non-significance. CIT retains a significant main effect as little of its impact can be considered as indirect. The index of external involvement has a strong main effect and adds an additional 7% to variance explained in product development performance.

In Table 4, Models 2 and 5, the effect of adding external involvement by customers (CPD) is compared with that for suppliers/partners (SPD). External involvement by customers adds 4% to variance explained and involvement by suppliers/partners adds 6%.

Significant levels of variance in product development performance are explained by a troika of internal elements of a composite model of product development. However, co-involvement by external companies (customers and suppliers/partners) in NSD adds significantly to multiple R squared. Thus, external co-involvement and internal practices are important as predictors of NSD performance in this dataset. These results support Hypotheses 1a and 1b.

15.4.3. Contingency effects

It was hypothesized that there would be a contingency effect between the company's innovation strategy and the degree of C&SPD. No interactions with novelty were observed with external involvement. Therefore, no support was found for Hypothesis 3 in the analysis presented herein. In

Table 4:   Regression of NSD performance on internal practices and customer vs. supplier involvement.

	Customer (CPD)				Supplier/partner (SPD)		
	M1	M2	M3	M4	M5	M6	M7
Ext. involvement	—	0.25*	0.22*	0.24*	0.39**	0.35**	0.37**
OTS	0.26**	0.14	−0.33	−0.55*t*	0.12	−0.31	−0.56*t*
IDC	0.22*t*	0.14	0.16	0.12	0.01	0.04	−0.01
CIT	0.24*	0.25*	0.21*	0.28**	0.31**	0.26**	0.34**
New	0.15	0.17*t*	−0.51	0.18*t*	0.14	−0.48	0.16
TKV	0.00	0.02	0.03	−0.60*t*	0.05	0.07	−0.55*t*
OTS × NEW	—	—	1.03*	—	—	0.95*t*	—
OTS × TKV	—	—	—	1.09*	—	—	1.06*
R^2	0.46	0.49	0.52	0.52	0.52	0.54	0.55
R^2 Adj	0.41	0.43	0.46	0.46	0.46	0.48	0.48
F-ratio	8.8**	8.3**	7.8**	7.8**	9.1**	8.4**	8.5**
F-ratio Δ		3.6*	2.9*	3.1*	6.2**	2.5*t*	3.1*
ΔR^2		0.04	0.03	0.03	0.06	0.02	0.03

$**p = 0.01$, $*p = 0.05$, $t = 0.10$.

addition, no interactions with TKV were observed with external involvement. Therefore, no support was found for Hypothesis 4.

OTS, however, has an interaction effect with a strategy of product novelty as shown in Model 3 in Table 3. Similarly, Model 4 in Table 3 shows an interaction effect between OTS with value-added by tacit knowledge. Parallel results are observed if involvement of customers and suppliers/partners is disaggregated, as shown in Table 4.

15.5. Discussion

This research has confirmed the importance of both customer and supplier involvement for NSD performance. Based on previous research from the goods literature, this was to be expected but it is satisfying to see the results confirmed. Recently, research has been exploring the role of the customer in NSD (e.g., Kristensson *et al.*, 2004), however, there is still a dearth of literature covering the relationship with suppliers. Both upstream and downstream activities are important but it appears that the involvement of suppliers has a relatively greater influence over the NSD process. This may be a result of service companies being less knowledgeable about managing their relationship with suppliers than they are with customers. Further research is needed in this area.

The level of involvement by external customers and supplier/partners in PD decisions is predicted by two of the three elements at the core of the composite model, OTS organization and IDC process. Moreover, these two elements also have a significant interaction effect on C&SPD (Customer & Supplier involvement in product development). Thus, OTS and IDC may be interpreted as internal capabilities enabling enterprises engaged in NSD to more effectively co-involve external companies in decision making. OTS enables firms and NSD teams to move out of their inward functions focusing thought-worlds and to openly engage with external partners. To be effective, the integration of external players needs to be formally controlled. Hence, IDC is important for involvement. This is supported by the buyer–supplier integration and supply chain management literature which stresses the need for appropriate safeguards and controlling mechanisms (Petersen *et al.*, 2005).

Surprisingly, Computer Information Technologies (CIT) has a slightly negative effect on the involvement of suppliers in product development. It may be that service companies find incompatibility problems between the company's information systems and its suppliers. This has been found to inhibit supplier involvement in NPD (McIvor and Humphreys, 2004). Similarly, the extent to which the company's offering is based on tacit knowledge also has a slightly negative effect on SPD. Tacit knowledge-based services are inherently more uncertain and this lack of specificity may make supplier/partner involvement relatively more difficult. It may be the case that for services development on extensive explicit knowledge supplier involvement may be higher. This may require support form extensive CIT.

OTS is the cornerstone of the composite model because it requires the transformation of the enterprise from a hierarchical integration of functional activities to a project-based company, adding value by integrating value chains horizontally. OTS was found to be contingent upon two factors, a strategic focus on generating novel products and exploitation of a tacit knowledge base. The logic is that organizing the creativity of people is more necessary for developing new products and those with tacit rather than explicitly defined features.

Although parallel interactions were hypothesized for C&SPD, none were observed. This is surprising. It may be the case that for service firms facing rapidly changing markets/technologies, there may be advantage in delaying as much as possible supplier involvement in order to capture the latest technology (Handfield *et al.*, 1999; Peterson *et al.*, 2003). Looking solely at C&SPD in the development of delivery processes, it was found to have positive interaction effects on product development performance. Each interaction adds approximately 3% to variance explained in performance.

It was hypothesized that the basis for competitive advantage (i.e., tacit versus explicit knowledge) would have an impact on the degree of importance for external involvement in NSD. However, this was not shown to be the case. C&SPD is highly important, irrespective of the approach taken in the market. This suggests that this field is worthy of further study.

15.6. Conclusions

This paper elaborates upon a composite model of product development effectiveness that has proven predictive of performance in two goods studies as well as the service dataset of 70 service companies in New York further analyzed herein. Results of analysis suggest that the composite model, as well as perhaps others focusing strictly on internal elements of the system, may be suboptimal in an increasingly interconnected world where company boundaries are more porous. By adding C&SPD (co-involvement of external customers and suppliers/partners in NSD decision making) in multiple regression analysis, additional variance in product development performance was explained over and above that predicted by internal elements.

Two elements dealing with organization and process form the axis of a composite model of product development. Organic team structure and in-process design controls predict co-involvement of external companies in NSD. This duo also has an interaction effect on the level of C&SPD. Thus, organic team structures and in-process design controls are postulated as additive as well as multiplicative capabilities enabling co-involvement of external companies in NSD.

In accordance with contingency theory, the need for OTS is moderated by the degree of uncertainty in the environment. Uncertainty was measured herein as a strategic focus on novel product creation and exploitation of tacit rather than explicit knowledge bases. Organic team structures (OTS) is the cornerstone of the composite model and enables people to be relatively more creative in the face of uncertain tasks. Consistent with contingency theory, interaction effects were observed between OTS and a novel product development strategy and the exploitation of tacit knowledge.

In summary, this paper argues for more holistic models of new service development effectiveness that span external as well as internal input into NSD. However, certain internal capabilities are probably critical for effectively integrating external input. These likely include ways of organizing human creativity in disciplined, yet flexible ways.

References

Adler, P and B Borys (1996). Two types of bureaucracy: Enabling and coercive. *Administrative Science Quarterly*, 41(1), 61–89.

Alam, I (2002). An exploratory investigation of user involvement in new service development. *Journal of the Academy of Marketing Science*, 30(3), 250–261.

Avlonitis, GJ, PG Papastahopoulou and SP Gounaris (2001). An empirically-based typology of product innovativeness for new financial services: Success and failure scenarios. *Journal of Product Innovation Management*, 18(5), 324–342.

Blau, PM and RA Schoenherr (1971). *The Structure of Organizations*. New York: Basic Books.

Bonner (2005). The influence of formal controls on customer interactivity in new product development. *Industrial Marketing Management*, 34(1), 63–69.

Bonner, J and O Walker (2004). Selecting influential business-to-business customers in new product development. *Journal of Product Innovation Management*, 21(3), 155–169.

Brown, SL and K Eisenhardt (1997). The art of continuous change: Linking complexity theory and time-paced evolution in relentlessly shifting organizations. *Administrative Science Quarterly*, 42(1), 1–34.

Burns, T and GM Stalker (1961). *The Management of Innovation*. London: Tavistock.

Callahan, J and E Lasry (2004). The importance of customer input in the development of very new products. *R&D Management*, 34(2), 107–120.

Clark, KB and SC Wheelwright (1993). *Managing New Product and Process Development: Text and Cases*. Cambridge, MA: Harvard Business School.

Collins, PD and FM Hull (2003). A replication and extension of the composite model of concurrent engineering effectiveness. *ICE Conference Proceedings*, Helsinki, 16 June.

Collins, PD and FM Hull (2002). Early simultaneous influence of manufacturing across stages of the product development cycle: Impact on time and cost. *International Journal of Innovation Management*, 6(1), 1–24.

Collins, PD, J Hage and FM Hull (1988). Technical systems: A framework for analysis. In *Research in the Sociology of Organizations*, Bacharach, S and N DiTomaso (eds.), pp. 81–100. Greenwich, CT: JAI Press.

Cooper, RG and S Edgett (1999). *Service Product Development*. Cambridge, MA: Perseus.

Dabholkar, PA (1994). Technology-based service delivery. In *Advances in Services Marketing and Management*, Schwartz, TA, DE Bowen and SW Brown (eds.), 3 Greenwich, CT: JAI Press: 241–271.

Daft, RL (1978). A dual-core model of organizational innovation. *Academy of Management Journal*, 24, 68–82.

Damanpour, F (1991). Organizational innovations: A meta-analysis of effects of determinants and moderators. *Academy of Management Journal*, 34(3), 555–91.

Drew, SAW (1995). *Accelerating Innovation in Financial Services, Long Range Planning*, London, 28 August (4).

Duncan, RB (1976). The ambidextrous organization: Designing dual structures for innovation. In *The Management of Organization Design*, Killman, RH, LR Pondy and D Slevin (eds.), pp. 167–188. New York: North-Holland.

Edvardsson, BAG and I Roos (2005). Service portraits in service research — A critical review. *International Journal of Service Industry Management*, 16(1), 107–121.

Edvardsson, B and J Olsson (1996). Key concepts for new service development. *The Service Industries Journal*, 16, 14–64.

Edvardsson, B, L Haglund and J Mattsson (1995). Analysis, planning, improvisation and control in the development of New Services. *International Journal of Service Industry Management*, 6(2), 24–35.

Eisenhardt, K and B Tabrizi (1995). Accelerating adaptive processes. *Administrative Science Quarterly*, 40(1), 84–110.

Fleischer, M and JK Liker (1997). *Concurrent Engineering Effectiveness: Integrating Product Development Across Organizations*. Cincinnati, OH: Hanser-Gardner.

Froehle, CM, V Aleda, RB Chase, Voss and CA Roth (2000). Antecedents of new service development effectiveness: An exploratory examination of strategic operations choices. *Journal of Service Research*, 3(1), 3–17.

Fruen, MA (1993). Better products in half the time. *Best's Review*, Oldwick, September, 94(5).

Galbraith, J (1977). *Matrix*, New York: Wiley.

Garvin, D (1995). Leveraging processes for strategic advantage. *Harvard Business Review*, 73(5), 76–89.

Gatenby, DA, PM Lee, RE Howard, K Hushyer, R Layendecker and J Weaver (1994). Concurrent engineering: An enabler for fast, high-quality product realization. *Bell Technical Journal*, 34–47.

Gerwin, D and GI Susman (eds.) (1996). Special issue on concurrent engineering. *IEEE Transactions on Engineering Management*, 43(2), 118–123.

Graessel, B and P Zeidler (1993). Using quality function deployment to improve customer service. *Quality Progress*, November.

Griffin, A and J Hauser (1993). The voice of the customer. *Marketing Science*, 12(1), 1–27.

Gruner, K and C Homburg (2000). Does customer interaction enhance new product success. *Journal of Business Research*, 49(1), 1–14.

Gustafsson, A and M Johnson (2003). *Competing in the Service Economy*. San Francisco, CV: Jossey-Bass.

Handfield, R, G Ragatz, K Petersen and C Monczka (1999). Involving suppliers in new product development. *California Management Review*, 42(1), 59–82.

Hartley, JR (1992). *Concurrent Engineering: Shortening Lead Times, Raising Quality, and Lowering Costs*. Cambridge, MA: Productivity Press.

Hull, FM, PD Collins and JK Liker (1996). Composite forms of organization as a strategy for concurrent engineering effectiveness. *IEEE Transactions on Engineering Management*, 43(2), 133–142.

Hull, FM (2004a). A composite model of product development: Application to services. *IEEE Transactions on Engineering Management*.

Hull, FM (2004b). Innovation strategy and the impact of a composite model of service product development on performance. *Journal of Service Research*, 7(4), 167–181.

Hull, FM and J Hage (1982). Organizing for innovation: Beyond Burns and Stalker's organic type. *Sociology*, 16, 546–547.

Hull, F (1988). Inventive pay-off from R&D: Organization designs for maximizing efficient research performance. *Sociology*, 22 (3), 171–93.

Hull, F (2003). Simultaneous involvement in service product development: A strategic contingency approach. *International Journal of Innovation Management*, 7(3), 1–32.

Jaworski, BJ and AK Kohli (1993). Market orientation: Antecedents and consequences. *Journal of Marketing*, 57(3), 53–71.

Katzenbach, JR and D Smith (1993). *The Wisdom of Teams*. Cambridge, MA: Harvard Business School Press.

Kristensson, P, P Magnusson and J Matthing (2002). Users as a hidden resource for creativity: Findings from an experimental study on user involvement. *Journal of Creativity and Innovation Management*, 11(1), 55–61.

Kristensson, P, A Gustafsson and T Archer (2004). Harnessing the creative potential among users. *Journal of Product Innovation Management*, 21(1), 4–14.

Lawrence, J and Lorsch (1967). *Organization and Environment*. Cambridge, MA: Harvard University Press.

Leonard, D and JF Rayport (1997). Spark innovation through empathic design. *Harvard Business Review*, 75 (6), 102–113.

Lievens A and RK Moenaert (2000). New service teams as information-processing systems: Reducing innovative uncertainty. *Journal of Service Research*, 3(1), 46–65.

Liker, JK, RR Kamath, SM Wasti and M Nagamachi (1996). Supplier involvement in automotive product design. *Research Policy*, 25(1), 59–89.

Liker, J, P Collins and F Hull (1999). Flexibility and standardization: Test of a contingency model of product design-manufacturing integration. *Journal of Product Innovation Management*, 16(3), 248–267.

Lovelock, CH (1996). *Services Marketing. Upper Saddle River*, NJ: Prentice-Hall.

Lovitt, M (1996). Continuous improvement through the QS-9000 road map. *Quality Progress*, February.

Lutz, RA (1994). Implementing technological change with cross-functional teams. *Research Technology Management*, 37(2), 14–17.

Magnusson, P, J Matthing and P Kristensson (2003). Managing user involvement in service innovation. Experiments with innovating end-users. *Journal of Service Research*, 6 (2), 111–124.

Matthing, J, B Sandén and B Edvardsson (2004). New service development — Learning from and with customers. *International Journal of Service Industry Management*, 15(5), 479–498.

McIver R and P Humphreys (2004). Early supplier involvement in the design process. *Omega*, 32, 179–199.

Melan, EH (1985). Process management in service and administrative operations. *Quality Progress*.

Meyer, MH and A DeTore (1999). Product development for services. *Academy of Management Executive*, 13(3), 64–76. Identified OPT as key practices.

Narver, JC, SF Slater and DL MacLachlan (2004). Responsive and proactive market orientation and new product success. *Journal of Product Innovation Management*, 21(5), 334–347.

Nevins, JL and DE Whitney (1989). *Concurrent Design of Products and Processes*. New York: McGraw-Hill.

Nonaka, I and H Takeuchi (1995). *The Knowledge-Creating Company*. Oxford University Press, New York.

Olson, EM, OC Walker and RW Ruekert (1995). Organizing for effective new product development: The moderating role of product innovativeness. *Journal of Marketing*, 59(1), 48–62.

Petersen, K, R Handfield and G Ragatz (2003). A model of supplier integration into new product development. *Journal of Product Innovation Management*, 20(4), 284–299.

Petersen, K, R Handfield and G Ragatz (2005). Supplier integration into new product development. *Journal of Operations Management*, 23(3/4), 371–388.

Polanyi, M (1966). *The Tacit Dimension*. Routledge & Kegan Paul, London.

Primo, M and S Amundson (2002). An exploratory study of the effects of supplier relationships on new product development outcomes. *Journal of Operations Management*, 20(1), 33–52.

Rayport, J and J Sviokla (1995). Exploiting the virtual value chain. *Harvard Business Review*.

Roach, S (1988). Technology and the services sector, America's hidden competitive challenge. Guile, BR and JB Quinn (eds.). In *Policies for Growth, Trade, and Employment*, Washington, DC: National Academy Press.

Rochfordt, L and W Rudelius (1992). How involving more functional areas within a firm affects the new product process. *Journal of Product Innovation Management*, 9(4), 287–299.

Roy, S, K Sivakumar and I Wilkinson (2004). Innovation generation in supply chain relationships. *Journal of the Academy of Marketing Science*, 32(1), 61–79.

Souder, WE, JD Sherman and R Davies-Cooper (1999). Environmental uncertainty, organizational integration, and new product development effectiveness: A test of contingency theory. *Journal of Product Innovation Management*, 15(6), 520–533.

Storey, C and FM Hull (2005). Service product development: A contingent approach by service type. Paper read at PDMA, San Diego.

Storey, C and J Easingwood (1998). The augmented service offering: A conceptualization and study of its impact on new service success. *Journal of Product Innovation Management*, 15(4), 335–351.

Susman, GI and JW Dean Jr. (1992). Development of a model for predicting design for manufacturability effectiveness. In *Integrating Design and Manufacturing for Competitive Advantage*. Susman, GI (ed.). pp. 207–227. New York: Oxford University Press.

Swink, M (1999). Threats to new product manufacturability and the effects of development team integration processes. *Journal of Operations Management*, 17(6), 691–709.

Swink, M (2000). Technological innovativeness as a moderator of new product design integration and top management support. *Journal of Product Innovation Management*, 17(3), 208–220.

Terrill, CA (1992). The ten commandments of new service development. *Management Review*, 81(2).

Tidd, J and F Hull (eds.) (2003). *Service Innovation: Organizational Responses to Technological Opportunities & Market Imperatives*. London: Imperial College Press.

Thomke, S (2003). R&D comes to services: Bank of America's path breaking experiments. *Harvard Business Review*, 81(4), 71–79.

Ulwick, AW (2002). Turn customer input into innovation. *Harvard Business Review*, 80(1), 91–97.

von Hippel, E (1994). Sticky information and the locus of problem solving. *Management Science*, 40(4), 429–439.

von Hippel, E (2001). User Toolkits for Innovation. *Journal of Product Innovation Management*, 18(4), 247–257.

Vargo, SL and RF Lusch (2002). Evolving to a new dominant logic for marketing. *Journal of Marketing*, 68(1), 1–17.

Walter, A (2003). Relationship specific factors influencing supplier involvement in customer new product development. *Journal of Business Research*, 56(9), 721–733.

Wynstra, F, B Axelsson and AJ Van Weele (2000). Driving and enabling factors for purchasing involvement in product development. *European Journal of Purchasing and Supply Chain Management*, 6(2), 129–41.

Zirger, BJ and JL Hartley (1996). The effect of acceleration techniques on product development time. *IEEE Transactions on Engineering Management*, 43(2), 143–152.

Zirger, BJ, A Modestom and Maaidque (1990). A model of new product development: An empirical test. *Management Science*, 36(7), 867–883.

Appendix A — Types of Companies in Service Sample

Category	Number
Banking/financial services	18
Retail — 5	
Credit card — 3	
Lending — 2	
Investment services — 2	
Private banking — 1	
Investment services — 5	
Construction	1
Consulting services	4
Distribution/logistics (*)	6
Education/training	1
Healthcare	8
Diagnostic services — 4	
Hospital — 2	
Pharmaceutical services — 2	
Insurance	8
Manufacturing related services (**)	4
Non-profit	3
Publishing	2
Retail	3
Travel/hotel	2
Telecommunications	5
Transportation	5
Total	70

*Utilities, engineering, distribution of product, etc.
**Credit, risk, etc.

Appendix B — Measures

Concept	Items
Performance	
NSD performance ($\alpha = 0.90$)	*To what extent have your service products changed during the past five years?* • New features • Upgraded features • Higher quality • Shorter time from concept to test market of service product • Shorter time from test market to full-scale delivery of the service product • Reduced cost of service product development
Organization	
OTS — organic team structure ($\alpha = 0.89$)	• Strengthening the role of project managers • Cross-functional teaming • Cross-training specialists • Increasing the influence of downstream functions in upstream decisions, for example, customer service input in product development • Reorganization of jobs to reduce hand-offs • Collocating complementary functions
Process	
IDC — in-process design controls ($\alpha = 0.84$)	*To what extent have you engaged in the following activities during the past five years in the development of service products?* • Benchmarking best-in-class companies • Using structured processes for identifying customer needs and translating into requirements (QFD) • Setting performance criteria for projects • Setting standards for the performance of products • Institutionalizing systematic reviews for development projects • Mapping processes to reduce non-value added activities

(Continued)

(Continued)

Concept	Items
	• Improving documentation of processes • Measuring conformance with processes • Institutionalizing continuous improvement processes
Tools	
CIT — computer information technology ($\alpha = 0.83$)	*To what extent have you emphasized the following kinds of activities during the past five years?* • Company internal communications via e-mail or other computer networks • Updating existing IT systems • Management Information systems/expert systems • Distributed databases on-line to multiple functions • Common software for project management • Common software for process mapping • Building on-line databases with lessons learned and best practice templates • Linking electronically (EDI) with externals, for example, suppliers, partners, etc. • Linking electronically with customers, for example, EDI, computer networks, etc.
Innovation strategy	
Novelty	*To what extent did your strategy for the past five years focus on:* • Developing novel service products
Knowledge Strategy[3]	
Tacit knowledge ($\alpha = 0.66$)	*To what extent do the following add value to your service products for which customers are willing to pay?* • Personal service • Convenience • Guarantees • Transactional changes

[3]The other factor dealt with explicit or codified knowledge, professional knowledge, knowledge bases, for example, research, hardware, software, and communications. Two kinds of value added grouped in a third, miscellaneous factor: leisure and transportation. Neither the explicit nor miscellaneous factor had any significant main or interaction effects.

Biographies

Intehkab (Ian) Alam

Dr. Alam is an Assistant Professor of Marketing in the Jones School of Business, State University of New York (SUNY) at Geneseo, New York, USA. He conducts research in the areas of New Service and Product Development, Global Marketing of Services, and Qualitative Research Methodologies. His articles have been, or are scheduled to be published, in several prestigious marketing journals, including the *Journal of the Academy of Marketing Science, Journal of Services Marketing, Journal of Product Innovation Management, Industrial Marketing Management, International Marketing Review, Journal of Marketing Management, Qualitative Market Research,* and *Journal of International Marketing and Exporting.* He has also published a chapter in the *PDMA Handbook of New Product Development* (John Wiley and PDMA, 2004).

Hans Björkman

Dr. Björkman received his PhD degree in Business Administration at the Stockholm School of Economics. He is associated as Senior Researcher with the FENIX Centre for Innovations in Management at Chalmers University of Technology in Göteborg, Sweden, and employed as a Senior Strategist at Sif, the major white-collar trade union in Sweden. Current professional assignments concern the development of environmental scanning strategies, research on segmentation strategies, and participation in a merger process involving two major unions. Dr. Björkman is the author of *Learning from members Tools for strategic positioning and service innovation in trade unions* (2005, Stockholm School of Economics) and of articles published in scientific journals on topics such as group creativity in innovation processes and trade union renewal through member involvement in innovation processes, but also on insider action research methodology. His research focuses on customer and market orientation, new service development, the creation of innovative cultures and climates in organizations, and on action research as a tool for organizational change.

Fredrik Dahlsten

Combining positions in academy and industry, Fredrik Dahlsten is Associated Senior Researcher, FENIX Centre for Innovations in Management at Chalmers University of Technology, Sweden, and Executive Support Manager, Marketing, Sales & Customer Service at Volvo Cars, Sweden. Adopting a collaborative research perspective, insider action research results include both change management projects for market intelligence and customer focused development at Volvo Cars as well as some five published academic articles. Research focus covers customer orientation development, with emphasis on customer knowledge creation for innovation and customer experience development.

Per Echeverri

Dr. Echeverri, who has a PhD in business administration at Karlstad University, Sweden, is a member of the CTF group. His research is oriented toward areas such as service encounter communication, group communication, inter-organizational relations, customer experiences of servicescapes, and issues linked to video-based methodology. During the years, he has developed a specific interest in industries such as public transport, voluntary organizations, and agricultural business. In addition, Dr. Echeverri has co-authored books, research reports, academic articles, and book chapters in service management.

Bo Edvardsson

Dr. Edvardsson is professor of business administration and director of the Service Research Center (CTF) at Karlstad University, Sweden. He is the editor of *International Journal of Service Industry Management* and a fellow at the Center for Service leadership at Arizona State University and at Hanken in Helsinki. Dr. Edvardsson is author or co-author of 15 books and has published 65 articles in scientific journals. In 2004, he received the American Marketing Association (AMA) Award for Leadership in Services. His research focuses on service quality, new service development, dynamics in customer relationships, and value creation through service and customer experiences.

Evert Gummesson

Dr. Gummesson is Professor of Marketing at Stockholm University, Sweden. His research interests embrace services, quality, relationships, networks, and qualitative methodology. In 1977, he wrote the first book on services in Scandinavia. In 2000, he received the *American Marketing Association (AMA) Award for Leadership in Services*, in 2004, the *AMA Award for Best Article on Services* (with Christopher Lovelock), and the *Chartered Institute of Marketing*, UK, includes him in its guru list of the 50 most important contributors to the development of marketing. His latest book is *Many-to-Many Marketing* with the subtitle, "From one-to-one to many-to-many in the marketing of the networked economy." Dr. Gummesson has 25-years of experience in business and is a frequent speaker at companies and universities throughout the world.

Anders Gustafsson

Dr. Gustafsson is professor of business administration at the Service Research Center (CTF) at Karlstad University, Sweden. He has authored or co-authored nine books, including *Conjoint Measurement — Methods and Applications* (Springer, 2003), Improving Customer Satisfaction, Loyalty and Profit: An Integrated Measurement and Management System (Jossey-Bass, 2000), and Competing in a Service Economy: How to Create a Competitive Advantage through Service Development and Innovation (Jossey-Bass, 2003). The latter two books have been translated into a number of different languages. In addition, Dr. Gustafsson has published over 70 academic articles, book chapters, and industry reports. His research focuses on customer and market orientation, new service development, and management of customer relationships.

Cornelius Herstatt

Dr. Herstatt (DBA, MBA) is a professor for Technology and Innovation Management at Hamburg University of Technology. He is director of the Institute for Technology and Innovation Management, leading a group of researchers. His research interests are the Front End of Innovation, user-innovation, user-innovation communities, and innovation systems. Prior to these activities, professor Herstatt worked for many years in managerial positions in both Industry and Consulting. Before joining TUHH, he was a faculty member at the Swiss Federal Institute of Technology (ETHZ), the University of Zurich, and the University of St. Gallen (Switzerland).

Christiane Hipp

Since December 2005, Dr. Hipp holds a chair as full professor for organization, human resource management, and general management at the Technical University of Brandenburg (Cottbus). Her areas of research include innovation process in services, innovation strategies, technology foresight, environmental management, and intellectual property rights. She is in charge of several research projects in the field of innovation process and entrepreneurship, and she has authored various publications on innovation processes in services.

Frank Hull

Dr. Hull (PhD, Columbia University, 1977) is a visiting professor at the Arizona State University and was previously at the Fordham University in New York City. He adapted a model of product development based on the principle of concurrency to services. At Fordham, he developed specialized graduate courses in new service development and strategic business product development to adapt best practices from goods industries to services. He then collaborated with a user group of leading service enterprises in the New York City metropolitan area to apply the model to performance improvement. These user group leaders help shape a survey of best practices for new service development for collecting the data analyzed herein. Dr. Hull lives in Manhattan and teaches in Europe during the summers where he is internationalizing his research studies.

Per Kristensson

Dr. Kristensson is Assistant Professor in Psychology at the Service Research Center (CTF) and the Department of Psychology at the Karlstad University, Sweden. He has a PhD in Psychology from the Gothenburg University and a Licentiate Degree from Luleå Technical University. Dr Kristensson has published over 30 articles in leading journals and peer-reviewed conference proceedings. His research mainly concerns topics on consumer behavior, management of technology, and cognitive psychology. In respect to user involvement, he has published articles in several journals such as the *Journal of Product Innovation Management*, *Journal of Service Research*, *Creativity and Innovation Management*, and *Journal of Services Marketing*.

Peter Magnusson

Dr. Magnusson is Assistant Professor of Marketing at the Service Research Center (CTF) at Karlstad University, Sweden. He holds an MSc in electrical engineering from the Chalmers University of Technology, an MBA in executive business administration from the University of Uppsala, and a PhD from the Stockholm School of Economics. He has 20 years experience in R&D in the computing and telecommunications industries. His research focuses on new product and service innovation, the management of technology, and organizing and managing creativity. He has received several nominations and rewards for his research. He has published in leading refereed journals and peer-reviewed conference proceedings.

Ulf Mannervik

Ulf Mannervik is managing partner of NormannPartners and Research fellow in Strategic Renewal Research Programme, Oxford University. He is a director of the board at The Knowledge Foundation, Sweden. He has worked with many clients across most sectors. His work and research focuses on business design, business innovation, and renewal processes. He holds an MPhil in Design theory from Chalmers University of Technology, and a BScBA from the Gothenburg School of Economics and Stanford Graduate School of Business.

Jonas Matthing

Dr. Matthing has a background in sales and marketing at Xerox and Gartner. He is a researcher at the Service Research Center (CTF), and teaches in marketing at the Karlstad University. Dr. Matthing (2004) presented a dissertation focusing on, and titled, Customer Involvement in New Service Development, and has published several scientific articles on this research theme in journals such as *Journal of Service Research, International Journal of Service Industry Management*, and *Journal of Services Marketing*. His research currently focuses on the future of telecom services by exploring customer involvement methods as well as lead user research together with Eric von Hippel.

Rainer Naegele

Rainer Naegele is head of the Competence Center "Service Management" at the Fraunhofer Institute of Industrial Engineering (IAO) in Stuttgart, Germany. The main research interests of Rainer are in the fields of service benchmarking, service innovation, and customer integration in new service development. He has been the project manager of 20 different research and consulting projects, especially projects with the following focus: service management: quality and service processes, service measurement and service benchmarking, service management: strategy development, restructuring of service portfolios, modularization of services, service engineering: redesign and development of services, and service engineering: customer integration in the service development process. Rainer Naegele is author of more than 20 publications.

Rafael Ramirez

Dr. Ramirez is currently Professor of Management at HEC-Paris, University Fellow of the James Martin Institute and Fellow of Templeton College and Saïd Business School at the University of Oxford, and Partner in Normann Partners in Stockholm. He is the author or co-author of five books and his academic articles have appeared in publications such as *Futures*, the *Strategic Management Journal*, *Harvard Business Review*, and the *European Management Review*. His research focuses on aesthetics, scenarios, business re-design, and value co-production.

Bodil Sandén

Bodil Sandén is a PhD Candidate at the Service Research Center (CTF), Karlstad University. Her dissertation is about customer involvement in new service development. Bodil also teaches marketing at the Department of Business and Economics at the Karlstad University.

Chris Storey

Chris D. Storey, BCom (Birmingham), MSc (Warwick), PhD (Manchester). Reader, Cass Business School, City University London. He is currently at Cass Business School since 1994. Chris Storey has previously held positions at Kings College, London (1993–1994) and Manchester Business School (1989–1994). Prior to an academic career, he held various marketing roles at one of UK's big four Banks. He has also held visiting positions at MacMaster University, Canada and Monash University, Australia. He has published numerous articles in leading Journals including the *Journal of Product Innovation Management, Journal of Business Research, European Journal of Marketing, Long Range Planning,* and the *International Journal of Service Industry Management.* His main area of interest is innovation as a source of competitive advantage in service industries. Specifically his research has centered on success factors, service offerings, multi-channel distribution systems, development processes, on-line banking strategies, evaluating development activities, and knowledge management in NPD.

Lars Witell

Dr. Witell is associate professor at the Service Research Center (CTF) at Karlstad University, Sweden. He performs research on product and service development, customer orientation, service infusion in manufacturing, and quality management. He has written about 20 book chapters and papers in scientific journals. He teaches in industrial marketing, customer focused product development, quality management and research methodology, and works as a consultant within development work and market research.

Index

1996